Praise for Nature's People

"Let me praise Tom Schaefer's extensive work, thoroughness, and encompassing scope of his beloved subject. He has included, via extensive interviews, much lively observation by those participating in the adventure called the Hog Island Audubon Camp, over its long history. Plus he's told the Todd-Bingham story well and in some depth. This is a grand history, full of facts and explanations one rarely finds in such a survey of an institution.

Thank you, dear Tom, for carrying the torch of Emily Dickinson into new territory. I'm very proud of your long persistence, and of having had a small role in the process… Yours is a fine persistence and achievement. Congratulations for making sure this piece of history isn't forgotten…. There are great stories embedded here that shouldn't be lost, and now won't be."

— Polly Longsworth
Dickinson scholar
Author of *Austin & Mabel: The Amherst Affair and Love Letters of Austin Dickinson and Mabel Loomis Todd*

"Tom Schaefer has given Hog Island enthusiasts, and those who have yet to visit, a deep dive into the lives and thinking of the Hog Island Audubon Camp's founders. His thorough research brings to life the challenges and personalities of the people who made the camp a thriving reality that continues to captivate not only educators and birders, but also environmental leaders, naturalists, teens, and families in ever-widening circles."

—Steven W. Kress
National Audubon Society Vice President for Bird Conservation *retired*
Hog Island Audubon Camp director *retired*
Author of *Project Puffin: The Improbable Quest to Bring a Beloved Seabird Back to Egg Rock*

"From the opening quotations to the historical set of illustrations, a major work of which you certainly should be proud. My very best wishes for your final assembling of the masterwork that provides history, insight, and personality to the Todd-Bingham-Audubon saga of a most important island. Well done!

—**Art Borror**
Long-time Audubon Camp staff

"For all who love Hog Island and its camp, *Nature's People* is a must read. It was hard to put down. All the praise is due. I was only planning to read chapter 7 but just took a quick look at the first chapter and continued through to the last chapter. I even read all the footnotes which I found to be a trove of information both scintillating and informative!"

—**Juanita Roushdy**
Friends of Hog Island Executive Director

"Tom Schaefer's recounting Hog Island's story is obviously a labor of love for the story itself, plus the impressive listing of resources shows the amazing amount of research completed via extensive interviews and substantial work with archives to be able to present this detailed account. Tom's long years of personal investment in this work show good effort."

—**Ted Gilman**
Greenwich Audubon Center & Hog Island Audubon Camp naturalist
retired

"*Nature's People* is a wonderful summary of the Hog Island's importance. Tom Schaefer has underlined the impact that one woman had on both the Emily Dickinson canon and Hog Island. Mabel Loomis Todd is certainly one of the most important figures in American culture because of the two wonderful persons (Austin Dickinson and Emily Dickinson) and the place that she loved."

—**James M. Hughes**
Dickinson scholar & poet

"The more I read and reread *Nature's People* the more astounding it is to me that Tom Schaefer has written such a thorough and fascinating history of Hog Island and the people involved in its preservation and maintenance. There is human drama here as well as underlying themes that cover conservation, environmental education, wildlife, and aesthetic values. I have spent time on this small bit of exceptional landscape and no one is more qualified to write the Hog Island story than Tom Schaefer. Tom's meticulous research, personal experience, and unbounded passion make this a story for the ages."
—**Paul Knoop, Jr.**
Aullwood Audubon Center & Farm Education Director *retired*

"Hog Island, long regarded as the 'mother church' of American conservation, played an equally storied role – heretofore largely unknown – in American literary tradition. Tom Schaefer has skillfully unlocked the secrets of both worlds, played out on a little Maine island that continues to captivate all who walk its rockbound shores and forest paths."
—**David Klinger**
Friends of Hog Island former president

"Great storytelling. A fascinating narrative. Not just the love story of Mabel Loomis Todd and Austin Dickinson, but all of the anecdotal stories which are told so vividly. Tom Schaefer's own way of phrasing things makes for avid reading of the narrative. Even the financial problems and conflicts between state office and National Audubon were rendered compelling. I absolutely love this book and know that other readers will love it, too."
—**Betsy Hughes**
Educator & poet

"There is a unique spirit and vision that led Mabel Loomis Todd and a few other Northeasterners to recognize and conserve precious parts of the natural world. Upon reading *Nature's People*, I realized that my husband's parents, in settling on their two-hundred acres in Austerlitz, New York, were motivated by that same spirit. Today descendants work to keep the rural estate as parents left it.

I thoroughly enjoyed the island itself, the Todds, and the others who made it happen. *Nature's People* is a great story."
—Phyllis M. Kittel
Benedictine University (Chicago) dean *retired*
Author of *Staying In the Fire: A Sisterhood Responds to Vatican II*

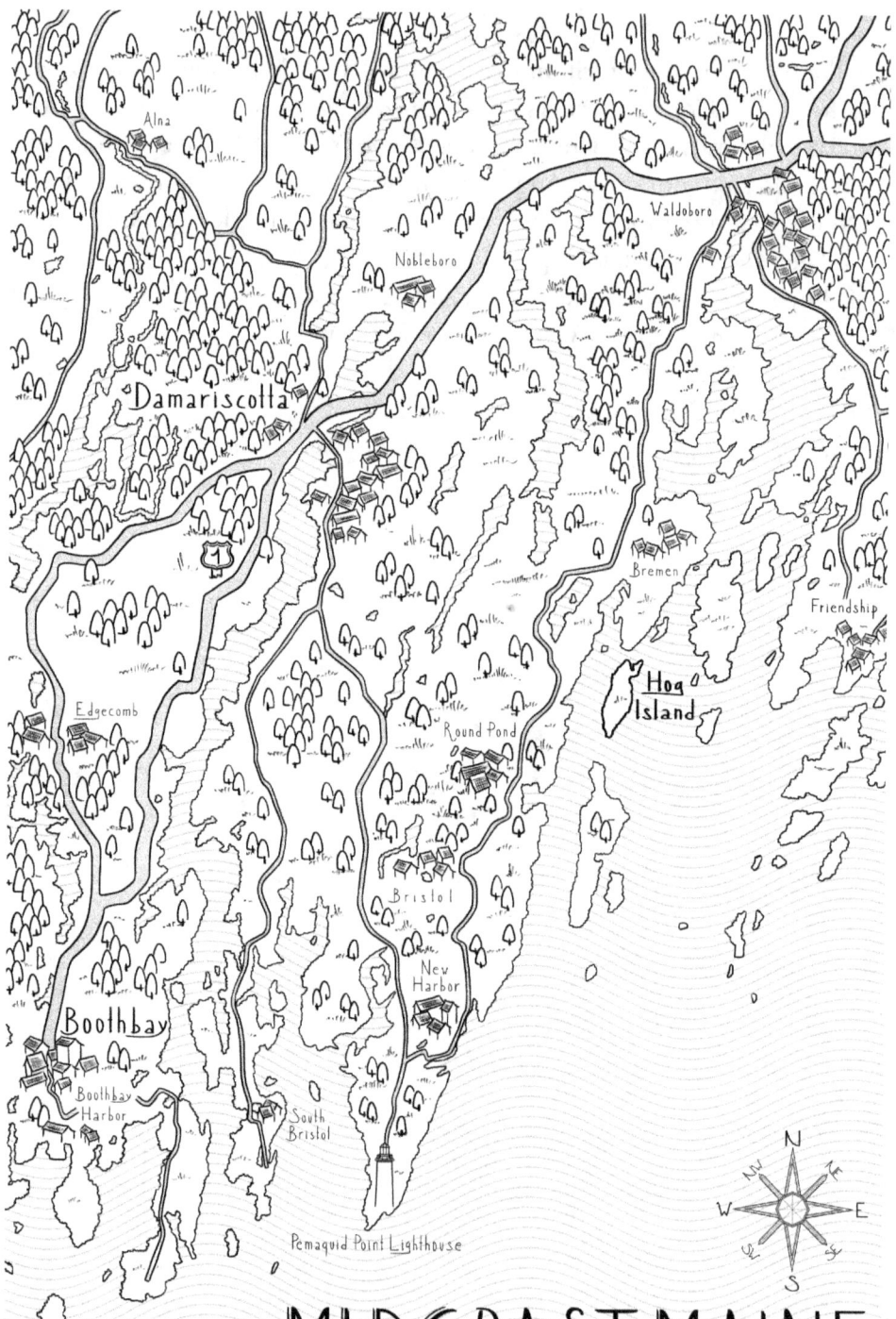

Alna

Waldoboro

Nobleboro

Damariscotta

1

Bremen

Friendship

Edgecomb

Round Pond

Hog
Island

Bristol

New
Harbor

Boothbay

Boothbay
Harbor

South
Bristol

Pemaquid Point Lighthouse

N

W · E

S

MIDCOAST MAINE

NATURE'S PEOPLE

THE HOG ISLAND STORY FROM MABEL LOOMIS TODD TO AUDUBON

TOM SCHAEFER

FOREWORD BY DR. STEPHEN W. KRESS
AFTERWORD BY SCOTT WEIDENSAUL

**Canoe Tree
Press**

4697 Main Street
Manchester Center, VT 05255

Canoe Tree Press is a division of DartFrog Books

To Bart and Ginny Cadbury, who, with a few other island stalwarts, had the foresight to organize Friends of Hog Island in order "to ensure the future of the island."

To Jim Hemmert and Jim Hughes, career mentors both, who turned me on to the wonders of literature.

To Cindy Lou Cooke, the light of my life, for the encouragement to pursue my dream of telling Hog Island's story.

Exultation is the going
Of an inland soul to sea -
Past the Houses -
Past the Headlands -
Into deep Eternity -

Bred as we, among the mountains,
Can the sailor understand
The divine intoxication
Of the first league out from land?

—Emily Dickinson
Franklin #143

N
NW NE
W   E
SW SE
S

Audubon Camp Buildings

Mussel Bar

Bingham Cottages/
Camp Mavooshen

Long Cove

① (circled)

③ (circled)

② (circled)

④ (circled)

Todd Wildlife Sanctuary
Dedication Plaque

Midden Cove

Sand Cove

⑥ (circled)

⑤ (circled)

⑦ (circled)

Hog Island Ledge

① West Camp Trail
② Center Camp Trail
③ East Camp Trail
④ Bingham Cottages Trail
⑤ East Shore Trail
⑥ Sand Cove Cross-Island Trail
⑦ West Shore Trail

Hog Island Bar

HOG ISLAND

Table of Contents

Foreword

I first heard about Hog Island in 1963 when I was working as a student assistant at the Audubon Camp in Greenwich, Connecticut. Hog Island was always mentioned in the most revered way—like an Audubon mecca. I was fortunate to have a direct source of the Hog Island stories when Carl Buchheister, then president of National Audubon, came to visit the Greenwich Camp. It never took him long to find his way to the working side of the kitchen to let the student assistants know how important they were to the operation. Usually the same evening he arrived, he would arrange for a gathering of the assistants at the home of Dur and Peggy Morton, who resided in a cottage located a short walk from the kitchen. Dur was then director of the Greenwich Audubon Camp.

Buchheister had a commanding presence and a booming speaking voice that completely pulled one into his storytelling. He always picked a topic that would enthrall this gathering of young naturalists. Like living among "walking peters" (Leach's storm-petrels) on Matinicus Rock, and his adventures on Isla Rasa in California's Sea of Cortez, where Audubon was helping to save the world's largest colony of elegant terns and Heerman's gulls. But all his ocean stories began with telling us about the "Mother Church"—his fond name for the Hog Island Audubon Camp. He was the camp's first director and held that position for two decades until he became president of Audubon.

It was certainly Buchheister's descriptions of Hog Island and its location as a gateway to Muscongus Bay's bird islands that led me to want to spend summers on this special Maine island. But why did he call it Audubon's "Mother Church"? This eluded me at first, but soon I had a theory: the three other Audubon camps that existed in 1963 (Connecticut, Wisconsin, and Wyoming) were all inspired by Hog Island—the first of the camps. Each occupied a different region of the country and habitat type, but the mission of all camps was the same—to

15

inform and inspire teachers about nature, so they could return to their communities ready to share what they had learned with their students and others.

Tom Schaefer's *Nature's People* offers new detail and the best overview to date about how Mabel Loomis Todd saved Hog Island from lumbering at the turn of the century, taking the first bold step for setting the stage for the Hog Island saga. Mabel was exposed to the values of Henry David Thoreau, an essayist, poet, and practical philosopher who was a family friend of her father, Eben Loomis. Always with a gift for drama, she liked to tell the story of how, as a child, she was held by Thoreau, absorbing his passion for nature.

Clearly, Mabel passed her love of nature to her daughter, Millicent Todd Bingham. Fortuitously, Millicent came to the idea of using the island to inspire teachers and to serve as a science center at the same time that John Baker, the new president of the National Audubon Society, was looking for a place to inspire teachers about birds and to teach ecology. The idea was surprisingly novel at the time. It is more important now than ever.

Certainly, a key feature of the experiment was the island nature of this first Audubon camp, as it contained not only the people but the enthusiasm of the teacher and students. The opportunity for educators and the public to live and eat in close company with the country's great naturalists was a unique experience and key to the profound success of the experiment.

There is another reason for calling Hog Island Audubon's "Mother Church." In this insightful Hog Island history (much of which is previously unpublished), Tom Schaefer points out that as a devout Catholic, Buchheister would not have used the "Mother Church" moniker lightly. Schaefer notes that Buchheister's goal of establishing an ecological program at Hog Island blended everything that was important to him: wildlife, citizens, education, conservation, sanctuaries, ecosystems, science, and fun. These were the best elements of life, all distilled into two weeks of dynamic, enjoyable, engaging teaching, with plenty of field experience.

In the dark hours of 2009 when the camp was shuttered—perhaps permanently—I felt that there must be a way to keep Millicent Todd Bingham and John Baker's vision alive, possibly via a new model that would play to the unique strengths of Audubon and this glorious location. I hoped that a program based on shorter, bird-focused sessions would not only sell well, but would carry on the tradition of renowned ornithologists teaching ecology through birds. That is why, in 2010, Project Puffin took on the management of the camp and reopened it with four ornithology sessions. These sessions were later supplemented by additional bird programs for teens and birding programs that stretched the season into the spring and fall, as well as other popular programs, including a family camp and an educator's camp. But it was the bird programs that made the camp's renaissance possible and permitted the residential programs to grow to fill most of the summer. Of course none of this would have been possible without a solid financial plan and a small army of helpers to look after the buildings and grounds. To this end, the Friends of Hog Island stepped up to raise funds and keep the buildings clean and well-maintained.

For various reasons, the other Audubon camps created in Buchheister's time no longer exist as summer-long residential facilities, but Hog Island lives on, re-invented several times over, often arising like a rebounding phoenix. It continues to captivate not only educators but also environmental leaders, naturalists, teens, and families in ever-widening circles. The recipe for environmental education invented by Buchheister endures. Today, after more than eighty-five years of operation, the list of Hog Island instructors is a veritable who's-who of famed naturalists, biologists, and environmental leaders who continue to reach out to an ever-expanding following.

Tom Schaefer has given Hog Island enthusiasts, and those who have yet to visit, a deep dive into the lives and thinking of the Hog Island Audubon Camp's founders. His thorough research brings to life the challenges and personalities of the people who made the camp a thriving reality.

The Hog Island camp was started by dreamers who wished to create an enduring place from which people returned to their communities as missionaries for our planet. Against all odds, this vision has taken root in this verdant oasis. Hog Island continues to attract visionaries, educators, and scientists as well as talented carpenters, chefs, kitchen helpers, gardeners, and boatmen. All these people who teach, assist, and attend Hog Island programs are enriched by the island experience. They are a growing force of stewards and healers of the planet. They are "Nature's People."

— Dr. Stephen W. Kress
Founder of National Audubon Society's Project Puffin and
Former Director of the Hog Island Audubon Camp
Ithaca, New York
September 2020

Introduction

An unexpectedly wonderful thing happened back in 1981 that changed my life. I am quite certain that I am not the only person who can make that statement, but in my case it was so clear, so quickly, and then I had two weeks to watch the magic unfold. In the middle of it all, I watched the Maine sunrise over Muscongus Bay each morning, most often with a copy of Emily Dickinson's poetry next to me on the rocks, my personal journal in my lap, and my special fountain pen at the ready to record thoughts about the natural beauty I witnessed in front of me. For a kid from the Midwest whose idea of big water is Lake Erie—and trust me that *is* big—having a couple of weeks at the Audubon Ecology Workshop in Maine, as the Hog Island camp was then known, made an impact that set in motion forces that made my life different from then on.

As cool as the whale-watching, puffin-spotting, and mud-flat-wading were, my wonder had followed me in a vector that started at my home in Ohio, budded in central Massachusetts, and then flowered at the Audubon Camp on Hog Island. At the time I was a veteran junior high school English teacher who had been encouraged to get working on a master's degree. At just that time, Wright State University in Dayton, Ohio, initiated a new master of humanities program that seemed to fit me to a tee. I did not want to be a school administrator, and the humanities focus would allow me to pick courses of my choosing and create a program of my own. Teaching had taught me I was a life-long learner and this humanities option seemed just right, since I hoped, before too long, to be teaching even bigger kids at the high school level.

The first two graduate-level quarters found me in night school working through the introductory workshops, for which I wrote papers focused on John Muir and Ansel Adams, both heroes of mine—an early indication I was making my way toward a program in nature-based topics. For the spring quarter, a favorite teacher from my undergraduate days encouraged me to take his Emily Dickinson workshop, which he thought would fit into my program nicely. I didn't understand, wondering what Dickinson had to do with the environment and conservation history, the direction I seemed to be heading. "Oh, she's connected to all sorts of mysterious things," was Mr. Hughes's response. And he was right. The seed of my life's change was sown.

During that spring quarter in 1981, two important events occurred that would further set my new course. A junior high school science colleague had been to the Audubon Camp in Maine the previous summer on scholarship from the local Audubon chapter. She had found the experience very beneficial and told me that university credit was available. I applied for a Dayton Audubon Society scholarship, none too sure they would grant one for a science-based Audubon camp to an English teacher. But after a harrowing interview with a couple of stern-faced chapter leaders, they did. Summer plans began to come together that would take my young family and me to the coast of Maine for two weeks.

As for Emily Dickinson, I was familiar with her poetry to some degree, but not much. A quote of hers, hanging in Mr. Hemmert's English class at Carroll High School, intrigued me ever since I encountered it as a teenager. I learned in the Dickinson workshop it came from a letter she'd written to Thomas Wentworth Higginson, the nationally published writer with whom she had corresponded and who had advised that her poems were *not* publishable. I wonder now if this was her response.

> "If I read a book and it makes my whole body so cold no fire can ever warm me, I know that is poetry. If I feel physically as if the top of my head were taken off, I know that is poetry. These are the only ways I know it. Is there any other way?"

So, when someone in the graduate workshop mentioned he had visited Walt Whitman's house along his travels, I thought, *What a great idea.* On the way to Maine, we could spend a night in central Massachusetts, and I would get a chance, in a sense, to visit Emily

Dickinson, with whom I had become smitten. By early July we were ready for our family adventure.

Yet when we arrived in Amherst, Emily's hometown, it was obvious the Dickinson homestead on Main Street was not open to the public. In those pre-internet days, acquiring all travel details before leaving home was more difficult. But all was not lost. The grounds were open to visitors, so I enjoyed taking pictures and with my wife tried to identify some of the varieties of flowers in the beds once so carefully tended by Emily.

But I wanted more. I had come for Emily and thought the best place to find her then was at the West Cemetery where she was buried. Finding the Dickinson plot that contained Emily, her sister, her parents, and the girls' grandparents wasn't too difficult, but the black-and-white photographs I intended to take would be. The family plot was cordoned off by a black wrought iron fence set very close to headstones, and one huge tree just west of the plot cast one headstone in complete shadow. Sure enough, that headstone was Emily's.

"Called back" Emily Dickinson's headstone
in Amherst, Massachusetts (Schaefer)

While my wife took the kids on a meander, giving their dad a chance to have a little time with Emily, I took a few pictures, even knowing they wouldn't work out well under my darkroom enlarger. Soon, though, I realized that as the sun settled into the late afternoon light, the tree's shadow had moved across Emily's stone and caused that stately fence to cast its own brilliant shadow. I still consider the photographs taken that afternoon the favorites in my personal portfolio.

The next morning we were finally off to Maine, where the family would stay with my wife's cousin up the coast an hour away, while I would begin my two weeks on Hog Island. Driving down Keene Neck Road toward the camp landing and reaching the top of the hill, we were greeted by Mary Johansen, wife of Audubon warden and camp boatman Joe Johansen. I was a bit apprehensive, not at all sure what I was about to get myself into, but Mary gushed over how cute my little girls were and immediately all felt better. Gear was loaded on the boat, my family said our goodbyes, and within a short time Joe motored a few of us across the narrows where I found myself ascending the gangplank up to the *Queen Mary* veranda for the first time.

I was assigned shared accommodations in the Porthole, the old island hotel, with a roommate I would meet later. I stowed my gear and had an hour or so before the first program began, so off I went, amazed at the lobster buoys dotting the bay and the fact that I had actually arrived at such a stunningly picturesque place. I prowled around the Fish House, the main meeting hall, looking at the book collection and pictures of classic camp scenes on its walls. I was most drawn to one display behind glass commemorating the island's history. There were a few artifacts, a dedication deed, and some old photographs, but there was something about one of those pictures that set off an alarm in my head. Then it hit me: The woman in the photo was none other than Mabel Loomis Todd, about whom I had learned in the Dickinson workshop was the dedicated prime mover who first brought Emily Dickinson's poetry to publication in 1890. The whole island, christened the Todd Wildlife Sanctuary by Audubon fifty years prior, was dedicated to her. I could feel the hair on the back of my neck stand up when I realized what I had just stumbled into.

To complete my humanities master's, I would need to develop an extensive nine-credit-hour project, meant to be creative, multi-media, and interdisciplinary, which would integrate my varied studies. Planning the trip to Maine, I had hoped some viable idea would make itself known while I was on Hog Island. I was there less than an hour and it was clear that Mrs. Todd and Emily Dickinson would somehow be the subject of whatever that project was going to be. The result, which earned me my graduate degree, was *The Road Past Amherst*, a slideshow-turned-video narrating my adventure, along with a four-chapter paper borrowing a title from Mrs. Todd, *The Epic of Hog*, with my original subtitle, *The Todd Bingham Family and the Establishment of the Audubon Ecology Workshop in Maine*.

The following spring, as the concept of the Dickinson/Todd humanities project was still taking shape, the Dayton Audubon Society invited me to give a presentation to their membership at the annual picnic. Holding my copy of Emily Dickinson's poems like my own personal Bible, I showed those gathered my slides and told them my amazing story. Before I left the building, the chapter president asked if I would serve on the board of directors. Over the next twenty-plus years I served the Dayton Audubon Society in a number of capacities, including as scholarship committee chair and president.[1] As a result, my interest in Audubon deepened. My wife and I and our daughters volunteered once a month at the Aullwood Audubon Center gift shop near our home. Later I found myself on a committee to create Audubon Ohio, Audubon's new state office, and served on that board for a couple of terms and for a time as a vice president.

But underneath it all, I really wanted to return to Hog Island to teach some kind of humanities track that would enhance the science that was the heart and soul of the Audubon camp's program. Surely the Mabel Loomis Todd influence and the Emily Dickinson connection could be developed into a nature literature component to complement the already top-notch offerings. I applied a couple of times through the 1980s, but Audubon wasn't interested.

In 1994 I thought I would try one last time. Don Burgess was Hog

Island camp director that summer, and though he didn't see how my idea would fit into his camp curriculum, he advised me that Audubon was looking for a director for their Greenwich adult summer camp, the Audubon Ecology Workshop in Connecticut. Would I be interested? I took a big gulp but decided to apply. Audubon camps coordinator Jean Porter flew me up for an interview and showed me around. I began to think I actually could do it and asked Jean if I could throw in some poetry along the way. She thought that would be a nice addition to the programming, and I have fond memories to this day of standing at one of those lovely New England agricultural stone walls, reading and then facilitating a discussion about Robert Frost's "Mending Wall." It was also during my two years as director of the Audubon Ecology Workshop in Connecticut that I came to know Ted Gilman, one of the finest naturalists I've ever had the privilege of meeting.

By the late 1990s, Gilman passed along word that the Friends of Hog Island (FOHI) was forming to do whatever it could to help the financially stressed Maine camp survive for future generations. I wrote a letter to the new organization's secretary, Ginny Cadbury, wife of the camp's second director, Bart Cadbury, telling her of my Hog Island interest. Soon I received a very nice handwritten response asking if I could come to the island that upcoming summer for a membership meeting. Over the next couple of summers, having remarried, my new wife and I traveled to Maine to join Ginny and Bart and a host of other charter FOHI members for annual meetings. Somewhere along the line I volunteered to redevelop the group's newsletter, *Across the Narrows*. After Maine Audubon took over the direction of the Hog Island facility in 1999, I served as FOHI president for a short time.

By the time I was getting ready to retire from teaching, I again floated the idea of a humanities track at the camp, this time to the then-director, Seth Benz. In their never-ending struggle to keep the camp financially viable, Maine Audubon had revamped the curriculum to include a multitude of mini-camp offerings that they hoped would attract not only teachers and birders but also the senior hostel crowd, Scout leaders, and others.

Benz had wanted to add a literary track, and, in 2002, signed me up to teach a fall offering called "Nature Literature and Journaling," hoping it would bring in a dozen or so campers. It did. That first fall of retirement found me, instead of teaching kids in Huber Heights, passing out journaling prompts to my Hog Island crew, mostly Girl Scout leaders. Life was good.

But underneath all of my Audubon activity and never-flagging affection for Emily Dickinson and Mabel Loomis Todd, I developed a sense that my twenty-year-old master's project, which few had or would ever read—its only copy shelved at the Dunbar Library at Wright State—really should be turned into a book available to a broader audience. I can remember standing in the Fish House one evening after talking about Mrs. Todd and reading a Dickinson poem, promising the Friends of Hog Island that I was, right then and there, committing myself to write that book. I wasn't sure exactly how it would develop, but I figured as a newly retired guy with all the time in the world to spend on projects of his own choosing, I'd find what it took to write it.

Twenty years later, I must say it has been a dynamic journey. After resurrecting all the documents filed after my master's was completed, I began collecting anything I could find by Mabel Loomis Todd, her astronomer husband David Peck Todd, and their daughter and Hog Island heir, Millicent Todd Bingham. I did online searches to see what I could find and was disappointed because, back then, Mabel Loomis Todd did not yet exist on Wikipedia. I went back to Amherst to poke through the public library and returned to the Sterling Library at Yale University to see if there were papers or photographs in the Todd Bingham archive I had missed the first time around. In New Hampshire I interviewed the daughter of Carl Buchheister, the first Hog Island camp director, and traveled to Williamsburg to talk with Duryea and Peggy Morton, Dur being a long-time Audubon administrator with deep Hog Island roots. I copied and transcribed a tape-recorded presentation given to campers by Millicent Bingham in 1950.

I knew the focus of the project had to narrow somehow, but how wasn't immediately clear. I thought for a time the title of the book would be

Mother Church, Carl Buchheister's affectionate name for Hog Island, since so many proud Audubon moments emanated from there. Eventually I decided to focus on Mabel Loomis Todd, and the title *Nature's People,* a line from a Dickinson poem, which felt right for a book that would compare Emily Dickinson with Mabel Todd as authentic nature lovers. Before long that, too, felt too all-encompassing since I really wanted a book about the founders of Hog Island, not the Belle of Amherst.

About that time, Lyndal Gordon wrote a book for the contemporary Dickinson renaissance entitled *Lives Like Loaded Guns: Emily Dickinson and Her Family Feuds.* By the time a reader gets through just a bit of this book, they can see how Mabel Todd figured prominently in Dickinson's family history and their infamous "war between the houses." Gordon called the globetrotting Mabel Todd a "dressy adventuress," and though that term felt pejorative, I rather liked the phrase, so I considered *The Dressy Adventuress* for a new title. Still, when I thought about how Hog Island needed to be the clear focus of the book, I wondered if this tangent, too, was not quite where I wanted to go.

About then the idea of *Nature's People* came floating back into consideration. This iteration of *Nature's People* would begin with the Dickinson-Todd complications in Amherst, then shift focus to Mabel Todd's buying a largely undeveloped Muscongus Bay island and how that action fit into the scope of summering and conservation/preservation thinking in turn-of-the-twentieth-century America. It reinforced the concept that not only were Mabel Todd and Emily Dickinson "Nature's people" but *all* who came to Hog Island.

Still, the book was difficult to birth. I kept researching, but no text was making it to my computer's memory bank. Over time, I came to realize that the only way for me to get anything done was to sequester myself someplace the family could afford. I rented a cabin at an Ohio state park for a winter week, at the end of which I felt better about finally having synthesized parts of that research into something I could include in my book.

With that modicum of success in mind, I had a great idea the following summer as I worked over dirty pots in the Hog Island kitchen as a FOHI volunteer. Restoration of the two remaining structures at the Todds' old summer compound on the island, Camp Mavooshen, was nearing completion—such a sequester *that* would be. Serving as a Hog Island artist-in-residence the following summer, in 2014, was an inspiration for me and the kickstart my book needed.[2] I worked for a month-long string of quiet days at the family camp without leaving the re-wilding side of the island. I slept in Millicent Todd Bingham's very own cottage and worked in her mother's much-loved camp building that once was "filled with books." I took evening meals in the camp dining room when in session, but for two of my four weeks I was alone, cooking dinners carefully on a one-burner stove perched on a stone hearth in that very old wooden building. Lunch was most often a cut-up apple dipped in peanut butter while I sat on the front porch watching lobster folk check their pots and juvenile osprey learn how to fish. After sunset I sat in lantern-light indoors listening to music, wondering if Mrs. Todd and Mrs. Bingham would approve, and in the vein of Emily Dickinson, wrote some original verse of my own inspired by this once-in-a-lifetime opportunity.[3] I could text home most days and use the Wi-Fi at the Audubon Camp, a brisk fifteen-minute walk away, but for days at a time I let it go. A newly installed solar electrical system offered enough power to recharge a laptop, a cell phone, and in my case, a little audio speaker. I had all I needed.

Truth was, though, I never really was alone. Staff still had lots to do even when camp wasn't in session. And since the island is an Audubon property, it is open to visitors, some of whom dropped anchor to walk the trails, then found themselves strolling right by my front porch. When I told visitors I was writing about summer life on the island in a place that had stood vacant for more than forty years, a few asked if I had felt any ghosts. Most were disappointed to hear I had not. Still, there were times when some of the book's seemingly unmanageable puzzle chunks just slipped into place. One day I was writing about the history of Waldoboro, the small town just north of Hog Island on the Medomak River, when kayakers paddled by and one mentioned loudly enough for me to hear that the town was proud of its heritage, having built the first five-masted schooner. A worthy reminder from a benevolent spirit, I thought, so I added it into the narrative.

Let me confess to all here and now that I have been in awe of this Hog Island history project since it hit me like a lightning bolt my very first afternoon there. When I decided to take up the broader challenge of writing a book about Mrs. Todd and Hog Island, I realized one of the essential research activities needed to bring the larger story to light would be a careful sifting through her personal diaries and journal entries which I knew existed only in original form archived at Yale. Travel expenses for that trip would put a pinch on our family budget.

To my pleasant surprise, I received an email from a FOHI member with a link to an article she had come across by Julie Dobrow, a Dickinson scholar focusing her research on how Mrs. Todd and Mrs. Bingham brought the Dickinson poetry and letters into publication. In emails with Dobrow, I learned that I could borrow the whole Todd collection of journals and diaries on microfilm. My request for that trove of documents was approved and after hours of deciphering Mabel Todd's handwriting in the Wright State library, not so unlike her own efforts transcribing Emily Dickinson's handwritten verses from the backs of envelopes, a rich collection of excerpts brought the Hog Island story into clearer and more colorful focus. Because of her meticulous record keeping, one can report with a good degree of certainty when she and family arrived at the Round Pond dock for pickup, when and how a new camp building was constructed, and the years when murals were painted in the eaves of her camp "living room."

Culling details from Mabel Todd's journals and Millicent Bingham's vast archive of family papers, along with parsing the Audubon camp record, brought Hog Island summers into a clearer historical perspective. And as an artist-in-residence, having worked on this story in the very space where the Todds enjoyed cool night fires while crafting my narrative on Millicent's very own desk, I am left humbled and honored by the opportunity to bring this notable family's story to public light.

Millicent Bingham's desk on Hog Island 2014 (Schaefer)

Huge thanks go to a bevy of souls who helped me complete this study. Perhaps most important was the encouragement offered by Polly Longsworth, an eminent Dickinson scholar who emailed *me* having heard about my project from a mutual Hog Island acquaintance. Special thanks to Julie Dobrow, who not only advised me on the availability of Mrs. Todd's microfilm but pointed me toward the best boxes of photographs in the Yale archive, many of which appear in this book. I still think it mighty cool that the first time I shook Julie's hand was on the front porch of Mrs. Todd's Camp Mavooshen just about the time her book, *After Emily: Two Remarkable Women and the Legacy of America's Greatest Poet,* had been accepted for publication by W.W. Norton.

Hugs to Shannon Wood and Sabrina Winchell for offering their summer rental at Lake Cumberland as a winter writing retreat; to Betsy Cadbury, Art Borror, and Jim and Betsy Hughes for early encouragement; to the Auduboners who put up with my interviews: Bart and Ginny Cadbury, Carl W. Buchheister, Joe Johansen, Doug and Elsie Morse, Duryea and Peggy Morton, Juanita Roushdy, Seth

Benz, Pete Salmansohn, Mary Carol Massinneau, Prentice Stout, Roland Clement, and of course, Steve Kress. Special appreciation to Chris Speh for his written recollection of 1950s summer life at the Osprey cabin and to Dr. Robert Parke for his shared story of actually sleeping in Emily's bedroom as a boy. Amazing but true.[4] Thanks, too, to the Dayton Audubon Society for my original Hog Island scholarship and to Wright State University's Masters of Humanities program for the opportunity to go where no historian had yet gone. Kudos to the guys in my writers' group: Jim Hughes, Andy Bergeron, and David Dominic, with special thanks to David for clearing the way for access to Yale's microfilm. I truly can't thank the brave souls enough who agreed to critique drafts: the aforementioned Polly Longsworth, Julie Dobrow, Steve Kress, Scott Weidensaul, Frank Graham Jr., Art Borror, Betsy Cadbury, Juanita Roushdy, Ted Gilman, and Jim and Betsy Hughes, along with Phyllis Kittel, David Klinger, Paul Knoop Jr., David Dominic, and Cecile Cary. Special thanks to Scott Weidensaul, too, for offering valuable guidance and suggestions that culminated in the first edition publication of *Nature's People*. And how can I say thanks warmly enough to my wife, Cindy Lou Cooke, for her support and for putting up with me for all the years it has taken to give life to this amazing narrative?

I am pleased to bring Mrs. Todd's and Hog Island's story to you. It is one worth knowing. It is one worth retelling.

— Tom Schaefer
Dayton, Ohio
Winter 2023

Introduction Notes

[1] Encouraging local chapters to employ new technology in promoting the Audubon Cause, *Audubon* magazine covered a handful of activists, including this author, using nascent cable television to spread the word. See Leslie B. Ware's article in the January 1986 *Audubon*, "Grassroots Television" (114–17).

[2] The first Hog Island artist-in-residence in 2014 was Rebecca Gillman, a Pulitzer Prize finalist who devoted her time there to *Woman of the World*, a one-woman play about Mabel Loomis Todd set on Hog Island, which premiered in New York City in 2019 with Kathleen Chalfant as Mrs. Todd. For more on the Hog Island artist-in-residence program, see: https://hogisland.audubon.org/programs/artist-residency-information.

[3] Some original poetry and photographs made their way through the island muses, as well, and were self-published in a little collection I called *A forest of ferns: Reflections on Hog Island*.

[4] Rob Parke, a church friend, explained how his great-grandparents purchased the Dickinson homestead in 1916. His grandmother was, in fact, the owner who would open up Emily's home on occasion for a Dickinson pilgrim who came knocking on the door. Rob's father, Rev. John Parke, was raised in the house and assigned Emily's bedroom as his own. As a child, Rob spent time there as well. The Parke family sold the homestead to Amherst College in the mid-1960s. The structure today houses the Emily Dickinson Museum.

CHAPTER 1

Of Nature & Dickinsons

Several of nature's people
I know, and they know me;
I feel for them a transport
Of cordiality...

—Emily Dickinson
from *Poems: Second Series* / 1891

Before the United States came of age and gave birth to transcendentalism, that uniquely American take on German and British romanticism that Ralph Waldo Emerson liked to say was the first truly American way of seeing the universe, the idea of *wilderness* was not a particularly warm and welcoming one. When explorers and colonists alike made landfall after spending weeks or months negotiating the treacherous and fickle north Atlantic in their surprisingly small ships, the seemingly endless expanse of North American forest they encountered manifested itself as anything but friendly. It was dark and populated by not only wild animals that went bump in the night, but increasingly hostile interactions with native peoples who were beginning to get the picture that the new kids in the neighborhood did not understand the concept of sharing.

Eventually, of course, the heart of the wilderness darkness retreated with the brutal diminishment of Native Americans, the subsequent clearing of trees and the planting of colonial farms and villages. Before long the idea of American wilderness meant Maine, western Virginia and New York, then the old Northwest Territory, followed by the Midwest's verdant prairie, the mountains and deserts of the far West, and finally, the wildness of Alaska. The Eastern wilderness had evolved from impenetrable forests with lakes and rivers teeming with fur-bearing critters into the raw materials that meant commercial success and prosperity for colonists, settlers, and their financial supporters.

Pockets of primary growth forests and undeveloped tracts of Eastern wilderness survived, however, providing touchstones for transcendentalists like Emerson and his protege Henry David Thoreau, who saw beyond the mere utility of raw materials into a universe where people and nature shared an inherent goodness. Emerson encouraged a thinking population to reach for "an original relation to the universe" that would sing with its own "poetry and philosophy of insight and not of tradition."[1] Nature was the primary medium through which this universal insight and wisdom could be realized, as was articulated by Emerson in his seminal work, the essay "Nature."

It was upon this world of nature awareness that Mabel Loomis Todd was weaned. Her transcendental roots began in her youth, spending her earliest summers in Concord, Massachusetts, where her grandfather, the Rev. John Wilder, was minister of the Trinitarian church attended by the Thoreau family. Upon Wilder's untimely death in 1844, the congregation embraced the new widow, Mary Wales Fobes Wilder, and her children as family of their own. Granddaughter Mabel wrote that when she arrived on the Concord scene years later, "I was adopted in the same affectionate way, and not told for years afterward" that the Thoreaus were, in fact, not blood relatives. Her affection for the Thoreaus and the depth of their relationship with her own grandparents and parents were commemorated in a pamphlet authored by Mabel Loomis Todd and published posthumously by the Thoreau Society in 1958.[2]

Given the loss of the family's income, however, Mabel Todd's mother, Mary Alden Wilder (known in the family as Molly), was one of three siblings hustled off to Cambridge, where their mother successfully ran a boarding house to keep the family afloat. At that time in Boston, the *American Ephemeris and Nautical Almanac*, a new endeavor attached to the Department of the Navy, was beginning publication. The almanac employed mathematicians to calculate information necessary for astronomers, surveyors, and navigators.[3] Among those human "computers," as they were known, were Molly's brother, John Wilder, and New York state transplant Nathan Loomis, and his son, Eben Jenks Loomis. Millicent wrote of those early Boston days when her grandfather took up residence in the Wilder boarding house, "Eben Loomis met the Wilders, and it was not long before he became part of the household." He and John became close friends and in July 1853, Eben and Molly were wed. They spent some of their first summer as husband and wife in Concord at the Thoreau home.

Molly Loomis was trained well in the domestic arts, excelled at embroidery, and was always concerned about the family budget. She adored her only child, Mabel, who would come to disdain housework but embrace her mother's love of fabric. Mabel assessed her mother's temperament as "tumultuous, volcanic, enthusiastic, appreciative, happy, disappointed, prejudicial, intense, and affectionate."[4] It was not those qualities that planted and sustained young Mabel's growing affection for nature. They came from her father.

Eben Jenks Loomis was born in 1828 in Morris, New York, and moved to Fairfax, Virginia, as a child. At age twenty-three, he followed his father to Boston and after taking a mathematics course at Harvard's Lawrence Scientific School, was hired as an assistant at the almanac office. In addition to studying math, Eben attended engaging lectures at the Lawrence School given by the likes of natural history giants Louis Agassiz and Asa Gray. In a letter to Mabel, Molly Loomis wrote, "Your father from a little child had an exquisite literary taste & love for nature & poetry, and not finding the *least* congeniality among his family, spent hours, alone, and made nature take the place of loved ones. To such a degree that he became an expert ornithologist and with a *few best* books such as Shakespeare, and the best poets, became a *critical scholar!*"[5] In truth, Eben Loomis was merely a common clerk with an avocation for nature and the classics, but that did not dissuade his daughter from addressing him in correspondence as "Professor Eben J. Loomis." Mabel loved her father. Growing up, she depended on his love, wisdom, and temperate guidance in ways she would later find in Emily Dickinson's brother, Austin.[6]

After the Civil War, Eben Jenks Loomis took a financial risk by investing almost all the family funds that Molly could muster in an agricultural concern in Florida. Within the year, all had been lost and he was back in Boston penniless, unable to find work. The *Nautical Almanac* office had in the meantime moved to Washington, and Eben had little choice but to take up work there again. Molly Loomis was not happy. She had little interest in raising her beloved daughter in a hot Southern city, still with dirt streets and poor sanitation. When the family did eventually regroup in Washington one year later, Molly took the opportunity every summer thereafter to escape with her mother and daughter to cooler and hopefully healthier northern climes. Some summers saw the women trek beyond Boston and Concord as far north as New Hampshire and the Maine coast, where they boarded until fall with willing farmers or fishermen. Eben stayed home to work and swelter in the heat, looking forward to annual autumn breaks when he could travel solo into the natural world he so loved.

Nature was of utmost importance to Mabel Loomis from her early years in Boston, through her formative years in Washington and those summer junkets to cooler places and eventually to the life she enjoyed in her adopted hometown of Amherst, Massachusetts. Walks with her father, whom she adored, always included bird identification and botanizing. Further evidence of her penchant for nature is found in her portfolio of oil, watercolor, and fabric paintings; her personal and public writing professing the divine in the natural, and three purchases of land she and her husband later made within their modest means.

David Peck Todd, soon to be Mabel Loomis's lifelong spouse, came into her life as a Washington neighbor in 1878. Born onto a five-hundred-acre tract of heavy woodland near Lake Ridge, New York, on March 19, 1855, David Todd's family traced ancestral connections to colonial preacher and theologian Jonathan Edwards. His father, Sereno Edwards Todd, was "a writer of note" who published a variety of works focused on economic and modern scientific farming practices.[7] His mother, Rhoda Peck Todd, hailed from a family of farmers near Greenwich, Connecticut, who relocated to Lake Ridge when she was a girl. David's parents married in 1844 and moved their family to Brooklyn when he was still a child.

At age fifteen, David entered Columbia College, where he had important personal decisions to make. What career field would it be: arts or sciences? He trained himself to maintain manual pump organs and over time became quite a player in his own right. Would he take up the study of the organ or another of his personal loves, observation of the night sky? Because of Todd's expertise in many things mechanical, Thomas Alva Edison, himself at the beginning of a career that would lead to his storied Menlo Park laboratory, offered him a job experimenting and engineering solutions to mechanical problems. Coming to understand that his greatest interest lay in the heavens, David Todd turned down Edison to pursue a self-directed career blending the arts of mechanics and photography with the science of astronomy.[8] And it surprised few who knew him that, because Columbia did not yet have a telescope with which he could make real-time observations, he built his own. Two years later, at the urging of his uncle, Todd transferred to Amherst College, where he would go on to use the school's 7.25-inch Clark refractor telescope for his study of the night sky, but especially the moons of Jupiter and the 1874 transit of Venus across the face of the sun.[9] David Peck Todd acquired both his baccalaureate and master's degrees from Amherst while being awarded an honorary Ph.D. from Washington and Jefferson College in 1888 following his successful direction of many important astronomical expeditions.[10]

By the time Todd completed his undergraduate work at Amherst in 1875, he had already made significant waves in the astronomy community through his published observations of the eclipses of Jupiter's moons.[11] One who noticed was Simon Newcomb, head of the US Naval Observatory in Washington, DC, who offered the young astronomer a temporary post there the summer following Todd's graduation. When Newcomb moved to the *American Ephemeris and Nautical Almanac* in 1878, Todd followed him as his chief computing and printing assistant.

At that time, the Naval Observatory was the place the country relied on to keep the nation's time straight in an era when such a significant public task was still largely a local chore. Exact local time, if anyone cared, varied from place to place. Time zones were not established in the United States until Congress enacted them at the behest of the railroad industry in 1883, making rail service more efficient. That plan divided the nation into the four standard time zones recognized today in the contiguous forty-eight states, whose boundaries still bear odd skirting around urban areas for purposes of commerce. There were different proposals for the determination of what time zones should look like in the United States, so one can imagine spirited discussions at the Naval Observatory as options were argued. David Todd, to be sure, was a proponent of precise clock tending. Near the end of his career he would get credit in the history of timekeeping for establishing standard time in Peru.

The late nineteenth century was an exciting time for astronomy. Modern observatories combined with the advent of photography made the field ripe for innovation, which was right up David Todd's technical alley. In the summer of 1878, the same year he moved with Newcomb to the *Almanac*, Todd not only earned his master's degree but was given charge of an expedition to Texas to observe a July 29 solar eclipse. It was there that he began developing the idea of a synchronized photographic apparatus to record the sun's corona at totality using multiple cameras. The glass plate images would permit coronal study like never before. This 1878 Texas trip would be the first of nineteen astronomical expeditions Todd participated in, most often as the expedition director.

Upon his arrival in Washington, Todd resided for a time at the Newcomb home, which was directly across the street from the boarding house engaged by Eben Jenks Loomis and family. David's first memory of Mabel, however, was of him spying on her on the steps of the *Almanac* offices wearing an old blue waterproof on a rainy workday talking with her father, one of his colleagues. David would make his first formal call across the street in November 1877.

By that time, Mabel had graduated from the Georgetown Female Seminary in Washington with the hope of continuing her studies in music. Her parents were able to afford some semesters for her pursuit in the arts, but budget limitations put a disappointing early end to those studies. Regarding relationships with young men, however, Mabel experienced no such disappointments. By her early twenties, she was well aware of her charms and their effects on people, especially gentlemen callers. While her mother and father voiced concerns about the motives and prospects of most, David Todd seemed to fit all the Wilder women's criteria. He was not only educated with good earning potential but handsome, charming, and articulate.[12] And while clean-shaven at the time, by summer 1878, his tonsorial practice changed with the addition of a mustache and beard, some version of which he groomed for the next forty years.[13]

Both Mabel Loomis and David Todd had had some experience in relationships that could have culminated in marriage, but nothing as serious as this new bond. When Mabel traveled north in late spring 1878, as she always had, she thought her absence a strong test of their relationship. As David directed the eclipse expedition to Texas that summer, nearly one hundred letters passed between them. Both were pleased, as well, with the advancement of David's career. The two were married in a small ceremony on March 5, 1879, in the Washington boardinghouse the Loomises called home. The couple's only child, Millicent, came along the following February.

In 1881, Amherst College President Julius Seelye offered David Todd a position as director of the college's observatory, an exciting career advance for a proud alum. What interested Todd most about this opportunity was the promise of a new observatory with upgraded optics, compared with the device on which he had honed his skills as an undergraduate. Over time, however, the expected financial gift failed to materialize. It became a point of decades-long irritation to him that it took until 1904 for the new building to be constructed using funds procured primarily by the astronomer himself.[14]

Nevertheless, when David Peck Todd triumphantly returned to Amherst, a small central Massachusetts college town steeped in New England civility, he brought with him his spirited twenty-four-year-old wife "full of ambition, and fresh from a vibrant, social girlhood" who "brought zest and color to the quiet elegance [of Amherst], and soon became a leading figure in many branches of the town's activity." From her initial wariness about making a life far from an active urban cultural center, Mabel Todd quickly warmed up to the town. Just two months after her arrival, she wrote in her journal, "Do you know, I think Amherst is in many respects quite ideal. I always did like a college town, with its air of cultivation." Before Mabel Loomis Todd's long run in Amherst was over, she would perform in local theater, serve as a church soloist, give music and painting lessons, help found the local chapter of the Daughters of the American Revolution, and saw the Amherst Woman's Club well on its way. Dickinson biographer Richard B. Sewall concluded, "Mrs. Todd made an immediate impression on Amherst, as did Amherst on her."[15]

To make adjustments easier for the new faculty couple, their two-year-old daughter Millicent stayed behind for a time in Washington with grandparents while Mabel and David made their first Amherst home in a simple boarding house, not unlike the ones in which she had grown up. And to her continued surprise, she found that "living in the country, amid the luxuriance of nature, and yet of having refined & educated society at the same time" suited her tastes better than anticipated. Her enthusiasm for her new life was enhanced by her being "taken in" right away by the college community, who she reported invited her "constantly ... for weeks."[16] But when the college treasurer and his wife stopped by for a welcoming visit to the residence of the new astronomer and his spouse, complicated relationships began that would impact all parties involved forever.

The home of that college treasurer, William Austin Dickinson, was known throughout the town as a lively hub for the arts. The musical performances, literary readings, and soirees held at that home, known in town as the Evergreens, were orchestrated by his wife, Susan, and provided just the kind of stimulation Mabel Todd craved.[17] As a regular guest at the house, Mabel not only performed but "put herself forward with a vivacious charm that enabled her to attract the attention of the gathering in any room she entered."[18] In a very short time Susan's Evergreens became the center of Mabel's universe. By mid-October, Mabel wrote that Susan "appreciates me completely, and I love and admire her equally. She is a rare woman, and her home is my haven of pleasure in Amherst."[19] The women came to realize how much they had in common.

Both had come from modest families, had similar tastes in literature, and aspired to ascend socially through the arts. Along the way, Susan shared some poetry sent to her by Austin's sister, Emily, a secretive soul who lived next door with the other Dickinson sibling, Lavinia. Though the poetry was unusual by contemporary standards, both women recognized in much of the verse a unique power and genius.

With all of her gifts and abounding energy, Mabel Todd made an immediate impact that rippled through the Dickinson family. One of the first to feel it was the oldest Dickinson son, Edward, known to the family as Ned. Five years Mabel's junior, the young man was smitten by her early on. He showed his enthusiasm by eagerly serving as her escort whenever possible. His mother encouraged the interaction, hoping Mrs. Todd might help Ned develop important social skills. Mabel did indeed embrace the attention at first, welcoming the charming and chivalrous Ned in an innocent way. Only twenty-five years old, she was used to suitors and loved attention. But by mid-winter she became concerned when Ned's calling became a daily occurrence. Upon reflection she allowed that she should have seen it coming, but life was good and she in truth was devoted to David. "I love him better every day," she wrote. "I have made the perfect marriage."[20]

Over that first year in Amherst Ned wasn't the only Dickinson male to take notice of young Mrs. Todd. The father of the household, Austin, often a reticent attendee of social gatherings, took an interest in her as well, walking her home from Evergreen soirees on occasion, and if the family and friends took off on a carriage ride through the country, insisting she sit next to him. She rejoiced in finding he cared as deeply as she did about nature. He was "someone who loved the landscape, welcomed all weather, and was genuinely stirred by the chirping of August crickets."[21]

But besides serving as a mecca for the arts, the Evergreens was also port in a maelstrom of squabbles that plagued the Dickinson family. Just a short time after coming to town, Mabel Todd had already seen and heard enough about them to write they were "a family quarrel of endless convolutions." Sometime later she wrote that Lavinia and Susan "hate each other black and blue," perhaps because of Lavinia's perception of Susan's treatment of Emily.[22] Mabel would later hear from a confiding Austin that from the time he and Susan courted, he had felt trapped in the relationship. He confessed that on his wedding day he felt as if he "were going to his own execution."[23]

Emily Dickinson and Susan Gilbert had been childhood friends, and at the time of Susan's engagement to Austin, with both in their twenties, all seemed acceptable. Over the years they had exchanged much correspondence and now and again Emily would send along an original poem.[24] But by Susan and Austin's wedding the two friends had become estranged over some kind of quarrel, apparently not their first. In any case, as family loyalties calcified in this "war between the houses," it would be Susan and the Dickinson children, most notably the two oldest, Ned and Martha, set against Austin and his loyal sisters, Emily and Lavinia, and eventually, Mabel Loomis Todd. As life at the Evergreens soured for Austin, he spent so much time talking with his sisters that Emily observed, "My Brother is with us so often each Day, we almost forget that he ever passed to a wedded Home."[25] Regarding his wife, Emily wrote, "Sue—you can go or stay—There is but one alternative—We differ often lately, and this must be the last. You need not fear to leave me lest I should be alone, for I often part with things I fancy I have loved."[26] Though there would be moments of recovery, as when the family grieved the untimely death of Austin and Susan's youngest child, Gilbert, the rift between the once–best friends never healed.

On September 11, 1882, Austin came by the boardinghouse to escort Mabel to a gathering at the Evergreens. When they reached his home, instead of going in, they walked on down Main Street engrossed in a conversation of a much more personal nature. Of that night they both recorded the word "Rubicon" in personal correspondence, recognizing it as their "going by the gate," the formal beginning of a love affair of complete intimacy they would both grapple with and cherish for the next thirteen years. They went on to record their affection in an archive of clandestine letters sent back and forth between them, celebrating their love as "of the ages" and on par with the likes of Antony and Cleopatra. As Mabel wrote years later, "No love story approaches it."[27]

Susan was aware of her husband's initial interest in Mabel Todd and didn't seem to mind, thinking perhaps he was at "a kind of dead center in his life" and could use some "sprucing up."[28] She also encouraged Ned to escort or partner with Mrs. Todd whenever possible, unaware of the degree of his growing infatuation. Susan Dickinson saw Mabel Todd as an accomplished young artist and thought her relationship with her family was energizing. Mabel continued to be welcome in her home, and it was on a February afternoon in 1882 when Susan first shared with her poems written by her reclusive sister-in-law. It was Mabel's first exposure to the verse she would in time come to know so well and bring forward to an appreciative and enthusiastic public.

Before long the chivalrous yet flirtatious son, Ned, sensed something going on between his father and Mrs. Todd and told his mother so. The ensuing confrontation did not go well, but Austin was an important man in town, and the Dickinsons did everything possible to keep the affair secret. Whatever the neighbors saw or surmised, they kept to themselves, except when Mabel was given the cold shoulder by judgmental townsfolk.

Such was not the case next door at the Dickinson homestead. Mabel and Austin met there secretly countless times. Lavinia and Emily were aware of their brother's effort to find happiness in an otherwise dreary home life and were happy he had found at least a modicum of it with Mrs. Todd. Still, the stress between the two Dickinson houses brought on by the affair and other slights grew into a "loaded gun" ready to cause generational damage, which it eventually did.

The night before their "Rubicon" walk, Austin and Lavinia invited Mabel to the Dickinson homestead to play piano and sing for their bedridden mother and hermitic sister. Based on what she had learned about Emily from the poet's two siblings, and had experienced in prior performances there, Mabel expected Emily would not come out to meet her but instead sit by herself on the stairs, "hearing every word," then follow the performance with sending out a glass of sherry and a small present or poem in appreciation. She did that night, as well.

In describing the odd Dickinson sister in a letter to her parents not long after arriving in Amherst, Mabel wrote, "I must tell you about the *character* of Amherst. It is a lady whom the people call the *Myth*. She is the sister of Mr. Dickinson and seems to be the climax of all the family oddity." Mabel was already aware at that early date of the whispered stories around town that Emily dressed "wholly in white" and wrote "finely, but no one *ever* sees her." Scuttlebutt was that Emily had not been "outside of her own house in fifteen years, except once to see a new church, when she crept out at night and viewed it by moonlight." She continued in the same letter to say, "No one who calls upon her mother and sister ever see her, but she allows little children once in a great while and one at a time, to come in, when she gives them cake or candy, or some nicety, for she is very fond of little ones. But more often she lets down the sweetmeat by a string, out of a window, to them." She concluded, "Isn't that just like a book? So interesting."[29]

Though Mabel went on to perform on occasion at the homestead at Emily's request, the reclusive resident never came forth to greet her. Mabel wrote, "She wanted me to come and sing to her, but she would not see me."[30] The two never met face to face. Still, there is a record of correspondence that gives some insight into the nature of their relationship. Mabel's notes and letters to Emily, as well as all others, were destroyed by Lavinia per the poet's request upon her death in 1886. Emily's correspondence to others, however, was collected and published, though much has been lost.[31]

Perhaps a reflection of her own reticence to be with people, yet a hope that things might flower at a later date, Emily's first note to Mabel came in the autumn of 1881, just weeks after David had taken his position on the faculty and, it would appear, following an early performance by Mabel at the homestead. "The parting of those that never met, shall it be delusion, or rather, an unfolding snare whose fruitage is later?"[32] Not long after, Mabel responded to Emily by sending her an original watercolor of an Indian pipe, a ghostly white wildflower. The poet replied quickly and enthusiastically in a note, writing that it was one of her favorite plants. "That without suspecting it you should send me the preferred flower of life, seems almost supernatural, and the sweet glee I felt at meeting it, I could confide to none." Dickinson's letter continued with a personal self-reflection that readers of her poetry would later find so engaging. "I still cherish the clutch with which I bore it from the ground when a wondering Child, an unearthly booty, and maturity only enhances mystery, never decreases it." And though Mabel never met Emily personally, it is clear her young daughter did. In the closing line of that letter, Dickinson responded to little Millicent in a way that was surely endearing to her mother. "I trust you are well, and the quaint little Girl with the deep Eyes, every day more fathomless."[33]

The scope of Emily Dickinson's correspondence to Mabel Todd spans eleven documents, with another six addressed to Mabel's parents in Washington, one of those composed following a Loomis trip to Amherst for a fall 1884 family visit. Emily wrote Mabel's parents, "The atmospheric acquaintance so recently and delightfully made, is not, I trust, ephemeral, but absolute as Ether." Apparently the Loomises had sent along some small gift, to which Emily replied, "Thank you for the Beauty—Thank you too for Boundlessness— that rarely given, but choicest Gift. To 'know in whom' we 'have believed,' is Immortality."[34]

The first Dickinson poem Mabel Todd received came not long after the September 1882, pre-"Rubicon" performance. "Dear friend," Emily wrote, "I cannot make an Indian Pipe but please accept a Humming Bird.

> A Route of Evanescence
> With a revolving Wheel —
> A Resonance of Emerald —
> A Rush of Cochineal,
> And every Blossom on the Bush
> Adjusts its tumbled Head —

> The Mail from Tunis probably,
> An easy Morning's Ride —
> E. Dickinson"[35]

Most of the correspondence from Emily Dickinson to Mabel Todd included a verse or lines of prose that could be taken as poetry. Though most were addressed to "Friend," two were addressed to "Brother & Sister's dear friend," a greeting that indicates familiarity, but not a particular personal closeness. Indeed, though Emily and Mabel never met physically, they had some modicum of a relationship, one that was not only reflected in Emily's correspondence, but anchored in a shared love for the well-being of the current family patriarch, Austin Dickinson. Much of what Mabel Loomis Todd would come to know about Emily came to her through conversations with Austin.

Fall 1882 proved a fateful season for the Dickinsons and the Todds. Surely "Rubicon" on September 11 would forever be remembered by Austin and Mabel as the beginning of a love that could only have been ordained in heaven. By mid-October, Susan and daughter Martha packed off to Grand Rapids, Michigan, for a family wedding. Austin stayed home. And about that same time David Todd packed up for Mount Hamilton, California, where he would photograph the Transit of Venus on December 6. Time unencumbered by family gave Austin and Mabel the space they needed to deepen their bond. Much later, Millicent Todd Bingham confided in Richard Sewall that her father conceded, "I never should have left her."[36]

Throughout the following winter, Mabel and Austin authored a flurry of correspondence reinforcing their love. In December she wrote, "You reached out your hand without knowing it, almost—in the darkness—and you met another—warm and tender. You clasped it—knowing it was your fate.... Good night, beloved. Love me. Love me every minute, and think of me. The stars are shining brilliantly. I see many bright things for us in the future."[37] Sweetness in tone and a hope for a future together flowed from the older gentleman, as well. On one occasion, Austin wrote, "Remember my dearie darling that I love you, love you and that I am going to fly through eternity with you tacked close under my wing."[38] Both quickly realized notes and letters like this, if found, could have dire family consequences. Mabel encouraged Austin to burn the letters she sent. He did, but only after recopying them in his own hand, placing them in an envelope, then passing them along to Lavinia with a note that said, "Vin—If anything happens to me, burn this package at once—without opening. Do this as you love me."[39] Dickinson historians are pleased Lavinia never followed through with her brother's demand.

By the time David Todd returned from California, a chill had permeated the Todd-Dickinson relationships. Mabel had, indeed, made it clear to Ned that his romantic interest was out of line and would not be reciprocated. She hoped they could remain friends, but her pronouncement left him feeling angry and jilted. Ned accused her of caring more for his father than himself, which was the truth. Ned talked with his mother about Mrs. Todd's prurient interests and accused Mabel of being a flirt. When Susan heard that news, she defended her beloved Ned and became jealous herself. Mabel and Susan would come to have a long conversation, including words about Mabel's relationship with Austin. "Sue had always known that her husband was fond of me and was very glad," Mabel journaled about the event, though she gives no indication there was any discussion of anything beyond a general friendship. When all was said and done, Mabel felt the meeting was "conducted with fairness (in general) on both sides."[40] Mabel would continue to be invited to some gatherings at the Dickinsons over the next few years, but the old cordial, frank relationship shared between the women never rekindled. It would be another decade before enough fire passed between them that the two considered each other unforgivable.

A few words are needed here about David Todd and little Millicent. Were they aware, as time went on, of Mabel's developing entanglement—her affair—with Mr. Dickinson? Records indicate that, yes, indeed, all were aware, including Millicent's live-in nanny, Grandma Wilder. The little girl was afraid of the hard-faced Mr. Dickinson and was witness to many a closed door. She had a hard time understanding why neighbors treated her and her mother so curtly. Only later in life did she learn that when she heard her father whistling a special song coming home from the observatory at night, it was a signal to Mabel and Austin that he was coming. Later, in her own thorough treatment of the Dickinson family biography, Millicent Todd Bingham, who had never approved of the affair, only hinted at her mother's involvement with Austin Dickinson. It would take other Dickinson biographers to reveal the depth and scope of what little Millie had witnessed firsthand.

David Todd found himself in a personal and professional pickle with Austin Dickinson as his boss and his wife as his boss's not-so-secret lover. Very aware of Austin's influence on campus, David nonetheless respected him and was delighted and flattered by the frequent visits. In time, David recognized Austin as one of his dearest friends. "I loved him more than any man I ever knew," David wrote.[41] The two men shared such a deep affection for Mabel that in the summer of 1885, while she was off traveling in Europe, Austin went so far as to propose to David a *menage a trois* where *all* would be shared. Though such a fantasy was never recorded, the three of them still enjoyed time together on local outings, theater road trips to Boston, occasional meetings in New York, and even as late as 1893, a trip to the Chicago World's Fair.[42] The real bottom line for David was that he loved his wife dearly and wanted her to have what she needed to be happy. If that meant sharing her with Austin Dickinson, so be it. He had come to realize how deeply his wife was involved, and he made up his mind to live with it.

Another factor in this true-life version of a Victorian soap opera was David Peck Todd's proclivity to fall in love. He truly loved his wife and was devoted to her happiness, but there were many others. Mabel once wrote that David was her "sweetly unmoral child." He would discover a new, interesting woman and find nothing the least bit wrong with starting up a sexual relationship with her, then come home and share some details with his wife. Mabel wrote in 1911, "I really believe he thinks I am as much interested in [a new love] as he is. He always expects me to like the person because he does, but *sometimes* I cannot enter in."[43] She complained to him that his occasional "low tastes" disappointed and somehow "contaminated" her. This was not an idle concern. David would go on to contract syphilis long before the miracle of penicillin was developed. He was relieved of his teaching duties as paralytic dementia overtook him and was institutionalized by 1920. Still, he helped direct the imaging of a solar eclipse from an airplane in 1924, so all apparently was not lost. Mabel wrote of visiting her "sweet David" hoping all was better, but then witnessing an unprovoked manic behavior bout that would keep him hospitalized until his death in 1939.

As for herself, Mabel Loomis Todd thought she could love "two men at once, though each in a different way." She never seemed to dwell in her writing about the social mores she and Austin broke but expounded more on how beautiful her life was with him in it. "Nothing stirs me from him [Austin], or alters my conviction for one moment that he is my absolute mate for all eternity. My dear David gives me all he has, but Austin's is a kind of love which David does not know." She continued, "The situation is certainly most exceptional. I understand it, and I appreciate both my dear men. I know what one is, I know what the other is, and two entirely separate sides of my nature go to them."[44] In their heart of hearts their only hope was that each would outlive their partners. David and Susan never gave them that satisfaction.

The next significant milestones in the Dickinson drama occurred, first in 1883 with the death of Austin and Susan's seven-year-old son Gilbert, known as Gib, and following in 1886 with the passing of his sister Emily. Gilbert was dear to Austin and perhaps the only one of his children who didn't side with their mother in holding deep-seated resentments against him. When Gib died, Austin took it hard, driving him ever deeper into the comforting arms of Mabel. Then with the passing of Emily and the discovery of her unknown cache of more than 1,500 poems, the ensuing interactions in the family became testy and passionately difficult.[45] Perhaps the most far-reaching skirmish of the "war between the houses" was about to ignite in earnest.

Lavinia Dickinson picked up the gauntlet of determining what to do with the mass of her sister's poetry, and loving Emily's memory dearly, she would not rest until she found a viable resolution. She concluded that publication must be the answer but did not know who had the tenacity and drive to sort through not only the seemingly completed poems but also the enormous number of verses scratched out on envelopes and paper scraps. Whereas Lavinia saw the task as merely *recopying* Emily's text, the fragments, changing handwriting, and various versions of some poems made the task much more of a grind than Vinnie seemed to understand.

The first choice for editor was the single person in Emily's life who had probably received the most letters and verse, her old best friend and sister-in-law Susan. But Susan's prolonged inaction drove Vinnie wild. At last, concluding that money was too tight and that they would never sell anyway, Susan decided nothing should be done with the poetry. Austin didn't understand the scope or importance of his sister's work and did not appear to care much one way or the other.

Realizing Susan was finally out, and possibly right, Lavinia turned to her second choice, Thomas Wentworth Higginson, the abolitionist writer who engaged in occasional correspondence with and actually visited Emily once. But he, too, was wary of the poetry and unwilling to take on the portfolio of verse. Which led Lavinia to her final alternative, a woman whom she knew recognized special qualities in Emily's poetry: Mabel Todd. Vinnie told Mabel she was sure Emily's friend Higginson would write a preface, "and somebody would be willing to publish them, and the desire of her heart would be accomplished."[46] Mabel could have said no. She was plenty busy with her own art and literary affairs, teaching and giving lessons, as well as participating in various Amherst community activities. She and David at the time were actively preparing for their first epic sailing adventure to Japan to photograph a solar eclipse. In addition, she was fully aware that her efforts on the part of the Dickinsons would raise the level of antagonism with Susan a few notches. But she said yes, and the literary world and lovers of poetry everywhere are forever grateful.

Over the following months, Lavinia encouraged Mabel to hurry on and get the poems in shape, partly because of her fear that if too many of their old friends died, there would be "no one left to welcome" the publication. When Mabel got a closer look at the collection, she assessed the heap of work as "appalling." The apparently completed poems, some sewn together in packets, were one thing, but the myriad fragments made it especially hard for her to know how to proceed.

Mabel decided to put poems she perceived to have popular appeal into an "A" stack while placing others in "B" and "C" categories. Higginson did, in fact, agree to help with publication and was "much impressed" with both the poems selected and Mrs. Todd's process. Though he was unsure of the poetry at first, he became more of a fan upon hearing Mabel's reading them aloud. He demoted some while promoting others into the collection and made additional editorial changes, some of which Mabel overrode. Against her better judgment, Higginson won the argument to place titles on all the poems. By late 1889, the first collection of Emily Dickinson's poetry, complete with a preface by established author Thomas Wentworth Higginson and a cover image of an Indian pipe by Mabel Loomis Todd, was ready to find a publisher.[47]

Higginson hoped Houghton Mifflin, a publisher with whom he had a relationship, would accept the manuscript of poems, but they declined. Instead, it was Roberts Brothers of Boston who embraced the Higginson gravitas and agreed to give the poems a try, though not everyone at the publishing house was sold on the idea. Mabel tried to upgrade the collection before publication by sending in a few more poems, but Thomas Niles, their prime contact at Roberts Brothers, did nothing to include them, aggravating both Mabel and Lavinia. He wrote to Mabel, "It has always seemed to me that it would be unwise to perpetuate Miss Dickinson's poems. They are quite as remarkable for defects as for beauties and are generally devoid of true poetical qualities."[48]

Nonetheless, *Poems* by Emily Dickinson was published in November 1890, and the rest, it is fair to say, is history. The first collection of 115 poems went through eleven printings in two years. *Poems: Second Series* followed in 1891, running into five editions by 1893, while *Poems: Third Series* appeared in 1896. One reviewer in 1892 wrote, "The world will not rest satisfied till every scrap of her writings, letters as well as literature, has been published."[49] Mabel Todd assisted in that effort by collecting and editing *Letters of Emily Dickinson,* which saw first publication in 1894.

Working intently to determine the mind of Emily Dickinson in both her poetry and letters made an impact on Mabel Loomis Todd. The Amherst that had so thrilled her not ten years before, was now oppressive and almost intolerable, especially when Austin was not around to sustain her. But in Emily's words Mabel recognized a "suffering yet resilient spirit" and "a tumultuous inner life" so in contrast with the apparently placid exterior that had evolved into the popular *Myth* of Amherst. Enriched by the stories told her by Austin, Mabel learned of a different Emily than her neighbors knew. Mabel found a woman who exhibited "a defiance of convention and orthodoxy" that mirrored her own situation with Austin. She came to see Emily's career as "the normal blossoming of a nature introspective to a high degree, whose best thought could not live in pretense." As she worked, a sense of spiritual kinship, however one-sided, grew. Mabel would go on to write, "The poems had a wonderful effect on me, mentally and spiritually. They seemed to open the door into a wider universe than the little sphere surrounding me which so often hurt and compressed me. They helped me nobly through a trying time. Their sadness and hopelessness, sometimes, was so much bitterer than mine that 'I was helped / As if a Kingdom cared.'"[50]

The next and terribly significant watershed in the Dickinson drama came in 1895 with the death of Austin Dickinson.[51] Apparently Mabel Todd was not compensated well for her work with the letters and poems, and in conversation with Austin, had been promised as payment a piece of Dickinson property just across from the homestead known as the Meadow. In their care not to have any correspondence discovered, however, that promise was never documented. Still feeling she had earned what was promised her by Austin, Mabel slipped in a document for Lavinia to sign amid a stack of other documents relating to publication. Lavinia signed. But when Mabel acted to secure title to the property, the "war between the houses" took on a different perspective when Lavinia, with no memory of signing any such thing and with Susan's quiet support, took Mabel to court to prevent the transfer.

The 1898 trial did not go well for Mabel Loomis Todd. Not only was the property transfer denied, but ownership of the entire Emily Dickinson catalog was awarded to descendants. Mabel Todd got nothing except the deep pain caused by her loss of Austin and the retribution of Amherst by having her reputation dragged through the mud in public. The decision left her no legal right to bring the Dickinson material still in her possession into print. Her work with Emily's writing was apparently over.[52]

After the court made its decision, the Emily Dickinson collection of originals primarily resided in three locations: one part at the Evergreens in Sue's possession, another portion at the homestead under Lavinia's jurisdiction, and the third component still with Mabel Todd. In truth, neither Susan nor Lavinia knew exactly what Mabel had, so in response to her rejection by both Dickinson houses, Mabel Todd did not return anything but gathered up what letters and poems she had and locked them away in a camphorwood chest, not to be opened until 1929 when she invited Millicent into the fray to complete the release of the remainder of Emily Dickinson's work.[53] It was not until 1955 that all of the Dickinson poetry would finally be published in a three-volume set, the Thomas Johnson edition completed under the auspices of Harvard University where the Dickinson papers had been gifted for archiving. Millicent Bingham would later come to learn how far Harvard's legal arm could reach when she requested terms for publication of her own treatment of the Emily Dickinson narrative using the sequestered materials her mother never surrendered.

Mabel Todd was disappointed by the court's decision, but in reality the loss was just a temporary setback. The loss of Austin, however, was real and remained poignant to her for the rest of her life. She most often made a note in her daily record each August 16, the anniversary of his passing. Just months after his death she wrote, "Nothing on earth has power to really thrill me any more. One old brown coat and a big hat used to be enough to set every drop of blood in my body tingling and racing through the veins in tumultuous rush.... After fourteen years I thrilled to his coming or his voice or his distant figure just as in the first wonderful months when we were finding out that each was for the other *forever*."[54] Ever headstrong, however, Mabel went on writing and entertaining audiences on repeated lecture tours, discussing topics ranging from her travels to Japan to her insider's view of Emily Dickinson's world.

With a sharper contemporary focus placed on Austin and Mabel's extraordinary relationship, it is easy to overlook or dismiss that Mabel and David Todd were, in fact, a pretty well-made, complementary pair. She wanted to grow and excel as a woman having little to do with domestic chores, which suited David well enough. He sought notoriety by hauling his cameras around the world to photograph celestial phenomena, which was fine with her. They supported each other in professional and practical ways. When he returned from California after having been one of the first to photograph the transit of Venus in 1882, daughter Millicent reported, "Mrs. Todd copied his articles and his observations of the transit for the printer, and thus begins the record of a dual life—of her own activities, literary and artistic, combined with help to my father in his scientific work."[55] David returned the favor, in part, by helping his wife decipher Emily's handwriting and then proofreading letters and poems to confirm accuracy. On a more personal note, Mabel recorded in her diary how much she appreciated David's pampering, being especially fond of his warming her clothes by the winter fire and then dressing her in bed on cold mornings. After that he encouraged her to spend her day doing whatever made her happiest.[56]

Aside from the reverberations of the Dickinson family drama on their lives, both Todds pursued individual careers that grappled with arts and sciences in different yet convergent ways, producing the array of professional accomplishments for which they are noted today. David Todd's claim to fame, as mentioned earlier, came from his blending of astronomy with the nascent technology of photography, inventing equipment that recorded multiple frames of transient celestial events on glass plates. Such events rarely occurred on the Eastern seaboard, so based on calculations made years in advance, he organized and directed more than one dozen expeditions to destinations like Japan, Indonesia, northern

Africa, Russia, and South America. Delicate optics were packed carefully and shipped by boat months prior, then intercepted at the destination by Todd's team and lugged to often remote locations. Living quarters, a commissary, and structures to protect the apparatus from inclement weather were constructed. David made many of the expeditions a family affair by including his wife, daughter, and, on a few, Grandpa Loomis.

In Mabel's case, her personal penchant for the arts, nature, civic responsibility, and her own regular practice of diary and journal writing provided the avenues to her success. She authored multiple articles for *The Century* magazine and *The Atlantic* on topics ranging from the specter of witchcraft in New England to the construction of world-class astronomical observatories. In that time before radio and television, she lectured not only throughout New England but across the country. As a painter, her most impressive public recognition came when, in 1889, noted entomologist Samuel Scudder used her full-color study of the monarch butterfly as the frontispiece of the prospectus for his *Butterflies of the Eastern United States and Canada*.[57]

A transcription of a lecture she gave at the annual meeting of the Connecticut Board of Agriculture in 1902 illustrates, again, her nature-based priorities and prescribes a lesson in civic responsibility. Titled "The Village Beautiful," her talk came at a time of heightening awareness of the new concept of urban planning. While the City Beautiful movement was prompting planners to rethink their responsibility in the "quest for urban beauty," the movement included a key goal of driving home a "middle-class morality and a sense of civic responsibility in the masses."[58] Cities would learn the benefits of attractive building lines and landscape plantings through the leadership of civic-minded people, an idea that came through loud and clear in Mrs. Todd's address.

Though she penciled a note in the margin of her archived copy that the stenographer had done a poor job of transcribing the talk, the report eloquently suggests nature-based civic concepts that were novel at the turn of the twentieth century. She lamented misguided farmers who dumped construction junk and general refuse into picturesque rural dells with no thought for the hosts of wildflowers and ferns that used to thrive there.

Dirt village streets were a target of her concern, as well, being either loose and powdery in the driest months, or too sloppy and muddy during the wettest. Nor was she happy with those who had no interest in preserving roadside trees for their natural aesthetic, or for public officials who built the cheapest structures they could with no consideration given to line, form, or landscape gardening. She punctuated her talk by proposing that what the country needed most was the cultivation of a love of the beautiful. "The public must be educated to the fact that it is worthwhile to preserve these pretty spots," she said. She was sure the observance and understanding of the truly beautiful would teach important values, leading civic leaders to preserve, plant, and design in ways not only best for the community of today but that of tomorrow.

She had a few things to say about summer places, too. Quaint rural settings had become destinations for summer people and others in the well-heeled class who could afford to raise their families away from the cities in which they worked. "Dirt and refuse are allowed to accumulate in [the countryside's] beautiful places, its natural beauties have been dispelled, and the summer transient is fast coming to the conclusion that he does not care to include it in the list of his or her stopping places."[59] In addition, she told how one civic-minded person saved a standing forest from harvest by offering the landowner payment that matched the income he would have received from the cut lumber. "In almost every case they have been perfectly willing to sell," she reported. "In this way he has become possessed of some 1,400 acres of land around that little town, and one immediate result of his patriotic effort is that the town has become famous for its rural beauty.... The land has increased in value and the result is that there is more competition every year for land for summer homes than there ever was before. Land in that place which could have been bought for ten dollars an acre a few years ago is now being sold by the foot to many people for summer cottages."[60]

While Mabel Todd exuded a well-documented spiritual interest in the wonders of nature, she had a more personal reason for calling attention to the beautiful countryside. By the first decade of the twentieth century (it is not clear exactly when), the Todds had purchased a little bit of heaven they affectionately called Fairhaven, a fifty-acre wooded plot with dwelling located on the east shore of the Acushnet River, opposite the old whaling port of New Bedford, Massachusetts. The towns of Fairhaven and New Bedford share a harbor, with whalers going out from both ports when the industry was at its peak in the first quarter of the nineteenth century. Over the years, New Bedford grew into prominence as the commercial whaling center, while Fairhaven complemented the industry as the residence of shipwrights, ship chandlers, rope makers, and sailmakers. Ship owners and ship captains, too, built homes and raised families there. Folks like the Todds made the repurposed Fairhaven a family retreat destination with camping and lodging at their very own place at the shore.

It was a bit of a trek, an all-day trip or longer, to get to Fairhaven from Amherst. First it meant a train to Boston, which never seemed to be a problem, for there were always big-city errands to run. Perhaps there was an overnight. The journey concluded with the last leg of the rail trip down to the shore. The Todds were most often picked up at Fairhaven station by a gentleman recorded only as "Phin," a friend who offered essential transportation to their place, the occasional dinner out, and leisurely evening drives through the Massachusetts coastal countryside.

Though she complained of clouds of mosquitos on occasion and had some trepidation about staying in her little house in the woods by herself, Fairhaven was a treasure for Mabel Todd. Following some structure upgrades, she jotted down in her diary, "Lovely, lovely wood, blue water, & no mosquitoes. It all looks exceedingly well, & is a very livable little house. It is nice to have it done."[61] Having been a boarder in someone else's establishment most of her life, she pondered further that summer, "There is something deliciously satisfying about actually owning land which is truly one's own."[62]

While Mabel Todd left a long and detailed paper trail of much of her life to biographers, she didn't make everything perfectly clear. No detailed written record of hers, neither journal nor diary, says much more about Fairhaven nor the origins of the next significant purchase of recreational land the couple made. Mabel had apparently been in communication with a friend from Boston, Etta H. Glidden, whose family hailed from the Muscongus Bay area around Bremen, Maine, about the purchase of an undeveloped island just off the shore. By the turn of the twentieth century, Maine was viewed more and more as a summer respite from New England heat and was evolving into a regional "vacationland." Mabel, of course, had enjoyed summers in that region in her childhood. Glidden had developed a summer boarding operation on her Martin's Point property and proposed she and the Todds become partners in buying the nearby island with the unusual name of Hog Island. Though the Todds would be primary owners of the undeveloped part of the island, the northern peninsula of Hog held some old commercial structures that just that summer had been upgraded into a resort called The Point Breeze Inn and Bungalows. Terms must have been agreeable because the paperwork was signed in Wiscasset in early July 1908.

Perhaps due to its proximity to Amherst, the Todds continued to retreat to Fairhaven after the Hog Island purchase. In August 1909, just a month after her first visit to the Maine property with her husband and Etta Glidden, Mabel wrote, "I may not get to Fairhaven at all, but I need it very much. The complications of this summer make my head actually snap.... The last two years have nearly annihilated me."[63] Six days after she thought her trip to the shore had slipped off her schedule, she had, in fact, arrived at Fairhaven. Not long after, obviously feeling better, she recorded, "We woke in the dewy morning ... with a lovely view of the sparkling bay. This is an outdoor bedroom indeed, of uttermost charm."[64]

There was something about Hog Island's potential, though, that eclipsed the lure of Fairhaven. One of the last references made to their place on the shores of Buzzard's Bay was in the summer of 1912, when its contents were crated up and shipped to Maine. Just days before setting out for Hog Island, Mabel wrote at Fairhaven about David's "clearing brush & shingles, reconstructing boxes & trunks," and her sorting "things to go back to Amherst, things to Hog Island." She further indicated they may have planned to rent their Massachusetts property out when she wrote about deciding on "things to leave in the house and arrange, & things…to stay but not be used except for us."[65] It is not clear after this point just how the Todds used Fairhaven before it disappeared from Mabel Todd's record-keeping upon its sale in May 1914.[66]

Following the packing up at Fairhaven, the summer of 1912 was a busy one for the Todds on Hog Island. The northbound shipment of furniture and household goods was destined for a barn in Round Pond for a season or two before ferrying at high tide over the Hockomock Narrows to the family campsite that Mabel would affectionately name Camp Mavooshen in honor of a Native American term for the region. Along with the tents they had packed along, the only existing storage or habitation at their preferred island location was in a small wooden shack standing on a granite outcrop near the shore. Traveling that year with her father, Eben Jenks Loomis, and daughter Millicent, the family boarded for one month at the Point Breeze, permitting Eben to entertain the ladies there with his stories and botanical knowledge. The new landowners worked days making their camp livable while thirty-something Millicent blazed a trail down the west side of the island. Meals and evenings were spent in the company of Point Breeze residents.

The little shack by the shore that was the center of the family camp in those early summers had served as cover and sleeping quarters for local clammers and perhaps lumbermen. Before the Todds could call the place home, however, they had to persuade a number of nature's people, large and small, to relocate. After the whole family worked at stuffing cracks in the little building, David set a pan of sulfur aflame inside and everybody stood back as "a squirrel ran out, & then a large rabbit." The next morning when they opened up the building, still "rather strong with sulfur," David continued the improvements by knocking out "sleeping bunks which had been built in it."[67] The newly animal-free, whitewashed building would go on to serve as the camp kitchen for many summers to come and, along with a grove cleared of downed and pruned limbs, was the biggest improvement to the camp during their first couple of summers.

Mabel Todd gets credit for the purchase of one more tract of undeveloped land, though this one had little to do with relaxation and everything to do with the modern concept of conservation. In 1909, one year after President Theodore Roosevelt took the bully pulpit to promote the concept of conservation at the Governor's Conference in Washington, DC, and just a year after purchasing the family share of Hog Island, Mabel Todd found it in her heart and the family's pocketbook to purchase the summit of Mount Orient, a landform known to Amherst locals as Pelham Knob. After observing that summer in her diary that the eighty-seven-acre tract was "a good deal of primitive woodland," she heeded her own civic advice and purchased the land to save the hilltop's trees from "the woodsman's axe and other forms of commercial exploitation" at the cost of about one thousand dollars.[68]

As with Fairhaven, Mabel Todd didn't have much to say in her personal record about Pelham Knob in the years that followed. Millicent did, however, when on the occasion of gifting the tract to Amherst College in 1961, she remembered her mother's "deepest source of happiness was her love of nature, from great trees to the smallest flower of spring." Millicent reminisced how "we used to drive out to the Pelham Knob in the month of May and climb to the place the arbutus grew— *Epigaea repens*, my mother always called it. So, too, did Emily Dickinson. 'Hush,' she exclaimed, 'Epigaea wakens!'"[69] The very small and very lovely trailing arbutus is the state flower of Massachusetts.

Henceforth known as The Mabel Loomis Todd Forest, the Mount Orient hilltop preserve that stayed in the family for over fifty years morphed from being merely a place where nature could be engaged into an environmental laboratory. "Today," Millicent continued in her dedication address, "another wild, wooded area rescued by my mother long ago is assured" to remain a perpetual preserve. "In our country such samples of original natural areas are needed as outdoor laboratories," she said. "This rugged hilltop, the Pelham Knob, ... is an ideal place in which to explore the complex interlocking dependence of all forms of life within the area. For here, undisturbed, plants and animals will be able to live out their natural lives."[70] The Pelham Knob purchase and its subsequent preservation illustrate what can happen when idealists of even modest means act to save unique environments in their natural state, whether to preserve them for the native beauty they contain, or to hold them for extended periods of ecological study.[71] Two such idealists were Mabel Loomis Todd and Millicent Todd Bingham.

In 1910, with land acquisition highlighting the new conservation ethic in the Todd household, Mabel added *A Cycle of Sunsets* to her published portfolio. Set in the Amherst area in the shadow of the Berkshire Mountains, the book is a record of nature observations casually taken at the end of each day for one calendar year, though the year is not specified. Mrs. Todd's ability to conjure words of color that described the changing sky and cloudscape was memorable. At summer solstice she wrote, "Despite a brisk breeze the air seems filled with faint mist, now like powdered gold dust. Everything visible seems fashioned from an impalpable yellow powder, glorious, transfiguring, opulent." She admitted that at times natural beauty escaped the ability of language. "Quite beyond the power of verbal description, I am still tempted to write on and on, hoping that by some turn of expression I may put the translucent picture into words that will at least suggest the strange beauty of this rich world, wealthy tonight beyond commerce."[72]

Along with the imagery of multiple sunsets, the text is spiced with descriptions of "nature's people" like hummingbirds, butterflies, daisies, and tree toads. She gives almanac reports ("For the first time in nearly two months heavy, refreshing rain has fallen all the afternoon") and follows the summer behavior of Marigold, a young female friend who is on the exciting journey of deciding on a life partner. "It will simply amaze you that such a king among men could look at me," the younger woman said. "I would go through fire and smoke for him. He is my earth, my heaven, and my hope for immortality."

Though *A Cycle of Sunsets* veers from descriptions of natural history into some "girl talk," end-of-day solar events and the region's seasonal cycle are central to its themes. Mrs. Todd describes rainbows and the song of the orchard oriole, the appearance of a luna moth, and the song of summer crickets. She ticks off details of kingbirds, Saint

John's-wort, and "the majesty in the western sky" in vocabulary she could have learned from her father. She highlights Pelham Knob in mid-summer, where "the whole superb scene, this conflagration of the sky, occupied not more than fifteen minutes, but it burned its way into immortal memory."[73] Surely Mabel Todd had a knack for the dramatic and one wonders if her thoughts about "immortal memory" somehow blended a young woman's idea on new love in a reflection through time on her own longing for Austin Dickinson.

In the scholarly assessment of Mabel Loomis Todd's impact on the literary world, her contributions to the Dickinson canon are surely recorded as foremost. In her later years she continued to travel the world with her astronomer husband, write about those travels, and when at home, lecture to multiple groups weekly on a wide variety of topics. Although the Emily Dickinson work was on a thirty-year hiatus, the woman still kept up a dizzying professional pace. Through it all nature remained her touchstone. One Todd biographer concluded that although Henry David Thoreau may have only literally touched her briefly while she was an infant, the imprint of his views on the natural world put her on a path "toward a life-long appreciation of the environment and set the stage for the development of her progressive beliefs about environmental preservation" that would be manifested over the next quarter century on an island just off the coast of Maine.[74]

Chapter 1 Notes

[1] Ralph Waldo Emerson, "Nature," 1.

[2] Millicent Todd Bingham worked with The Thoreau Society to have *The Thoreau Family: Two Generations Ago* by Mabel Loomis Todd published in 1958. In the foreword Millicent writes, "Toward the end of her life my mother, Mabel Loomis Todd, began to write down her memories of the Thoreau family starting with her earliest childhood...." While some revision to the manuscript was attempted by Mrs. Todd "to smooth out some roughnesses," her reflections on the Thoreaus was one of the unfinished written works left to her daughter. As editor of this piece, Millicent Bingham thought the "earlier draft ... better, because it comes straight from 'those old grounds of memory'—as fresh and as much her own as if no one had ever written about Thoreau before."

[3] In an industrializing world, the *American Ephemeris and Nautical Almanac* offered precise data utilized in varied technical fields to a uniquely American audience. The first section of the early issues begun in 1852 was provided by *The Nautical Almanac and Astronomical Ephemeris* in London grounding calculations on the prime meridian. The second section of the American version used Washington, DC, as its meridian. Calculations included data on the sun, moon, lunar distances, Venus, Mars, Jupiter, and Saturn. Times for eclipses and other celestial phenomena were included. The publication is currently called *The Astronomical Almanac* and is available online via the U. S. Navy website. See: http://aa.usno.navy.mil.

[4] Polly Longsworth, *Austin and Mabel: The Amherst Affair and Love Letters of Austin Dickinson and Mabel Loomis Todd* (Farrar, Straus, & Giroux, 1984), 18.

[5] Longsworth, *Austin and Mabel*, 14–15.

[6] Longsworth, *Austin and Mabel*, 15.

[7] Sereno Edwards Todd, David's father, wrote and published broadly on agricultural best practices. In 1860, S. Edwards Todd authored *The Young Farmer's Manual*, a book with a subtitle that said it all: *Detailing the Manipulations of the Farm in a Plain and Intelligible Manner. With Practical Directions for Laying out a Farm, and Erecting Buildings, Fences, and Farm*

Gates. Embracing also The Young Farmer's Workshop: Giving Full Directions for the Selection of Good Farm and Shop Tools, Their Use and Manufacture, with Numerous Original Illustrations of Fences, Gates, Tools, etc., and for Performing Nearly Every Branch of Farming Operations. Other Sereno Edwards Todd publications include *The American Gardener's Assistant* (1869), and *Todd's Country Homes and How to Save Money: A Practical Book by a Practical Man* (1885). No direct evidence exists in David's writings, but it is fair to assume the son picked up practical construction tips for Hog Island buildings through his father's teaching and writing.

[8] The meeting between contemporaries David Peck Todd and Thomas Alva Edison took place in 1876 while Todd worked with Simon Newcomb at the Naval Observatory. Polly Longsworth concluded that David Todd was more interested in the 26-inch refractor telescope at the Washington Observatory, then the largest telescopic lens in the world, "than about electricity and the prospect of life in Newark." Longsworth, *Austin and Mabel*, 42.

[9] David Peck Todd was named after his uncle David Todd, who, at the time of young David's work at Columbia in New York City, was an ordained minister overseeing a church in rural Massachusetts not far from Amherst. Knowing about the observatory availability at Amherst College, Rev. Todd encouraged young David to transfer, which he did.

[10] David Peck Todd's early biography was gleaned from his obituary published in *Popular Astronomy* (November 1939) and the *Guide to the David Peck Todd Papers* at Yale University (MS 496B). Thanks to Polly Longsworth's many details provided in *Austin and Mabel: The Amherst Affair and Love Letters of Austin Dickinson and Mabel Loomis Todd.*

[11] David Todd's observations of Jovian moons was published in *Astronomische Nachrichten* prior to his graduation in 1875.

[12] Julie Dobrow, *After Emily: Two Remarkable Women and the Legacy of America's Greatest Poet* (W. W. Norton & Co., 2018), 16.

[13] Longsworth, *Austin and Mabel*, 38.

[14] Though a new Amherst College observatory did not come about as planned, David Todd supervised the construction of a new observatory at nearby Smith College, where he also taught math. A David Peck Todd

achievement, the Smith Observatory opened in 1888, the same year he picked up his honorary Ph.D. from Washington and Jefferson College.

[15] All citations in this paragraph from Richard B. Sewall, *The Life of Emily Dickinson* (Farrar, Straus, and Giroux, 1980), 171–72.

[16] Sewall, *Dickinson*, 172.

[17] Longsworth, *Austin and Mabel*, 10.

[18] Sewall, *Dickinson*, 174.

[19] Visitors to The Evergreens included the likes of Ralph Waldo Emerson, Harriet Beecher Stowe, Samuel Bowles, Henry Ward Beecher, and Helen Hunt Jackson. Dobrow, *After Emily*, 30, 33.

[20] Sewall, *Dickinson*,174.

[21] Longsworth, *Austin and Mabel*, 62–63.

[22] Various quoted in Sewall, *Dickinson*, 161–168.

[23] Sewall, *Dickinson*, 168.

[24] Some modern Dickinson scholars propose Emily and Susan were lovers.

[25] Sewall, *Dickinson*, 178.

[26] Sewall, *Dickinson*, 163.

[27] For an analysis of Austin and Mabel's love letters, see Longsworth, *Austin and Mabel*.

[28] Sewall, *Dickinson*, 176.

[29] Sewall, *Dickinson*, 216.

[30] The "on the spot" Dickinson poem written to Mabel Todd on Sept. 10, 1882:

Elysium is as far as to

The very nearest Room

If in that Room a Friend await

Felicity or Doom —

What fortitude the Soul contains,

That it can so endure

The accent of a coming Foot —

The opening of a Door —

Franklin #1590 Sewall, *Dickinson*, 217.

[31] The Emily Dickinson Museum estimates only ten percent of Emily's

prolific personal correspondence was ever collected and published (ED Museum website).

[32] Thomas H. Johnson, ed. *Emily Dickinson Selected Letters,* #736 (Belknap Press, 1958).

[33] Johnson, *Selected Letters.* #769.

[34] Johnson, *Selected Letters.* #953.

[35] Johnson, *Selected Letters.* #770.

[36] Sewall, *Dickinson,* 176.

[37] Sewall, *Dickinson,* 177.

[38] Longsworth, *Austin and Mabel,* 243.

[39] Sewall, *Dickinson,* 178.

[40] Sewall, *Dickinson,* 175.

[41] Sewall, *Dickinson,* 179.

[42] Amherst College eventually built a home for the observatory director's family. Called the Dell, the building was designed in part by Austin Dickinson, the college treasurer, who wanted a secluded door and stairway installed that would make his own comings and goings more of a private matter.

[43] Various quotes, Longsworth, *Austin and Mabel,* 45–50.

[44] Dobrow, *After Emily,* 64.

[45] Mabel Todd wrote to her mother regarding Emily's funeral, "pall bearers took out the dainty, white casket into the sunshine where it was lifted by six or eight Irish workers, all of whom have worked about the place or been servants in the family for years, and all whom Emily saw and talked with occasionally, up to the last. They carried her through the fields, full of buttercups, while the friend who chose, followed on irregularly through the ferny footpaths to the little cemetery." Source: Letter on display at an Emily Dickinson display at the Jones Library in Amherst.

[46] Sewall, *Dickinson,* 219.

[47] Sewall, *Dickinson,* 220–221.

[48] Sewall, *Dickinson,* 221.

[49] Quoted in Wikipedia under "Emily Dickinson." Willis J. Buckingham, *Emily Dickinson's Reception in the 1890s: A Documentary History* (Pittsburgh: University of Pittsburgh Press, 1989).

[50] Sewall, *Dickinson*, 220 and 226. Dickinson verse drawn from Franklin #323.

[51] Mabel Todd was not welcome at the Evergreens for Austin's wake. Ned, however, made an effort to invite her over for a final private good-bye when other family members were out of the way. Another intriguing event at the time of Austin's death was the delivery of a red Columbia bicycle to Mabel on the day following his passing. The gift listed no sender. Upon asking the bike shop who shipped, she was told they had promised anonymity to the giver. Mabel never learned who sent the bike, but as she rode that summer to ease her grief, she always thought it was from Austin. For the bike story, see Dobrow, *After Emily*, 164.

[52] After Susan Dickinson's death, her daughter Martha Dickinson Bianchi, knowing then the popularity of Emily's poetry, went on to publish her own editions that helped keep Dickinson's verse in the public's eye.

[53] Sewall reports that after the disastrous trial results, Mabel Todd "determined to have nothing more to do with things Dickinson, put the manuscript materials, including some 665 of Emily's poems, in the famous camphorwood chest and shut the lid, as she thought, forever." With Mabel out of the publication picture, Martha Dickinson Bianchi had a "clear field" to take over the Dickinson canon. Sewall claims that under Martha's guidance, the poems came out "piecemeal, unprofessionally edited." (Sewall, *Dickinson*, 234).

[54] Sewall, *Dickinson*, 185.

[55] Mabel Loomis Todd Forest booklet (unpublished).

[56] Longsworth, *Austin and Mabel*, 59.

[57] Sewall, *Dickinson*, 173.

[58] Mabel Loomis Todd, "The Village Beautiful" (Annual Report of the Secretary of the Connecticut Board of Agriculture, 1902), 283.

[59] Todd, "Village," 285.

[60] Todd, "Village," 288–89.

[61] Mabel Loomis Todd diary, August 20, 1908.

[62] Todd diary, July 20, 1908.

[63] Todd diary, August 8, 1909.

[64] Todd diary, August 15, 1909.

[65] Todd diary, August 6, 1911.

[66] Julie Dobrow email to author, February 17, 2014.

[67] Todd diary, July 3, 1911.

[68] Mabel Loomis Todd Forest booklet (unpublished) and various Todd diary entries, July 1909.

[69] Todd Forest booklet (unpublished).

[70] Todd Forest booklet (unpublished).

[71] It is not clear when the nomenclature changed, but Pelham Knob is no longer known as the Mabel Loomis Todd Forest. Sometime after the 1961 dedication by Amherst College, the holding was absorbed into a larger body of land to incorporate surrounding areas in the Town of Amherst Community Conservation Area. Worthy of note is the twenty-six-mile-long Robert Frost Trail that passes over the knob and through the larger preserve.

[72] Mabel Loomis Todd, *A Cycle of Sunsets* (Small, Maynard, & Co., 1910).

[73] Various quotes from Todd, *Cycle of Sunsets*.

[74] Julie Dobrow, "Saving the Land: Thoreau's Environmental Ethic and Its Influence on Mabel Loomis Todd and Millicent Todd Bingham" (Thoreau Society, unpublished), 1.

CHAPTER 2

Of Artists & Rusticators

The place is usually first discovered by artists in search of sketches, or by a family of small means in search of pure air, and milk fresh from the cow, and liberty ... in the matter of dress.

—Edwin Lawrence Godkin
"The Evolution of a Summer Resort" / 1895

When Mabel Loomis Todd took the train from Boston on a July morning in 1908 to Wiscasset, Maine, to sign the papers for the purchase of her share of Hog Island, she not only became more deeply a part of the state's "vacationland" history, but she did so in the middle of a year recognized by historians to be one that catapulted the country into the modern world.[1]

It would not be too much of a stretch to credit Theodore Roosevelt as a driving force in this change. He was entering his last year as the nation's president, flexing both his political and cultural muscles. To prove his point regarding America's military might, he had sent out the navy's Great White Fleet in the waning days of 1907 on a year-long worldwide tour of ports that was designed to demonstrate to potential immigrants and world powers alike that America had turned away from global isolation and was more prepared to take an active role on the world stage.

To augment his legacy as a Progressive trustbuster and defender of the working class, he reserved unique, publicly held lands as national monuments and forests while convening a three-day Governors' Conference on Conservation in May 1908. Influenced by the country's first-ever chief of forestry, former Pennsylvania

69

governor Gifford Pinchot, the two men promoted the relatively new concept of conservation at the conference, which was attended by forty-one of forty-six governors as well as all nine Supreme Court justices, most of the president's cabinet, and industry and labor leaders. This amazing gathering of national power brokers promoted a concept new for the era that sought to deter the wholesale destruction of natural resources. A nation of plenty that had traditionally used up natural materials and then moved on to new horizons was introduced to the "gospel of efficiency," which promoted using only what was necessary and planning for future generations.

Besides Roosevelt's influence, other Americans were accomplishing great technical feats in 1908 that amazed and entertained the population. New Year's Day that year was the first time a lighted ball was dropped at Times Square to indicate when the celebration could begin. Just five days after Mabel Todd took the train to Wiscasset, Admiral Robert Peary set out for his third attempt to be the first man to reach the North Pole. On August 8, Wilbur Wright showed French observers at Le Mans that he and his brother Orville had indeed mastered the technical skills of flight by piloting their Wright 1907 Flyer through a series of banks and turns, looping the field twice, amazing all present, then being tagged by the local press as the most celebrated American since Benjamin Franklin. By the end of the year, still in France, Wilbur improved on his own family's record by staying aloft for a grand total of two and a half hours, the longest airplane flight made to date.

Henry Ford changed America's concept of personal transportation that year by opening a factory in Highland Park, Michigan, that mass-produced his famous Model T, a car affordable for the masses, which would change forever how America moved. While about half of the nation's population still lived on farms with primitive utilities, many Americans enjoyed the highest per capita income in the world and lived in places blessed with rail service, the telegraph and telephone, and homes and businesses powered by electricity and gas.[2] Though a prolific letter writer, Mabel Todd reported from Fairhaven later that summer that she got "a good many things accomplished by telephone," so even in a place where a busy university family retreated for rest and relaxation, Alexander Graham Bell's invention had already made significant inroads.[3]

Aside from the technological advancements of the era, Americans were developing a deeper awareness and appreciation for nature. While Roosevelt's business conference on conservation and his establishment of national monuments like Devil's Tower and the Grand Canyon confirmed this national direction, a neophyte national association with local and state roots, using the Audubon label, was turning the nation's attention to depleted populations of shorebirds and wading birds being hunted for their meat and plumes and was lobbying for precedent-setting legislation and wardens to protect them.[4] Railroad companies advertised luxurious and comfortable lodges in destinations like Yellowstone and Glacier national parks, drawing those of means away from industrialized centers out into spectacular settings in the West.

If most of America had the West to move toward as it attempted to define itself, New England had Maine. Considered part of Massachusetts until the Missouri Compromise in 1820, when it came into the Union in its own right, Maine was a resource-rich, hardscrabble land populated mostly by farmers, fishermen, lumberjacks, and shipbuilders.

Waldoboro, the town just north of Hog Island on the Medomak River, provides a good example of how a Maine coastal village evolved into a successful industrialized community. With a large German population, it reached its prominence as a shipbuilding center starting in 1810 and hit its heyday in the mid-1800s. As welcome signs there note today, Waldoboro's forebears constructed the first five-masted schooners. [5] Between 1820 and 1840, historian Samuel Llewellyn Miller reports that "shipbuilding and trade were drawing many citizens hither and every branch of industry was prospering." In its prime Waldoboro was home to thirteen companies building and outfitting wooden sailing ships while dozens of packet ships made regular runs between Waldoboro and Boston.[6] Local merchants listed in the town business directory included a druggist, a stove and tinware seller, two lumber dealers, two cabinet makers, a harness maker, a sawmill, and five attorneys. The town nearly burned to the ground in mid-summer 1854, but with the help of neighbors and a booming economy, it was rebuilt within a year and "presented a better appearance than before."[7] The population of Waldoboro reached its peak in 1860 then started to decline after the Civil War with the advent of steel ship construction. The timber-rich area could not compete with some of her neighbors, like Bath, which is still the home of the Bath Iron Works, a historic shipyard. After nearly a century of prosperity, it was a declining shipbuilding region that Mabel and David Todd found when they came to spend the summer at the Point Breeze Inn and Bungalows in 1910.

Though shipbuilding declined, fishing and farming remained, but both were difficult and locals all along the coast became at least reluctantly interested when folks from East Coast cities came north to escape the heat of summer looking for places to board. Pre-1850 saw sportsmen, mountain climbers, and river adventurers like Henry David Thoreau immerse themselves in Maine's wild country. Artists and "natural scientists" found boarding with willing families along the coast.[8] By mid-century the word was getting out about the restorative recreational value provided by the natural beauty of Maine. Some visitors found the locals brusque and territorial, but more natives were learning that money made from the summer folk went a long way to supplementing their farm and fishing incomes. These earliest summer visitors and the hordes to follow coalesced into a financial force that helped Maine evolve into Vacationland.

Historians credit painters like Thomas Cole and Frederick Church for generating interest in summer travel to Maine.[9] When New England audiences recognized the natural beauty depicted on seascape canvas was just up the coast a piece, those who could—often college folk with a summer break—wanted to witness it for themselves. Recognizing how accessible it was by steamship and eventually rail, newspapers from Washington, DC, to Boston followed by sending travel writers and illustrators to bring the story home to their readers.[10]

Enough summer people traveled to Maine coastal destinations through mid-century that they were given a name all their own.

According to the *Dictionary of American Regional English*, the term "rusticator" was first used in print in 1869 in a *Harper's Magazine* article describing "a vacationer, especially a summer boarder." Surely in use for some time before then, the term described folks trying to get away to "recharge their batteries amid this dreamy world of the recent past, where noble, simple Yankee folk went about their lives, in harmony with their surroundings, God, and one another."[11]

To accomplish that recharge, some packed up tents along with cooking and sleeping gear before escaping to remote destinations, but the visitors who made the biggest difference to local economies started out as boarders, finding lodging with agreeable fishing and farming families. Before too long, however, summer folk gravitated to larger resort communities with more amenities and more interesting things to do than walking the beach or taking rides in buckboards. The culminating stage of rustication, which developed rather quickly, saw resort visitors with financial means constructing summer cottages of their own with scenic views in more private settings, which in turn left the resort towns for the middle class.

This rustication evolution began with families like the Loomises, ones of modest means seeking to escape hot and busy lives. Mary Loomis was eager to get her daughter Mabel out of a city she considered fraught with pestilence in those post–Civil War years. Summering for them, as mentioned, frequently saw three generations of Loomis women head north back to Concord, or perhaps farther into New Hampshire, or all the way to Casco Bay, Maine. It is clear Mabel Loomis Todd knew the Maine coast from her youth. At Harpswell she enjoyed meeting and talking with eccentric seafarers who had adventurous stories to tell.

In an 1895 essay with a subtle negative tone, David R. Godine wrote, "Nothing is more remarkable in the history of American summering than the number of new resorts which are discovered and taken possession of by 'the city people' every year." He credited this seasonal migration in part to the "rapid increase in the means of transportation both to the mountains and the sea."[12] Still a dozen years away from the Model T's mass production, it was rail and coastal steamer routes that brought most of the influx.

Local farming and fishing families charged $5 to $7 a week for each adult guest, along with meals whose menu the host family guessed at. Undaunted by crude accommodations and simple food, which was often fresh catch they could not have gotten at home, first-year boarders didn't complain "but enjoy[ed] the open air and admire[d] the scenery." By the end of summer, once-reluctant hosts were surprised by how much money they had taken in and realized that tending boarders enhanced tight family budgets. In subsequent years they might even advertise for more "intellectual or cultured people" after enlarging the dining room, adding on a wing, and relieving the "wife of the cooking by hiring a woman in the nearest town."[13]

Little by little the reluctant host became a hotel keeper. Neighbors saw such successes and followed suit. Before long these collections of boarding houses became resort communities "with girls and boys in white flannel, lawn tennis, a livery stable, stages, an ice cream store with a soda fountain, [and] a new church ... with strange names taken out of books for the neighboring hills and lanes and brooks."[14] As mentioned, Mabel Loomis Todd's camp on Hog Island would be named Mavooshen, a Native American term for an extended region of Midcoast Maine.

By its heyday in 1890, Bar Harbor boasted eighteen grand hotels that could accommodate over two thousand guests at a time. The "rich and famous" were said to have incorporated the town into their lives, but changes were afoot.[15] Godkin observed that a resort town seemed to peak within thirty or forty years. Enter the next stage of the Maine vacation evolution, the cottager.

Outsiders invading the coast and countryside didn't sit well with all the residents, especially families who had owned land since their ancestors acquired original deeds in the eighteenth century. Godkin described cottagers as "what the red squirrel is to the gray, a ruthless invader and exterminator." Almost all cottagers began as boarders, he continued, "on whom the scenery has made such an impression that he quietly buys a lot with a fine view." Then, of course, comes the cottage construction and a revised summer experience with a more independent schedule and perhaps more luxury. A cottager still took part in the larger resort community, but gradually, Godkin observed, "separates himself from his fellow boarders. The community is now divided into two classes, one of which looks down upon the other."[16] Escaping to vacationland, it would seem, could not take Americans far enough away from home where class consciousness and Progressive reforms sought to level the social playing field of the Gilded Age culture of which the Todds were such a vibrant part.

While Mount Desert Island and the town of Bar Harbor serve as perhaps the best examples of the evolution of the resort town into one of expansive cottages, other notable summer communities grew up on offshore islands. The most famous, Monhegan, was once a colonial British fishing settlement then had a brief history with pirates. By the mid-nineteenth century, an artists' community bloomed there that gave inspiration to the likes of William Henry Singer, Edward Hopper, and Jamie Wyeth.[17] Farther south in the Gulf of Maine in the Isles of Shoals group, is Appledore, ironically also named Hog Island in years past. By the late 1800s, Mabel Todd's "dear friend" Celia Thaxter, once considered America's most popular female poet, reigned over an arts community on Appledore in a settlement owned by her family that hosted such luminaries as Nathaniel Hawthorne, Harriet Beecher Stowe, and none other than Henry David Thoreau.[18]

Audubon's Hog Island also turns out to be a good example of Maine's cultural evolution from working coastal industry to vacationland. The thirty-acre northern peninsula eras past used to accommodate the occasional homesteader and by the end of the nineteenth century hosted a store, known as a chandlery, that resupplied fishing boats moored in the area. In 1908, as fate would have it, the Point Breeze Inn and Bungalows opened to summer guests for the first time. Joseph H. Ambrose, a stonemason from North Monmouth, Maine, and his wife, Nellie L. House Ambrose, purchased the peninsula in the hope of operating a successful island resort. They upgraded the existing waterfront building and the farmhouse just beyond while adding other structures they hoped would attract a dignified summer clientele with good food, comfortable lodging, and refined programming in a serene setting unique to bay island living. By 1910, the Todd family joined in that summer community as they made plans to build their own cottage farther down the western shore on the larger three-hundred-acre southern section.

Eons before the Point Breeze, the Todds, and European settlers, native Wabanaki people had used Hog Island seasonally for food gathering, creating at the island's southern tip a fairly large midden of shells and other kitchen waste. Settler ownership began in 1670 when a deed for "Hogg Island" was signed over by native sagamore Samoset to Richard Pearce, a man said to have been "active in the Pemaquid region in the mid-seventeenth century." The island already had its name at this date, though it is not clear if it emanated from nameless early settlers or local Native Americans. Records show domesticated livestock were introduced to the region three or four decades prior to the deed signing. Richard Pearce accepted the deed in the name of his children, though all seemed lost in 1676 when the conflict known as King Philip's War broke out between Natives and the English across northern New England, causing all settlers, including the Pearces, to flee.[19]

For nearly fifty years after this war, European settlers were absent from the region. The next indication of their activity came in the 1760s when Shem Drowne of New Harbor had his name on the Hog Island deed. It would be his son, Thomas, who made a significant transfer of ownership in 1769 when the peninsula was signed over to Jacob Keene "of Hog Island, husbandman."[20] Such is the first mention of a citizen apparently living on Hog Island, and there were very few to follow. A 1772 map indicates a homestead on the peninsula.

In the deal with Jacob Keene, Thomas Drowne retained rights to cove access, probably for the purpose of taking timber off the larger southern part of the island. By 1774, however, Drowne was out of the picture, having signed the bulk of the island over to Mark Keene. By the time of the American Revolution, all of Hog Island was under the control of the Keene family.

The census of 1790 showed seven residents on the island, but by 1800 that number was down to one, a gentleman named Billingham, who is assumed to have been a caretaker. Two agricultural stone walls about 150 feet long indicate some attempt at husbandry over time, but apparently not successful enough to support residents. Other islands in the immediate area, some smaller, were successfully settled with working families by that time. Why not Hog?

Researcher Charles B. McLane proposes two reasons. First, the Keene clan retained ownership of the property, and although new deeds fragmented the island over time through inheritance, it remained largely a Keene family operation. Second, Hog Island was logged over frequently, which left little inducement to settle. McLane makes the conservative estimate that the island gave up at least four full harvests from the late eighteenth century through the end of the nineteenth. Bremen town records from 1876 indicate commercial activity on the island centered on a store on the peninsula, along with lumbering operations on the larger part of the island where a "main road" from the "head of the island" ran down to Long Cove. By 1877 the store was under the management of Joseph Lermond of Loud's Island, who paid Hog Island taxes on twenty-five peninsula acres, a homestead, and a half share of a boat. Mr. Lermond made some enemies of his Keene neighbors by selling alcohol at the island store, and around 1900 sold the peninsula and its buildings to Joseph and Nellie Ambrose for development into the Point Breeze Inn and Bungalows.

In the fall of 1937, Millicent Todd Bingham chatted with Myra Nash, the wife of Charlie Nash, who owned the family farmstead at the end of Keene Neck Road.[21] Myra was a Keene, born on Peake Island in Casco Bay in 1859 and adopted by William Keene five years later. Father William, as she affectionately referred to him, had lost his own father, Abden, when the ship he was captaining ran into a squall off Marblehead on a Waldoboro-to-Boston run. Fourteen-year-old William was cooking over an open fire below deck, as was the technology of the day, when the ship was overtaken by a wave. Grandfather Abden and the only other member of the crew were lost overboard. The boy knew enough to hoist the distress flag and eventually was towed into port but, as Mrs. Nash lamented, "He was all alone."

William did just fine, however, as he would come to own a fleet of five ships, including the two-masted schooner *William Keene*, and engage in commercial fish drying. He cleared his mainland farm's expansive east-facing hillside opposite Hog Island, from the farmhouse to the shoreline, for a complex of drying racks with good sun exposure. The dried "fish flakes" were then shipped to Boston. Myra spoke of a cranberry bog at the bottom of the hill and shared her memories of watching an indigenous man she knew as Big Thunder paddling through the narrows on his way to Sand Cove, where he camped and fished in the spring, she said, to support himself.[22]

In putting her stories of Hog Island together, Myra Keene Nash relied on details passed on by a family friend, Byron Studley. He told of an old seafarer who knew the coast of Maine well and that the open field Father William cut (and that Myra's husband Charlie "put his life into") was the only thing like it for more than one hundred miles. He also recalled how farmers swam horses, cows, and sheep from a point on the Keene peninsula to a low tide spit near Long Cove. Hog Island hosted up to five hundred branded animals at a time, Studley remembered, though he never mentioned pigs.

Grandfather Abden Keene was one of four siblings who lived on or near the end of the Keene neck. His daughter, Lydia Keene Trowant, William's sister, had a daughter of her own, Elizabeth. In 1870, a Canadian from Nova Scotia named Joseph Duryea asked William Keene if he could board for the winter in exchange for work. Duryea, whom Myra remembered as a "smart man," would marry Elizabeth Trowant and build her a house "out there at the turn of the road, and a store." Duryea later apparently burned both that house and the store for an insurance settlement. ("Don't say that," Millicent recorded Myra as saying in her draft.) He then built a house and a store on the tip of Hog Island's northern peninsula to serve local fishing operations. Duryea burned that store, as well, before rebuilding it in the 1880s. Turned out Joseph Duryea was a "terrible rascal," according to Myra, who "couldn't be trusted." He skipped back to Canada while his wife Elizabeth, the Keene who held the deed to the peninsula at the time, sold the property to Joseph Lerman and took her family to Worcester, Massachusetts. Lerman, the new proprietor of the Hog Island store, expanded inventory to include alcohol, though Myra Nash would conclude "he wasn't so strict as he might have been." Lerman then sold the peninsula property to Joseph Ambrose, a man Myra Nash found to be "awful smug." When Audubon's John Baker became involved in the purchase of the peninsula, Myra was glad his name wasn't Joseph. "We'd had enough of them."[23]

The Point Breeze Inn and Bungalows, also referred to in a Bremen business directory as The Point Breeze House, was comprised of buildings old and new. The old farmhouse became the inn, while the waterfront store became the resort's gathering room and casino. More guest rooms were provided in a hotel-like structure called The Annex, while a couple of bungalows down the east shore provided a bit more room and privacy.

A final cottage on the east shore of the peninsula, known these days to Audubon campers as the Crow's Nest, began as the Slade cottage. Not part of the original Point Breeze operation, the building was constructed by the Slade family of New York. The Ambroses agreed to let the family build their cottage under the condition that after five years they would either offer the Ambroses payment or leave the building to the Point Breeze resort to rent. The Slades did buy an eighty-foot-square section of the peninsula within five years and made their cottage their summer home complete with a hired boy to help with maintenance tasks. From the first summer of Mabel Todd's involvement with the Point Breeze, she mentions the Slades as "nice people." She would make her way to their cottage many weekends when Miss Nellie Slade facilitated a Sunday service. On one occasion Mabel's father, Eben Loomis, who also boarded at the Point Breeze for two summers with his daughter and son-in-law, read a few of his original poems and promptly sold ten copies of his collection to interested summer ladies who, the story goes, were smitten by his charm and knowledge of the natural world.

By 1919 the Point Breeze Inn and Bungalows had run its course. World War I and America's new love affair with automobiles brought tough economic conditions the Ambroses could not endure. When the resort shut down, many who summered there, including the Slades, moved up the coast to Cape Rozier, a small seafaring community in the town of Brooksville in Hancock County. Mabel Todd's diary mentions her occasionally sailing up to see her old friends, who in turn sometimes came back to Camp Mavooshen for a visit, but when the Point Breeze closed, the Todds were alone on Hog Island.[24]

A prime mover in bringing most of Hog Island under Todd-Bingham family control was Etta H. Glidden, a woman born in the area who had transplanted to Boston. Though it is not recorded how she and Mabel met, somewhere along the line they discussed making an investment together in a tract of Maine that would not only preserve it from development but provide a setting for a summer camp for the globetrotting Todds. Glidden had already invested in a summer boarding destination at Martin's Point near Friendship, Maine. Their plan, when Glidden found an appropriate location, would see Mabel Todd buy the biggest share and Glidden cover a portion. After Hog Island was decided on, Etta Glidden's cousin, Chester Glidden, decided to buy in with a quarter share. By 1909, Mabel Todd bought Chester's parcel and, with Etta's quarter, the women became proprietors of the largest undeveloped forested island on the Maine coast.[25]

When it came time to sell a share of Hog Island to a cottage builder, all parties concerned gathered in Wiscasset mid-summer 1908 to make the transaction official. Present were Etta and Chester Glidden; Nellie Ambrose, wife of the Point Breeze innkeeper; and Mabel Loomis Todd, a fifty-something dressy adventuress who, along with her husband, wanted to set down summer roots. Chester Glidden, perhaps, was looking for an investment opportunity near his home that he saw changing from traditional coastal industries. Etta Glidden enjoyed her Martin's Point property, complete with its paying summer boarders, enough to encourage a friend to join in and become a neighbor. Nellie Ambrose, representing Point Breeze interests, was there, perhaps, to assure the others that their investment would not be compromised by activities or development at her family's tip of the island. And it was Mabel Loomis Todd, an artist who came all the way from Amherst to Maine's Midcoast to purchase island property, not only to preserve its magnificent trees but to reserve a little bit of nature for a simple complex of cottages that would provide a summer haven of solitude, relaxation, and plenty of work for her family for decades to come.

Chapter 2 Notes

[1] Jim Rasenberger comprehensively develops the defining elements of the era in narrative format in his book, *America, 1908,* recommended for those who want a fuller picture of the nation the Todds were participating in.

[2] Jim Rasenberger, "1908" (*Smithsonian,* January 2008), 44.

[3] Mabel Loomis Todd diary, August 20, 1908.

[4] For a comprehensive history of the Audubon movement, see Frank Graham Jr.'s *The Audubon Ark.*

[5] The five-masted schooner in question was the *Governor Ames,* built in 1888. Other Waldoboro five-masters included six ships built by George L. Welt: *Fannie Palmer, Baker Palmer, Paul Palmer, Dorothy Palmer, Singleton Palmer,* and *Harwood Palmer.* The Palmer fleet was built between 1900 and 1904 and ranged between 1700 and 2400 tons. The Waldoboro town limit sign celebrates this feat. For more on this period of Waldoboro's history, see Samuel Llewellyn Miller's *History of the town of Waldoboro, Maine* (Emerson, 1910).

[6] Packet ships were medium-sized boats designed for domestic mail, passenger, and freight transportation. Miller, *Waldoboro,* 119.

[7] Miller, *Waldoboro,* 135.

[8] Charles and Samuella Shain, ed. *The Maine Reader: The Down East Experience from 1614 to the Present* (David R. Godine, 1991), 351.

[9] While Thomas Cole's paintings stirred interest in Maine travel in the 1840s, it is said that it was Frederick Church's 1850s painting "Fog Off Mount Desert" that inspired the first rusticators to make the long trip to Mount Desert Island. Bunny McBride and Harald E. L. Prins, *Indians in Eden: Wabanakis and Rusticators on Maine's Mount Desert Island, 1840s–1920s* (Down East, 2009), 25.

[10] In an online article, the Penobscot Marine Museum reports, "Rusticators from large East Coast cities gravitated to specific Maine towns: New Yorkers to Mount Desert Island, Bostonians to North Haven, and Philadelphians to Camden."

[11] Colin Woodard, *The Lobster Coast: Rebels, Rusticators, and the Struggle for a Forgotten Coast* (Penguin, 2004), 20.

[12] Shain, *Maine Reader*, 352.

[13] Shain, *Maine Reader*, 354–55.

[14] Shain, *Maine Reader*, 355.

[15] Shain, *Maine Reader*, 351.

[16] Shain, *Maine Reader*, 355.

[17] Wikipedia, "Monhegan."

[18] Mabel Loomis Todd refers to Celia Thaxter as her "dear friend" in the unpublished essay "Island Tragedies" included in her *Epic of Hog* collection.

[19] Using recorded deeds, federal census data, and local tax records, The Island Institute published *Islands of the Mid-Maine Coast, Volume III: Muscongus Bay and Monhegan Island* by Charles B. McLane in 1992. The bulk of the earliest Hog Island history included here comes from this source.

[20] Early deeds show the family name spelled Keen, though in time Keene became the more popular spelling. Keene is used here throughout for simplicity.

[21] Millicent Bingham is the ultimate Hog Island historian. She took it upon herself to not only learn the story of folks who owned Hog Island from Mrs. Nash but then typed it up and edited it carefully. Unfortunately her penciled-in revisions don't copy well from the archival original and are thus illegible. Mrs. Bingham's notes on her talks with Myra Nash are unpublished and reside in the Todd Bingham Family Papers archive at Yale University.

[22] Myra Nash's memories of Big Thunder to the contrary, other Wabanaki people scrambled to find livelihoods on a rapidly changing Maine coast. By 1850, it was reported that it was "not unusual" for a native camp to be in close proximity to a new homestead. "Facing poverty and hunger, Wabanakis increasingly depended on cash, which they earned as hunting and fishing guides to white sport hunters, as day laborers on wharves loading and unloading ships, and as loggers or river drivers." Some earned their keep as seasonal farm workers, while others made and sold baskets, handcrafted items, canoes, and moccasins. "Indian doctors" capitalized on indigenous healing practices. At Mount Desert

Island, summer crowds flocked to "Indian shows" featuring the likes of "Big Chief Thunder" Loring, a well-known showman, hunting guide, and canoe instructor who shared medicinal treatments. In brief, Native folk were drawn to locations that offered the best prospects for marketing traditional skills. McBride and Prins, *Indians in Eden,* 21–25.

[23] Myra Nash told more Keene stories than fit into this Hog Island narrative. She spoke of Jacob Keene, brother of her father, who had sons involved in all aspects of sailing, including one boy who sailed out of Gloucester for the Grand Banks in a ship with sixteen men. It was never seen again, not even wreckage. Life was rugged in that country.

[24] Details gleaned from multiple unpublished sources from the Todd-Bingham archive at Yale's Sterling Library.

[25] Millicent Bingham made the assessment that Hog Island was the "largest undeveloped, forested island in the region" in the unpublished text of a talk to Audubon campers on June 26, 1936. In a 1960s document she claims the island to be the largest of its kind "on the coast of Maine."

CHAPTER 3

"God's own heaven"

This island is so beautiful it really makes my heart ache! Why, it seems to me God's own heaven can hardly be more perfect.

—Journal of Mabel Loomis Todd
August 9, 1924

Although Mabel and David Todd's early married lives in Amherst were much influenced by the Dickinson family, they were able to travel to places far from that town's first family. David's astronomical expeditions "frequented strange regions, unknown to tourists," taking him and his wife to Japan, Africa, and the Dutch East Indies, all by 1901. Later they would travel to South America and Russia, but Mabel admitted "we had little time to go for restful vacations" during those years when professions were made.[1]

But some leisure summer family travel was achieved, most notably in Maine, where "we did, occasionally, go back to Harpswell" where Mabel sought the invigoration she felt as a child on Casco Bay. While there she continued a practice of her youth by making friends with ex-fishermen and sea captains, which as far as she was concerned kept her and her husband qualified as "Maine *habitués*."[2]

Knowing Mabel Loomis Todd's love for the coast of Maine and her affection for nature and its venerable stands of trees, it is not surprising to learn that she certified herself as a bona fide preservationist by not only buying Pelham Knob on Mount Orient but by securing a majority share of a three-hundred-acre Midcoast Maine island. Exactly who was the prime mover in closing the deal is a point of contention in the often-told stories that have become Hog Island history.

While Mabel Todd is celebrated as the single most important person responsible for Hog Island's preservation, it is unquestionably her daughter, Millicent Todd Bingham, who not only worked out the agreement with the National Audubon Society to perpetuate that preservation but who ordered and archived her mother's records and authored histories of her own that tell the tale of how all came to pass over a century ago. Over the years of that storytelling, much of it oral, given in talks at the Audubon Camp during summers when she was in residence on the island, there are some inconsistencies. One of the biggest was both published and repeated often enough by Mrs. Bingham that it has become one of the first things folks mention when the origins of the Audubon Camp story are retold.

The year after the Audubon Nature Camp for Adult Leaders opened in 1936, Millicent Bingham published a short piece in *Natural History* magazine that Audubon reprinted for years and passed out to campers when they arrived to familiarize them with the island's background. Her mother's first acquaintance with the island, Millicent wrote about and spoke of so many times, was in the summer of 1908 when she and her father sailed by and noticed a forty-acre clearcut of trees on the south side of Long Cove. Apparently knowing nothing else about the forested island, the story is told that her mother was moved on the spot to do something to save it. "Piles of dead brush and stumps gave to it an air of desolation," Millicent wrote in "Rescuing an Island." "There were rumors that the whole island-forest might be similarly ground to a pulp. My mother was shocked. She determined to do what she could to prevent it."[3] Story goes the couple stopped by the Point Breeze that day, chatted with the Ambroses, and within the year signed deeds and Hog Island became a Todd family treasure.

Well, not quite so. Upon examination of Mabel Todd's diary, a continuing document she regularly kept throughout her adult life, all that happened summer of 1908 regarding Hog Island was the train trip to Wiscasset on July 1, where Etta Glidden and company met her, hopefully had lunch, and signed ownership papers. In a letter to the directors of the National Audubon Society in August 1960 gifting the bulk of Hog Island to Audubon, Millicent got the first detail mostly correct when she wrote that her parents made first footfall on the section of Hog Island where they were majority owners in July 1909. Millicent recorded the titanic event as happening on July 10, though Mabel wrote in her diary that on that day she was at work in Amherst finalizing details on the purchase of the eighty-seven-acre tract on the top of Mount Orient she was trying to preserve. Mabel recorded the magic on Hog Island started for the Todds on July 14. But it was most certainly *not* 1908.

Perhaps it is worthwhile here to consider Millicent Todd Bingham as a storyteller. One wonders if she was merely retelling a yarn her mother had spun over the years about the island she so loved or if the daughter just got a few important details wrong. Mabel *did* love nature. Millicent, only too aware of her mother's contributions to the Emily Dickinson whirlwind, says she "cared most of all about the world of nature, particularly about the preservation of forests and their wild inhabitants."[4] Perhaps the daughter sought to add a little sparkle to her mother's already illustrious career. Millicent had from her earliest histories of Hog Island credited Etta Glidden with the tedious footwork of contacting multiple island landholders, assembling the paperwork, and being her mother's partner in the preservation venture. She does not, however, give Etta H. Glidden proper credit for locating Hog Island in the first place.[5]

It is unclear when the idea of an Etta Glidden/Mabel Todd cooperative preservation buy originated, but Todd writes in both diary and journal that Glidden not only did the paperwork, but also located the property. On July 25, 1909, just days after returning from Martin's Point and her first foray into the Hog Island regenerating wilderness, Mabel Todd wrote in her journal, "I had already promised to go in with her on an island if she could find one." And find one she did. Having family roots in the Bremen area undoubtedly helped Glidden clear the paperwork through the nine different local island tract owners.[6] When all was ready, Mabel concluded, "I bought half of it, and she and her cousin the other half—undivided," which meant there would be no property lines laid out like the old agricultural stone walls that separated grazing stock in past years. All current owners would have free access to all parts of the island, exclusive, of course, of the northern peninsula where the Ambroses owned and operated the Point Breeze. Mabel concluded her remarks that day by writing, "It is a wonderful place, and Millicent is most deeply interested."[7]

In August after the papers were signed, Etta Glidden wrote to Mabel Todd, wondering how they should proceed on surveying the island. Now that the new deed was in order, they wanted to know if the "two-hundred fifty-seven acres, more or less" listed on the deed was accurate. Glidden suggested the island be plotted out in ten sections. She knew of a surveyor whose results were reliable and the work proceeded. Turns out the surveyor found the total acreage of their piece of Hog Island was closer to three hundred.

It was a foggy Tuesday morning in July 1909 when Mabel Todd and her husband were aboard "the little *Monhegan*," a packet boat out of Portland, steaming its rounds north to various coastal communities delivering both cargo and passengers. Their destination that week was Hog Island, but that day it was Friendship, where Etta Glidden's niece met them and took them by "a pretty sea country road" to her Martin's Point camp. There it was tea, a bit of a walk, and "All early to bed."[8]

On the following day, July 14, Mabel and David Todd took their first steps onto their Muscongus Bay island that would enchant them for years to come. They came by boat around Bremen Long Island and landed at Midden Cove. They "penetrated the deep, deep woods," climbed over granite cliffs, and finally reached the western shore. It was a "wonderful walk," she wrote, finding "richer beauty and more of it than I could have believed." They had lunch on the southern tip and at the end of the afternoon, Mabel thought the day "exquisite." The next morning started with a stop at Louds Island to pick up Chester Glidden, then more hiking at Hog and lunch at Sand Cove. The couple encountered the Long Cove clearcut that day for the first time, but Mabel does not offer any opinions in her diary.

A few days later that week they were sailing around the island when a thunderstorm popped up and they sought shelter in the Point Breeze "assembly room," where they witnessed "a *horrible* flash of lightning and a simultaneous clap." They lunched at the Point Breeze and Mabel Todd mentions first meeting "the Slades from NY." The sun came out again in the early afternoon and all were on their way.

The Todds spent a full week at Martin's Point that summer and visited Hog Island every chance they could. One day they found picnicking clam diggers at Sand Cove, who Etta Glidden reprimanded for not picking up their trash. Mabel found the day "wonderful" and "Hog Island more beautiful than ever." By week's end it was thank you's, a launch to Friendship, and back on the *Monhegan* to Portland by 4:00 p.m.

The 1910 Hog Island season started on August 6, seeing Mabel and David Todd board at the Point Breeze for five days. Etta Glidden met the pair in Portland and they shared passage to Round Pond, where Joseph Ambrose picked up the Todds "with his motor boat and took us on to his place, the little 'bulge' on the northeast corner of our own Hog Island." The short week started with the Todds exploring the Ambrose property on "many lovely paths" while noting that the Point Breeze "has *very* nice people only." The next day found Mabel "tired out, mind and soul," rising later than usual and glad of it. A walk onto the big island with David a bit later caused her to write in her diary, "Oh, this island is *radiantly* beautiful." Beyond that, the two had come upon "a site for a house as would bring ecstasy to someone who would appreciate it and had the money to build."

The Todds had hoped to sail out to Monhegan that week with new Point Breeze friends, but the day appointed was socked in with fog and all thought better of it. In the fog that morning Mabel sat on the rocks writing, then during a sunny respite at midday, headed into her woods where she "wandered about happily" taking an hour-long nap on soft moss. By evening the fog came in as thick as ever and she ended her day participating in a "progressive euchre party" at the Point Breeze. At week's end the two were ferried over to Waldoboro, where they caught the Bar Harbor to Boston train back home. She added in her diary that upon return to a rainy Amherst, she found a "big pile of mail and crowded desk" but was now "rested enough so it does not seem impossible as it did before I left."

Due to end-of-school-year responsibilities at Amherst College, summer vacationing usually began around the first of July for the Todds. In mid-June 1911, David took Mabel to Fairhaven for a weekend where after walking their fifty acres and having "a beautiful time," they collected tents for Maine. Trunks were packed back home and two weeks later found the whole family, including Millicent and Eben Jenks Loomis, in Portland ready for another coastal venture on the *Monhegan*. Again meeting Etta Glidden, this time with "a lot of nieces and nephews," the company steamed north to Round Pond, where Mr. Ambrose waited in his boat, *Breeze*. The day was uncharacteristically hot, but by the time Mabel reached the Point Breeze, she found it "very mossy and fragrant, and I am glad to be here."

During their first decade on Hog Island, the Todds were, indeed, Point Breeze people. Even though most of those years they camped on their side of the island, they kept in close contact with Point Breeze friends, rowing up to the northern peninsula for entertainment, meals, and Sunday services as well as having some of their favorites row down to have tea with them. Summer 1911 would see the family board for ten weeks at the resort while spending many days improving a beach site on the western shore that already had a small building and would within another season become their summer camp. The first order of business was to get the "little house" in better shape. Mabel was not happy it had been "camped out in, without leave" by unknown visitors. Dwelling improvements and more clearing of limbs took place, and on occasion Etta Glidden came by, joining the Todds for dinner at the Point Breeze.

Later that first week back at their camp, Frank Lailer came by. Known to Mrs. Todd as a carpenter, Lailer was a Boston man relocated to Bremen who would turn out to be one of the unsung heroes of her soon-to-be-named Camp Mavooshen. On this day he was called to put together an estimate on what materials it would take to build their first new structure. Over time Frank Lailer did countless construction and odd jobs to keep the camp up and running and ferried the family where needed in his boat, *Romany Girl*. He would, in fact, be on-site in the fall of 1932 when Mabel Loomis Todd fell on her porch and "crossed the bar" a few hours later.

David cut fresh timber "of the right size" for the new building's posts and with his father-in-law, motored up to Waldoboro to collect the other required lumber. Lailer brought a "boy" to help, and with all the family working, construction began on the camp's first new shelter located "on our north point." Mabel reported, as well, that David "made a complete path to the point ... to a cove landing just across from Ambrose."

That building and that cove landing are not known to Hog Island visitors today. A 1953 real estate assessment shows no buildings built in the summer of 1911. It declares a guesthouse was constructed in 1912, but Mabel Todd's diary speaks of nothing new in 1911. One wonders how much of the real estate document was reconstructed from faded memory, making building dates a little fuzzy. But one thing is for sure: Mabel Todd provided date-based details in her diary that described many things from foggy mornings and clearing dead branches from a favorite grove to lovely walks in the woods and community singing events at the Point Breeze. It is hard to rely on later documents to override her diary notations that seem to make her Hog Island story so clear.

As summer 1911 passed, Eben Jenks Loomis continued to make an impression on the ladies at the Point Breeze while Millicent made a significant island contribution of her own.[9] She was the trailblazer. In order for the Todds to get to their campsite from the Point Breeze, they often rowed along the mussel bar south through the narrows. Mabel writes a few times about slogging through a muddy shortcut across Long Cove at low tide to get back to their resort lodgings, but the Hog Island the family bought was without trails. Any forays they made on foot were products of bushwhacking through an island filled with ferns and encumbered by stands of trees and subsequent tangled tree falls. Surely they followed game trails whenever possible, but the place was without established footpaths. Enter thirty-something Millicent Todd. Her first conquest was a trail from their camp to Sand Cove, a lovely expanse of beach less than a mile south on the west shore. That summer she made it to South Point and eventually blazed the perimeter trail that completely encircles the island.

Spending over two months at the Maine shore that year gave the Todds ample opportunity to see and experience not only their island but other coastal destinations. They did get to Monhegan that summer, where Mabel writes of having coffee in "a very artistic bungalow" before going out to investigate "the wonderful cliffs on the east and south, 150 feet high, and a mile and a half from the houses." They visited a few studios where they found "wonderful paintings of surf and cliffs and sunshine and fog." Other islands visited included Wreck and Marsh. At the Franklin Island lighthouse they met the "keeper Larabee and his daughter Gertrude, a precious child of nine." They climbed the tower to its "fourth order light," where Mabel concluded all was "exquisitely kept."

Mabel Todd took a page from Henry David Thoreau's botany days by creating the first extensive list of the flora found native to the island.[10] A few of her favorites, according to Millicent, were June's pink lady slippers and the tiny twin bells of *Linnaea borealis,* followed later in the growing season by mushrooms and "the spectral Indian pipe," a watercolor version of Mabel's which had years before adorned the cover of the first series of Dickinson poetry.

Through the tough physical labor of forging a summer retreat out of an island returning to its natural state, Todd's enthusiasm for Hog Island never flagged. On August 4, after a wearying day of rowing and hauling tents and lumber, Mabel wrote of the nesting birds on the island that only "pass through Amherst." It was a day she said that was "so perfect that it is next to tears. Utterly still with such a richness of sunshine, such a brooding tenderness, such a sunset *enfolding* us as I never felt before, anywhere else in the world."

As August slipped into September, Point Breeze boarders departed. By then stone masons had improved rough steps and added a stone porch at the front of the Todds' newly whitewashed "little house" on the shore. "We have devoted a great deal of time and thought to this northern end this year," Mabel wrote, "but the west is glorious and the east and south almost best of all." By then David had transplanted "fifty little spruces" that were growing where the new building was coming together, cleared and reordered very heavy stones from the beach, and one evening gave a talk on Mars to the Point Breeze crowd. Mabel took care of family business by getting the checks written and pitched in at camp by clearing groves and burning dead and down limbs on the beach on cool days. One night she spoke to Ambrose boarders about their trip to Japan's Mount Fuji, and on another, Millicent regaled those gathered on Peru, the subject of a book she was writing. On September 13, with winter preparations at their nascent camp complete, the Todds boarded the *Breeze* for Round Pond, then back to Portland on the *Monhegan*.

The Todds were familiar with primitive camping and that's just what they were about to get themselves into full-time. Many of David's solar eclipse expeditions took the family to remote destinations, where they then traveled long distances to the totality track to camp for weeks prior to the event as equipment was shipped in, unpacked, set up, and calibrated. Clean water, food preparation, and sanitation in those places were always difficult, but in a world where many had no gas or electricity, only oil lamps and cooking fires or less, putting up with fewer conveniences was more commonplace.

Summer 1912 on Hog Island for the Todds did not begin until the second week of August and lasted only one month. In June, Mabel was working with her publisher on a new book, *Witchcraft in New England*. In July and again in early August, her diary shows trips to Fairhaven, where David was cleaning up building debris and packing household goods destined for Maine. Furniture was shipped and stored in Frank Lailer's barn in Round Pond until appropriate camp buildings were completed. Crated housekeeping items were transported to the island via Ambrose's motorboat and dory. On August 10, the whole family arrived at the Point Breeze, where Eben Jenks Loomis lodged again for the season while Mabel, David, and Millicent made their new camp their summer place. The little house appeared to be in good order, but Mabel was disappointed to find damage done by a strong July storm "that prostrated six superb spruces, large, green, full, straight—uprooting earth and rocks in their fall."

The next morning after breakfast at the Point Breeze, their camp came to life with the unpacking of utensils and supplies, "putting them on shelves in something like order." That night yet was spent at the Point Breeze lodging, but the next day was targeted as move-in day. When that morning dawned in heavy fog the Todds were tempted to postpone their venture, but realized "if we did not begin soon we should settle down and stay at the Ambroses." So off they went in the fog and before long they had dug up some clams "and had a camp fire in the rocks and very good things to eat several times during the day."

To say Millicent camped with her parents for the month would be only partially true. Still writing her book, *Peru: A Land of Contrasts,* she worked better at the Point Breeze at first, then tried tent camping with her folks. Bad weather and difficult writing conditions overall convinced her that her writing process worked better at the Point Breeze, where she returned for the rest of that summer.

More accomplishments were chronicled at the new camp that summer while days began and ended with domestic chores. Mornings began early with a row over to the Keene's for fresh milk and eggs while days most often ended with another row to the mainland and a walk into Medomak to pick up mail. Trips to Portland and Rockland secured more equipment needed to make the camp efficient and comfortable. David kept clearing stones from the beach using a roller log and lever system he devised. Mabel was amazed at her husband's stamina and what he could move, using such simple machines while she continued clearing groves of dead and low-hanging branches and making pillows filled with fragrant balsam fir needles. Frank Lailer set about construct-ing a second new building on the property, this one a "little house for trunks and stores" that included a toilet and woodshed. And in homage to their two excursions to Japan, a *torii* gate was erected as a welcome sign to nature's people.[11]

Up to this time, the Todds were reliant on others for water transport. Along with Frank Lailer's *Romany Girl* and Joseph Ambrose's *Breeze,* boats like the *Wotton* stopped by the resort float to pick up passengers for day trips around the bay. Just a few days into their summer 1912 stay, Mabel writes of heading over "to Greenland cove to inspect our great, splendid mahogany boat. She is a beauty. It will be a joy to go about in her." The boat needed a new engine that took a while to install, but when ready it was christened *Takusan* and gave the family good service for many years.[12]

A few new faces came by Hog Island that summer. One unnamed friend thought the island "very fine—far ahead of Fairhaven." Another, an Amherst woman recorded only as Ruth, stayed for the summer to assist Mabel with camp chores. One afternoon the two took a walk to Long Cove to the cut-over acres near their camp and "picked a lot of those queer currant-gooseberries" that Mabel said she "liked so much last year." The two made it back to camp taking one of Millicent's new trails. On their last day in camp that year, "Mr. Lailer and his wife and baby came over," and after locks were snapped closed, the party rowed over to the Ambroses' for "supper and the night."

Mabel Todd always seemed to have good things to say about her "island of beauty." Returning to camp from Portland, where, after shopping for camp supplies, she had given "a talk" to over one hundred people, she was "so glad to see it again!" A few weeks later she experienced a "wonderful night" with "phosphorescence, meteors, brilliant stars, and perfect stillness." But before the 1913 summer season began, the Todds would endure two crippling and painful family experiences that would change, at least for a time, their enjoyment of picturesque and wild Hog Island.

With the coming of fall and their return home to Amherst, Mabel Todd resumed her busy lecture schedule. In September she and David took a short break and headed back to Fairhaven for what appeared the last time. No mention of their property on Buzzard's Bay was ever made in her diary again. On a dark night that December with Mabel away from home on a speaking engagement, David called to report that her beloved father had died and gone, as she wrote, "to somewhere that I cannot follow." When she returned home, she found him "warm and dear—but I could not kiss him back to life." She had many notes to send while friends called to offer their sympathy. Throughout the day she "kept going up to that precious, peaceful figure lying there in his room."

As difficult as Mabel Todd found the loss of her father, she herself experienced a devastating blow six months later. While in preparation for returning to Maine, on July 2, 1913, she suffered a stroke, referred to later in her records as a "sunstroke." Her language, walking, and writing were severely impaired. Millicent reported the first thing her mother said when regaining consciousness several days later was, "Sue has finally got me."[13] Travel to Maine was out of the question. No diary entries were recorded for months while Mabel tried her hardest to get back into her rugged form. She was stubbornly committed to regaining her health and coordination. Still, her handwriting turned into an uneven scrawl, and when she resumed her diary entries in November, many were impossible to decipher. On occasion Millicent made entries in her mother's famous diary, including one the following February that reads, "Mamma was able this morning to get a hold of her hair brush with her right hand. It made her face violently red and she breathed hard, but she grasped it." Later that month Millicent reports, "Mamma cut her steak with her right hand" and was having success walking without a limp. She records her mother saying, "In a month more you'll see me doing wonderful things."

Still, Mabel Todd was convalescing summer 1914, which meant no Hog Island. Instead, she traveled with David and Millicent to Russia for the recording of a solar eclipse. Her island camp was in her thoughts, though, when she observed one day, "The loveliest of mornings along a shore as beautiful as Maine." In upcoming lectures she gave about this trip to Russia, she included that the family had to scurry out of the country as World War I had begun just weeks before eclipse day.

With Mabel's health improving, the Todds were back in Maine in 1915 as their camp swung into full operation. Their lovely boat, *Takusan*, "slid off the ways as I 'busted' the bottle of champagne on her bow," Mabel wrote. The next day the craft ferried those gathered on its first outing to Louds Island. Frank Lailer built a canopy on the shore building that, together with the stone porch, made "a little piazza" for the "Seaside Shack." In late August, Mr. Clarke visited and took the classic photograph of the Todd camp, which included the *Takusan* anchored with Japanese colors flying in full glory on the shore beyond. Just up the hill a bit, the *torii* gate erected in 1912 is visible, reinforcing the influence of Japan on the Todds' lives. In September, with the Slade sisters as guests, a larger *torii* of birch logs was erected elsewhere at camp. About that time too, David worked out a deal with Charlie Nash in which the camp boats, a small power boat and *Takusan*, would be wintered in the Nash mainland boathouse.

Mabel's diary entries were less frequent that summer due to her physical limitations. She mentioned that she spent more time at the Point Breeze than she wanted to but improving her coordination by walking the Ambrose trails would have been much easier than negotiating the rocks and roots at her camp. She mentioned, too, coming "home to Antlers," which is never clearly explained. By the early 1920s the camp would be known as Mavooshen, but perhaps for this summer the Todds thought of it as Antlers.

The next few summers provided Mabel and David Todd months of the work and relaxation that come with being vacation property owners. Millicent came up for a few weeks at a time, but she was completing her doctorate after finally publishing her book on Peru and providing an entry to *Encyclopedia Britannica* on that South American country. A new Eben Grove was groomed among the spruces to accompany the Emily Grove. A pagoda was erected down by the shore with a stone floor finished with crushed clam shells purchased specifically for that purpose.

Just about then, too, David Todd explored mainland junk in Round Pond and found old polishing bits from the shuttered Swanson Granite Quarry.[14] Not caring about their purpose, the astronomer in him saw *spiral nebula*. He collected a dozen or so of the spiral bits and transported them to the island by scow, where they were painted white and then hung in the gable of each camp building. Mabel soon called the mounted spiral her camp's insignia.[15]

The turn of the decade proved to be most auspicious for the Todds and Hog Island. After a sabbatical, which took Mabel and him to southern Florida, David Todd retired as professor and Director of the Observatory at Amherst College. The two vacated Amherst for Coconut Grove, Florida, where they bought "a lovely Spanish house" with the financial backing of Arthur Curtiss James, the same benefactor who had bankrolled the *Coronet* trip to Japan. With fond thoughts of their trips to the orient, Mabel called her new place Matsuba, which roughly translates from the Japanese to "in the pines."[16] Along the way Mabel made the acquaintance of Howard Hilder, an accomplished painter with roots in the Newport, Rhode Island, art scene. Hilder came north and boarded briefly at the Point Breeze in 1919, and after a walk from her camp to Sand Cove, she found him "absolutely enthusiastic over my dear island." Over the next winter, Hilder and Mabel Todd negotiated a deal that gave him ten acres of Hog Island on which to build a studio. Located down the west shore from her camp, Hilder's studio was built in 1921 and called Osprey.

During the summer of 1919, David was away in South America on a disastrous solar expedition while Mabel boarded at the Point Breeze one last summer.[17] During that same summer that Howard Hilder first visited, the main camp building that was to become its focal point was constructed. Frank Lailer was the primary framer with a crew of others while local masons disassembled an agricultural stone wall back in the island forest and transformed it into an impressive hearth and chimney. A story Mrs. Bingham often told that got a laugh from Audubon campers recalled when her mother questioned one of the masons, curious about the efficiency of the fireplace draft. Millicent said the man looked a bit peeved, turned to her mother, and in his unique Maine dialect, responded, "Ma'am, when I'm done with my *chimneys*, people worries about their *cats*."

World War I was hard on the Maine vacation trade. A country at war, or about to be, passed up vacations in those days while German U-boats were a concern for coastal shipping of both goods and people. The Point Breeze suffered and, except for temporary occupants, shut down in 1919.[18] As mentioned, summer regulars like the Slades looked for an alternative and settled on primitive Cape Rozier, just up the coast alongside Penobscot Bay. Mabel Todd sailed up to visit old friends from time to time and spent a summer there herself in 1922 following David Todd's long-term hospitalization, which she said left her feeling "stranded."

After the Point Breeze closed, the family and guests at the Todd camp were by themselves on Hog Island. For the first time in 1922, Mabel used the expression Camp Mavooshen in her writing to define her beloved summer place, which commemorated the Wabanaki influence on the island, most notably the extensive shell midden at South Point.

By that time Camp Mavooshen boasted seven buildings.[19] The existing whitewashed "little house" on the shore was now referred to as the lobster house. The first new building, the guest house constructed in 1911, occupied the flat area by their "north point," an area today full of ferns. The following summer the trunk house complemented the camp. No new construction occurred during the years immediately following Mabel's stroke. The most prestigious building came next in 1919, sometimes called the camp house but most often referred to by Mrs. Todd as her living room. Cases of books were shipped north, and in time she wrote, "Almost all of my favorite books are here." Stored furniture from Fairhaven was finally hauled over in 1920, and on cool nights a crackling fire enhanced her island home to make her camp "as serene as heaven." Howard Hilder painted the mural "Osprey Point" in the north eave of her living room that summer, followed in 1932 by "The Heronry" in the south eave.

Three of those seven buildings came in quick succession when Millicent's "own house" was built by Frank Lailer on a granite outcrop just south of her mother's living room in 1920. In time this structure would be called by Audubon "the writer's cottage." Next came "Hilder of Hog's" studio down the shore, Osprey, that Millicent would later say was not really part of her mother's camp. During that same time a "boys' house" was erected that lodged the summer help who cooked and performed odd jobs. The location of the trunk and boys' houses was not documented and is not known today.

The final building at Mavooshen came the same season as Mabel Todd's death. In 1932 diary entries she called it a dining room, but when Millicent and her husband took over management of the camp, this new building just behind the lobster house on the shore was known as the workshop. Walter Van Dyke Bingham would engineer a rain collection system on the roof of that building that provided gravity-fed water via a hose to the lobster house sink for much more convenient dishwashing.

Only two of the eight buildings still stand at the camp today. The guesthouse, trunk house, and "boys' house" were built on the ground without the benefit of stone footers or raised pilings and over time succumbed to coastal moisture and were demolished. Howard Hilder's Osprey exhibited construction shortcomings during his tenure and subsequent years with summer boarders and was disassembled sometime in the 1970s by island neighbors who repurposed the materials for their own use.[20] Both buildings on the shore, the lobster house and the workshop, were moved in the early 1980s to the north peninsula, where they were upgraded and are currently in use as Audubon Camp housing.[21] All that remains at Camp Mavooshen today are Mabel's living room and Millicent's private quarters.

It is worth a mention that all cottages created in the Maine vacationland continuum were not constructed equally. While Mabel Todd had good reason to be proud of the family's accomplishment in establishing a durable summer camp on a precious, minimally developed island, the Todd summer lifestyle was little more than glorified camping. While the building updates and new construction provided a working kitchen, protection from the elements, and a warm fire on cold nights, plumbing was non-existent and potable water was a most precious commodity. Evening light was by way of oil lamps and personal hygiene was a challenge. At Mount Desert Island, industrial titans like the Rockefellers, Vanderbilts, and Carnegies called their summer buildings "cottages," too, but theirs were lavish compounds that incorporated amenities that recreation for people of wealth required. The Todd family operation was much humbler and had more in common with Henry David Thoreau's rustic camping in the Maine woods than plush Down East country estates.

Hog Island's cast of characters changed after the Todds' first ten or so years. The Point Breeze community was gone, as were owners Nellie and Joseph Ambrose, who from the time they shuttered the inn, annex, and bungalows, tried to sell the peninsula to any interested buyer. By 1921, Millicent was married to Walter Van Dyke Bingham, who immediately became important in the camp's operation. David Todd was gone by then, institutionalized for the rest of his life suffering from mental deterioration due to complications of syphilis. Howard Hilder, ten years Mabel Todd's junior, became her "dear old pal" and, in her later years, her cherished caregiver. Through it all, however, Mabel Loomis Todd, Millicent Todd Bingham, Etta H. Glidden, Myra and Charlie Nash, and Frank Lailer were Hog Island constants.

As Mabel Todd's affection for Hog Island deepened, she wrote a few unpublished essays about the area. "Muscongus Island, Maine" focused on the rustic island just south of Hog Island now known as Louds Island. About the size of Hog, Muscongus was settled year-round and had a colorful history of disputes with the town of Bristol, the locality in which citizens voted and paid taxes. Mabel told of the seafaring families based on Muscongus and the proudly primitive way of life experienced there for generations, which shunned modernization and the influx of potential trade brought by summer people.[22]

As developed previously, the relationship between locals and seasonal visitors was tenuous as Maine transformed into a vacation mecca. Mabel Todd synthesized the controversy in this case by both acknowledging the Muscongus Island community for its efforts to retain the old ways while celebrating the potential contributions made by summer people. At the time of this undated essay, probably in the 1920s, Mabel noted younger generation Muscongus islanders considered selling out to city people. Such wouldn't be bad for the island community, she wrote, because the city people "would certainly brighten the summer program of the islanders if permitted to build and live there for three months, or even less." As a "foreigner" who found going "back to the island beauties and their green peace" a recharge from a hectic modern pace, Mabel Todd saw advantages in blending the old with the new and the outside world with the local.[23]

Most of what we know of Mabel Todd and company on Hog Island comes from her diary, not from her extensive compilation of more in-depth journal entries. The exception, however, is a collection of essays she called *The Epic of Hog*, written over a few summers in the 1920s. The rough literary gem is comprised of sixteen unpublished reflections highlighting what she found so endearing about living amid nature for months at a time. Topics range from nesting osprey to periwinkle "lids" to William Shakespeare.[24] The collection reads like observations made at Walden, in some ways written for no other reason than personal record. Mabel Todd wrote these undated essays later in life, which leaves one to wonder if *The Epic of Hog* might have ended up in print like *A Cycle of Sunsets* if timing and circumstances had been different.

The first essay in the collection is an eyewitness account of an osprey pair nesting high in a "Japanese-looking pine" on the "point nearest to us." The parents put up quite a racket when the nest was approached, she wrote, as "'we were distinctly told in fierce bird language to retreat." But upon rowing up quietly, the birds didn't seem to mind and osprey rearing was observed in greater detail. The style of these essays echoes the imagery of her sunset book but reset on a wilderness island by the ocean. "As the sweet, still sunset came on over the reflecting sea and above the dreaming hills, the pair abandoned their warlike attitude, and permitting us to float undisturbed near the point, curved with great sweeps around us, and became one with the calm evening." Howard Hilder was among those present and he watched "with undisguised admiration." That nesting event was remembered at the camp through his mural, "Osprey Point."

As mentioned, fresh water was a topic of dire interest on the island, being mentioned in the essays a few times. Mabel wrote about "delicious ice cold water from the hidden spring" near Osprey Point and another fresh water source down the shore near Howard Hilder's studio. Very important to island living were the rain barrels set at roof lines around camp to collect fresh water, albeit with a few spruce needles and the occasional dead critter. One morning after some particularly pleasant barrel-filling rain, Mabel was surprised to find a drowned flying squirrel in one. The animal's "wing-like forepaws, the curious back ones, and the bushy tail, alas, not bushy this morning," saddened her, not only for the loss of its life but because she didn't know the species at all and wished she had.

The flying squirrel story presents a theme prevalent in *The Epic of Hog*. Mabel Todd knew much about the scientific world, but she surely didn't know everything, and there were times when she wished she did. In her essay about the intricacies of spider web spinning, she observed, "Another subject which I ought to have pursued years ago! Only how was a young girl to pursue to specialist attainment all or even half the subjects which enthrall her!" She went on, "Botany, ornithology, biology, geology, the lighter aspects of geography, ethnology, anthropology, archeology, fishes, sea mosses, lichens, mushrooms, spiders, butter-flies—all the myriad subjects which make of this wonderful island a compendium of not less than half the exciting subjects of the world!"

A story of her mother's that Millicent Bingham enjoyed recounting to Audubon campers was "The Little Lids of the Winkle." On her many walks through the island, Mabel found small, rounded, jewel-like shapes that drew her attention. She found them "as beautiful as the finest tortoise shell" and was puzzled how they got to be just about everywhere. After talking with a local fisherman, she found that each was a periwinkle operculum. Crows and gulls would retrieve the succulent little creatures on the shore at low tides, then carry them high over the island, dropping them on hard surfaces, then landing to feed. The periwinkle's covering to protect soft flesh from the dangers in the sea did no good anymore and were in fact inedible. Thus, they were scattered like gems around the island.

Not unlike Audubon campers, the Todds made a practice of cruising out to Harbor Island for picnics and afternoons of seaside bouldering. As she waded into the water there, Mabel first noticed "hundreds of perfectly contented little snails, all in their gorgeous houses of yellow, shades of brown, white, and other dainty tints, all clustered on rocks where the retreating waves washed completely over them every few seconds and poured off in iridescent tints of rainbow beauty." Looking "a bit lower, nearer the waves," she discovered rocks covered with star-fishes. "Their colors were truly amazing," she wrote. "Several of brilliant vermillion, two or three delicate green, a dozen of lavender in varied shades, and finally one which was a real purple of most dainty shade, which, while I looked, resolved itself into pink, turning, while I gazed at him enthralled, to the most airy lilac, finally showing all the tints at once in rainbow colors the most wonderful." While Mabel Todd was, indeed, an eloquent writer skilled in recording detail, it doesn't take much imagination to hear in her writing voice the excited squeal of a youngster discovering amazing things at the beach for the first time.

Rational students of nature in this day and age try hard not to impose human values, or anthropomorphic tendencies, on what they observe in natural systems. Still thinking like the romantic she indeed was, however, when Mabel Todd saw "the cruel curve" of an adult osprey beak while bringing a fresh kill into the nest to the three young, she described the catch as a "hapless fish tweaked from his peaceful haunts in the quiet sea." As enlightened as she was, she did not comprehend yet that what she witnessed was a predator/prey link in the chain of life that would soon be a prime curriculum component at the Audubon Nature Camp that would come into fruition at the old Point Breeze a decade later.

As curious as the sea was for Mabel Todd, it was the forested island with its variety of life that drew her north every summer. She wrote about a "huge rock" found near their Camp Mavooshen "living room" that was "the pride and delight of all the dwellers in the enchanted isle. Like a little hill in the landscape, it stands like the guardian spirit of the inhabitants." Intrigued by the large boulder over many summers, she observed "several roots of fine ferns … caught in crevices, greening from year to year, and growing splendidly large. A little spruce has coyly rooted itself on the ultimate apex, a delicate wood daughter, prettily green and graceful." In addition, "A lovely variety of greenest moss covers the rock," she observed, making the monolith "a perfect adjunct to the Camp."

Just beyond the guardian boulder were a couple of small spruces that provided a kind of entrance into the forest, which had been "a joy to me" because they bore a "variety of lichen which has a curious significance." The growth was a "flat dull gray" that "in sunny, dry days … is hardly noticeable." When the fog rolled in, however, "the mysterious lichen comes at once into its own, for what was an uninteresting drab becomes almost immediately vivid green." The two small trees became "lovely with a sort of ruffled green garment, standing out in relief from their trunks, and turning momentarily a darker and richer tint. When it really rains it seems absolutely triumphant and grows more beautiful with every passing hour." She wrote of standing in the rain, quietly just watching the lichen unfold into refreshed being. And to finish this essay, a familiar refrain, "How I wish that I had made a specialty of lichens, studying them with that delightful old professor whose happy theme they were long ago!"

The early 1920s marked the beginning of Mabel Loomis Todd's last decade on Hog Island. Approaching seventy years of age, getting around on the island's uneven, rocky, and rooted trails became more difficult. Returning to Camp Mavooshen in 1923 after losing David to hospitalization, she hoped he could return to health enough to join her, but such would not be the case. Howard Hilder stepped into that breach and became a friend whom she helped by providing studios for him at both Osprey and in her garage at Matsuba in Coconut Grove. Others came to cook and help keep house, while Mabel's guest list was quite extensive. Walter Bingham kept *Takusan* in running condition and saw to it the boat was seaworthy for regular outings to Muscongus Bay islands or just for a sunset cruise on the water.

In an August 1924 journal entry, Mabel Todd summed up the restorative value she drew from her island retreat in a most superlative way. "This island is so beautiful it really makes my heart ache! To awaken in the utter stillness—no tooting horns, rushing automobiles, crazy trolley cars—no sickening heat & no arranged program for the day—but instead a soft sound of water, swishing trees, birds, and the savored loveliness of the quiet woods. Why it seems to me God's own heaven can hardly be more perfect."[25]

In 1926, for reasons not recorded but surmised, Howard Hilder vacated Osprey and moved his island studio to the Slade cottage on the northern peninsula. Mabel wrote that Hilder bought the Point Breeze, but conversations between Millicent Bingham and Nellie Ambrose post-1932 made it clear the Ambroses were still owners. Positioned on the western shore of Hog Island, Camp Mavooshen and Osprey are slow getting morning light.

Tall trees keep much in the shade, and it might be concluded that Howard Hilder preferred the brightness of the eastern shore. The Slade cottage had a wide veranda and an inner openness that might have offered an artist more of what was needed for morning production.

Though details are not clear, Hilder gave Osprey back to Mabel Todd, but since she considered deeds too much of an encumbrance in the first place, none was ever signed when the ten acres were transferred in 1920. Perhaps, as with the Slades at the Point Breeze, permission was granted to own on contingency if all worked out. The Slades bought their plot from the Ambroses, while Howard Hilder gave his cottage back to Mabel Todd, which she and her daughter would rent to friends for subsequent summers. In 1927, Mabel noted Hilder's studio at "Waban-aki," a destination that offered "fine steak dinners." When Mabel and her guests rowed to Waban-aki, she raved about the food and the delightful company. It's not a bad guess to consider Waban-aki the name Hilder gave his new cabin on the eastern shore.

In the late 1920s, Mabel Loomis Todd prepared her last Emily Dickinson publication. A reissue of Dickinson letters, first published in 1894, was updated with others that had been sequestered in Mabel's care since the court case that denied her the piece of family property promised her by Austin Dickinson. It is said she worked on editing those Emily Dickinson letters on the veranda of her beloved Hog Island camp house. Enlisting Millicent as co-editor, the new edition complemented an Emily Dickinson revival that left contemporary literary scholars to conclude that she, along with Walt Whitman, were perhaps the two most important and influential of all American poets to date. The new first edition of *Letters* sold out on the day of release, November 5, 1931.

The summer of 1932 was marked by Mabel Todd's first trip to Maine by car. Prior she had either steamed up the coast from Portland or taken a train to Waldoboro. In October the previous year, Howard Hilder had helped her decide on the purchase of a new Buick that he drove with her as a passenger and their summer gear to Maine. They stopped in Washington, DC, on the way for a short visit with Millicent and Walter Bingham.

By the end of July, Howard Hilder completed his painting of living room murals by installing "Heronry" in the south gable, which Mabel concluded was a "fine improvement." He went on to paint furniture in an upgraded guesthouse. No mention of *Takusan* that summer, but Frank Lailer was ready when needed for bay tours in his *Romany Girl*. The end of August was marked by a solar eclipse visible in Maine, where Millicent made arrangements for her father to meet her for the event. Mabel, frequently feeling dizzy, was unable to join them.

On October 14, 1932, seventy-five-year-old Mabel Loomis Todd crossed her final Rubicon. The week prior, she had accompanied Frank Lailer to Waldoboro to pick up shingles for the new building on the shore. The day prior she had supervised the completion of a new rock garden, while all along working diligently to complete the assembly of scrapbooks for Millicent that told their family story. But about midday, upon returning to the living room from a camp errand, she collapsed on the veranda and was gone a few hours later. One can only imagine that if Mabel Loomis Todd were given the choice of settings for the day she would join her beloved Austin, she would have picked Hog Island. If so, she got her wish. In a loving act of closure, Howard Hilder inscribed the final entry in her precious journal:

> "Finis. After a morning spent in happy diligence the end of an honored career of brilliant activities came suddenly soon after noon. Dear gallant soul. Adieu!"

Chapter 3 Notes

[1] Mabel Loomis Todd, "Muscongus Island, Maine." Manuscripts and Archives, Yale University Library.

[2] Mabel Todd, "Muscongus Island," 4.

[3] Millicent Todd Bingham, "Rescuing an Island" (*Natural History*, May 1937), 318.

[4] Millicent repeated this sentiment in a variety of ways over her history of establishing her mother's legacy. This particular quote comes from "Rescuing an Island," 318.

[5] Dickinson biographer Polly Longsworth included a 1933 comment made by Millicent Bingham in an *Austin and Mabel* footnote regarding her family's penchant for verbal fabrication. "One of the earliest things I can recall was a gradual awakening to the fact that both my mother and my grandmother distorted the truth, if necessary. Exaggeration, it was, rather than lying." Longsworth, *Austin and Mabel*, 13.

In a personal email this author received from Longsworth on this topic, she opined, "It's surprising for a person as fact oriented as Millicent was ('accurate to the seventh decimal' was her watchword), to be discovered gussying up the acquisition story. Yet, as you say, she did it with family references to her forebears and their achievements for the Biographical Record, so why not for the Audubon Society." As mentioned in an earlier chapter, the family also elevated Eben Jenks Loomis to the rank of "professor" after he had taken a few college classes when he was, in fact, primarily a nature-loving number cruncher who also loved poetry.

[6] In the unpublished "Appraisal Report and Valuation Analysis" Mrs. Bingham had done on her Hog Island property in summer 1953, the following June 1908 property owners of the island are listed as J. Melvin Genthner, Phillip W. Genthner, Arunah Weston, William H. Hilton, George T. Keene, F. Otis Kent, Susan C. and Lucy A. Weston, and G. L. Weston Kent. Use of commas and conjunctions in the document makes single- and multiple-owner sections unclear. In any case, there were nine owners of fewer than nine tracts.

[7] Mabel Loomis Todd journal, July 25, 1909.

[8] Mabel Todd had a lot to say in her diaries. For citation of the various comments inserted into this narrative, match comments with dates. All quotes taken from unpublished diary entries from Yale University archive microfilm.

[9] Millicent held her grandfather Eben in high regard, especially in his appreciation for nature. She remembers his having "a nature as open as the sunny meadows and as filled with light as the June sky." She referred to him as "a child of Nature." Quoted in Julie Dobrow, *After Emily: Two Remarkable Women and the Legacy of America's Greatest Poet* (W. W. Norton, 2018), 96.

[10] "Flowers Native to Hog Island," 1912. See Appendix B.

[11] It seems two different *toriis* were erected at Mavooshen. One early photograph in the family archive at Yale shows a rough version made of birch logs at the forest edge. Other pictures, including the 1915 "high tide" photograph, show a *torii* of smoother construction posted just up the hill from their "little house" on the shore. In Japan, *torii* gates are found at the entrances to Shinto shrines with a history of first being a perch, and thus a welcome, to birds.

[12] *Takusan* was a power boat that served the camp well. Still, Mabel Todd seemed to prefer being on the water under sail. On September 3, 1911, she wrote in her diary, "Sailing is so poetic! Motor-boating so merely convenient!"

[13] Quoted in Dobrow, *After Emily*, 205.

[14] Swanson Granite Quarry is mentioned by name in Mabel's diary entry for September 7, 1916. Millicent reported in her camp talks that stone from Swanson's was used in Grant's Tomb, among other important edifices. She claims demand for granite diminished when architects switched to concrete.

[15] Use of the spiral bits at the quarry: A bit was attached to a crossbar lowered onto hewn granite. Powered by horses, water and sand would work within the continually moving spiral to smooth the granite. Polishing aggregate would exit through the spiral's open end. Horsepower was eventually replaced by steam.

[16] Matsuba is also the name of a metallic-colored koi with a black netting or pinecone pattern on the body.

[17] Mabel reports in a March 30, 1920, journal entry from Matsuba that David's trip was a total washout. "It would appear David spent the whole summer down there with failed equipment, a hurricane, and a wrecked aeroplane." She concluded, "I am his mascot, really."

[18] Closing date for the Point Breeze is unclear. 1919 is recorded here based on research done by The Island Institute. Charles B. McLane, *Islands of the Mid-Maine Coast: Muscongus Bay and Monhegan Island,* Vol. 3 (The Island Institute / Tilbury House Publishers, 1992).

[19] The primary source for dates of Camp Mavooshen construction comes from a real estate appraisal Millicent Bingham had done in 1953 to ascertain the value of her property. The report itemizes the eight buildings reported here, but with multiple construction date errors when checked against Mabel Todd's diary entries.

[20] A surprised Steve Kress retells the story of talking to island neighbors when one said he was part of the Osprey's deconstruction and that materials from that building were used on his own property. The Osprey came down during the tenure of camp director Duryea Morton, who could not recall details of the cottage's demise. The chimney remained standing for some time before coming down in a storm.

[21] The lobster house and workshop were uprooted and floated to the Audubon Camp during Steve Kress's second tenure as camp director (1982–86). The lobster house was improved to become the Helm, while the workshop is now the Quarterdeck.

[22] The *Lincoln County News* reported the first flush toilet on Louds Island in 2009. By that time the school had closed, and the local community had abandoned the island to rusticators. The toilet was installed by a summer resident upgrading a farm property. Neighbors complained about the modernization, but the owner stated he was trying to avoid degrading the water quality that might harm local shellfish. After an investigation, no violation of his permit was found. Joe Gelarden, "A Historic First on Louds Island" (*Lincoln County News,* July 8, 2009).

[23] Mabel Todd, "Muscongus Island," 3.

[24] The gentle reader is encouraged to encounter Mabel Todd's unpublished *The Epic of Hog* in its entirety in Appendix A.

[25] Mabel Todd journal, August 9, 1924.

Todd-Bingham Era Gallery
Todd-Bingham Picture Collection (MS496E)
Manuscripts & Archives, Yale University Library

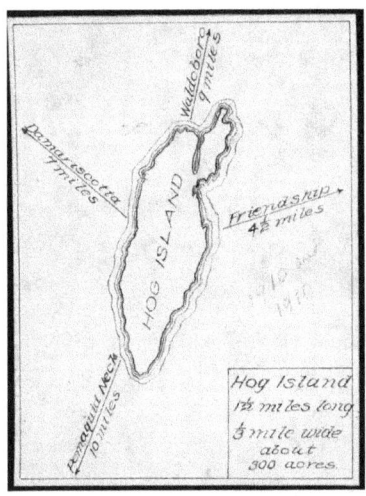

Map of Hog Island at the time of
the Todd purchase (Yale)

Mabel Loomis Todd on steps of the
Observatory House, Amherst, 1911 (FOHI)

David Peck Todd (Yale)

Amherst Station solar eclipse expedition equipment, Esashi, Japan, 1896.
Note Mabel Todd in the doorway. (Yale)

Mabel Loomis Todd in Japan (Yale)

Point Breeze Inn & Bugalows postcard (Yale)

Point Breeze bungalows (Yale)

The Point Breeze Annex, known today as the Porthole (Yale)

The Todds on their way to or from Hog Island ca. 1911. Seated, left to right:
David Todd, Millicent Todd, Mabel Todd, and Eben Loomis (Yale)

Site on the western shore selected for the Todd family camp (Yale)

Hog Island forest detail (Yale)

Primitive camping kitchen (Yale)

Building on site at time of the Todd purchase (Yale)

The Todds unload gear at high tide with Mabel's father,
Eben Loomis, still aboard (Yale)

David Todd and Eben Loomis engineer stone removal from the beach (Yale)

Stone masons unload equipment (Yale)

Work on the stone piazza (Yale)

Clammers cottage became known as the lobster house (Yale)

The family camp develops (Yale)

Meal with guests (Yale)

The Todd family camp with torii visible (Yale)

The torii is considered a welcome sign to birds and other wildlife (Yale)

Osprey and torii (Yale)

Improved lobster house kitchen (Yale)

"In bathing costume, she scans
the distant sea." (Yale)

Launch of the restored *Takusan* (Yale)

Takusan (Yale)

Mabel Todd on Muscongus Bay day trip (Yale)

Charlie Nash, along with wife Myra Keene,
original owners of the mainland farm (FOHI)

One of a few toriis erected over time (Yale)

Todd family camp at high tide with *Takusan* and Japanese flag ca. 1915 (Yale)

David Todd ferrys guests (Yale)

Millicent Todd (Yale)

Millicent's cabin ca. 1920 (Yale)

Camp Mavooshen visitor (Yale)

Mabel Todd (R) with camp guests (Yale)

Mabel and Millicent entertain island guests (Yale)

Todd camp building no longer standing (Yale)

Utility shed no longer standing (Yale)

"Rowley and (Frank) Lailer, 1920." (Yale)

Frank Lailer at one of many camp projects (Yale)

Mabel Loomis Todd on the veranda of her Camp Mavooshen main house (Yale)

Mabel Todd wrote how proud she was of the camp's front door (Yale)

Hearth built with stones from an island agricultural wall (Yale)

Mabel Loomis Todd at her summer home ca. 1930 (Yale)

Mabel Loomis Todd, 1931 (Yale)

Mabel Loomis Todd and Millicent Todd
Bingham (Yale)

Millicent Todd Bingham and Mabel Loomis Todd (Yale)

Left to right- Ida Slade, Walter Van Dyke Bingham, Dan Thomspson (cook),
David Peck Todd, and Millcent Todd Bingham (Yale)

Walter Van Dyke Bingham (FOHI)

Millicent Todd Bingham's portrait hanging in the Fish House inscribed to Carl Buchheister for his work creating the camp (FOHI)

Bingham cottages ca. 1932 (Yale)

"*Takusan* and 'Byron' on our float ca. 1939." (Yale)

Byron Studley, Hog Island storyteller (Yale)

The Osprey cottage (Yale)

The Osprey porch was directly over the shore trail (Yale)

Bingham cottages' float (Yale)

"Hog Island heronry, 1935 (Great Blue)." (Yale)

Mrs. Bingham in 1955, the summer following Hurricanes Carol and Edna (Yale)

Many mature trees lost around Mrs. Bingham's cottage (Yale)

Timber floated from the island to mainland dock area (Yale)

Timber transported to sawmill (Yale)

Interior of the main house ca. 1955 (Yale)

Millicent's Mavooshen ca. 1955 (Yale)

Mrs. Bingham (Yale)

Addition to main camp building now demolished (Yale)

Mrs. Bingham in her cottage (Yale)

Mrs. Bingham and the Carters, 1959 (Yale)

CHAPTER 4

Mavooshen's Men

Few are the branches of astronomy that have not been modified by photography and the spectroscope. It has become a measuring tool of the first order of accuracy.

—David Peck Todd
"Astronomy: A Living Science" / 1922

Any history of Hog Island must rely heavily on the remembrances of prime island historian Millicent Todd Bingham, which means there is no question about anyone other than her mother being responsible for the preservation of Hog Island and the rustic upgrades that evolved into Camp Mavooshen. At a time when strong American women were stepping up and playing more active roles in civic discourse, the preservation of Hog Island is, indeed, a tribute to the vision and activism of Mabel Loomis Todd, an accomplishment any daughter would celebrate.

Still, both Mabel and Millicent were married to published professional partners who both just happened to be proficient handymen capable of solving any number of practical problems that would inevitably come up at a summer camp on a coastal island that required not only water transportation to reach but had no reliable drinking water source, sanitation, or electricity. It is time for this Hog Island narrative to broaden to include the background of the seldom-mentioned men of Hog Island who had significant careers of their own yet still made vital contributions to the family compound that made the summer recreational life at Camp Mavooshen possible.

In turn, a focus follows on the professional accomplishments and worthwhile contributions to Hog Island by spouses David Peck Todd and Walter Van Dyke Bingham; camp artist and noted muralist G. Howard Hilder; and local jack-of-all-trades Frank Lailer.

David Peck Todd

Mabel Loomis Todd and David Peck Todd, as established earlier, were a complementary couple who assisted each other in their own unique and professional interests. David saw to it that his wife had a studio on the Amherst campus where she could pursue her interest in the visual arts and is also mentioned in the Dickinson legacy briefly as assisting his wife with proofreading chores.

Mabel, for her part, traveled with David broadly, sailing around the world as he chased the recording of data and photographic images of solar eclipses and signs of possible civilization on Mars while employing the most scientific and technical approaches to celestial science available at the time. On those trips, along with sketching coronal flares at totality, Mabel Todd's writing ambition blossomed as she chronicled the people and cultures of the places visited for an American readership back home hungry for stories of places little known and rarely visited. Her articles on family astronomical travels appeared in well-read and widely circulated periodicals of the day.[1] She also authored, co-authored, and edited publications about her husband's specialty, astronomy. When one defines David Todd's career, it would be difficult, in so many ways, to separate it from important work accomplished by Mabel Loomis Todd. When the accomplishments of one are highlighted, most often achievements of the other are not very far away.[2]

Five years into his tenure at Amherst College, David Peck Todd was no closer to being a famous astronomer than when he left the employ of Simon Newcomb at the Naval Observatory in the nation's capital. Funding for the promised new Amherst observatory had evaporated, though he was active in the construction of a new sky-watching facility at nearby Smith College, where he taught astronomy and mathematics part-time. If he hoped to have a new observatory of his own at Amherst, he would have to make a name for himself to have a serious impact on donors. Since he had had success managing the solar eclipse expedition to Texas almost a decade earlier, he thought to make his mark directing similar trips to upcoming totality destinations, targeting Japan in 1887 and West Africa in 1889. Once again assisted by Newcomb, Todd was named director of the American expeditions to both destinations with funding provided by the US Navy, while the Japan trip picked up additional financial support from the National Academy of Science.[3]

It is important to remember that for over two hundred years prior to 1853, Japan was an isolated nation under shogun rule that refused contact with the outside world, especially the West. After US Commodore Matthew Perry sailed into Tokyo harbor that summer and subsequently negotiated a treaty opening domestic ports to trade and the country to a foreign world, Japan fell into nearly two decades of interior conflict. It was not until 1868, when a Meiji emperor was restored as head of state, that national order resumed. When early Western visitors returned from Japan to report the beautiful and exotic wonders found there, the Pacific empire became a much-talked-about land of enchantment and mystery for America and the rest of the world to ponder.

As mentioned earlier, David and Mabel Todd were in the process of organizing the first long and arduous American solar expedition to the Land of the Rising Sun when Emily Dickinson died in the spring of 1886. By the time the expedition returned fall of 1887, Mabel was awarded the task of editing her poetry by default. But while in Japan, the Todds were both smitten by the land and the people so much that the Japanese influence in their personal lives would reach all the way to their summer camp on Hog Island, still twenty years down the road.

August weather in Japan is not ideal for clear skies, but it was the best tract for totality available as far as David Todd could calculate. Knowing this, he enriched the science potential of the trip by including "collateral work of such nature that, should the eclipse prove a failure, the labors of the Expedition might accrue to the benefit of science."[4] Along with the primary goal of photographing the sun's corona, he included a Ph.D. naturalist who would observe, note, and collect what flora and fauna specimens were permitted by a new government still trying to develop a viable foreign policy, not twenty years post-restoration. In addition, Todd negotiated permission for a team to ascend sacred Mount Fuji to conduct "an astronomical reconnaissance from the summit of the mountain, 12,400 feet high" to see if it were suitable for an observatory, a practice being duplicated then on tall mountain peaks all across the globe.[5]

While the eclipse was a total failure all along the line of totality, from Russia to Japan, a positive take away for the Todds was a co-authored article about their adventure together that appeared in summer 1892 in *The Century Magazine*.[6] "An Ascent of Fuji the Peerless" was primarily a narrative of the astronomy team's climb on the same paths taken over centuries by faithful pilgrims. At the highest point possible for celestial observation, they set up various equipment and were pleased with optical results even though the nighttime temperature became uncomfortably cold. Before they descended, some of the company, including Mabel Todd, walked down into Fuji's dramatic volcanic cauldron. She reported being the first "foreign woman" to reach the mountain's peak. One can only imagine the excitement the whole team felt on such a memorable exploratory adventure into and through a land of uniquely oriental appeal.

A few other expeditions and much personal history would come to pass in the nine years before David and Mabel Todd returned to Japan, a place not unlike Hog Island in that it renewed their spirits and captured their imaginations. The year following the first Japan expedition, 1888, was a milestone year for David Peck Todd. His efforts overseeing construction at Smith College were rewarded with the opening of their observatory. In addition, he was awarded his Ph.D., albeit honorary, from Washington and Jefferson College in Pennsylvania. And amid all of that professional hubbub, he and Mabel and eight-year-old Millicent moved into The Dell, their first real *house* together, located near the Dickinson homestead and designed with the assistance of Austin Dickinson.[7] The following year, 1889, marked two expeditions to capture images of the corona, one in January in the western United States, the second in December in Angola, West Africa, where David again directed the American expedition funded by the US Navy.

The tardiness of "An Ascent of Fuji the Peerless" not making print until 1892 was undoubtedly the product of Mabel Todd's attention to other publications in process at the time. The first two series of Dickinson poems came in 1890 and 1892, while the first edition of Emily's letters, letters Mabel Todd took responsibility for collecting, in 1894, the same year she published a contribution to the Columbian Knowledge Series, *Total Eclipses of the Sun.* Edited by her husband, Mabel notes in the preface, "Whatever in Professor Todd's writing, published or unpublished, could serve my purpose, I have summarily appropriated," meaning this document, too, was really co-authored by both Mabel and David.[8] In this text as in others, the two attempted to render complicated astronomical concepts understandable to the general public through the use of simple language and clear graphics.

By the time the Todds headed back to Japan in 1895 on what was billed as the longest yachting trek on record, their hearts were heavy with the death of Austin Dickinson earlier that year. Still, both were ready for the experience of a lifetime enhanced by what they had learned on their first trip. David was eager to put into play his new photographic apparatus, a system of glass plate cameras operated by a foot pedal and perforated tape that made possible several hundred pictures during the few critical minutes of totality. Par for the course, the weather clouded up and few usable pictures were generated. Still, he was pleased with his mechanism and would finally find success with it during totality in Tripoli in 1905.[9]

Mabel went on to publish a detailed record of the 45,000-mile New York to Esashi, Japan, expedition in *Corona and Coronet*. The book celebrated the ship's crew and owner, Arthur Curtiss James, an Amherst alum with deep financial roots in the mining and railroad businesses who captained his ship. In addition, the book called out the professionalism of the eclipse team and included detail of exotic ports of call like San Francisco, the Hawaiian islands, and Yokohama.[10] A book blurb by publisher Houghton Mifflin called it "A brilliant story of the longest yachting trip on record" with "entertaining chapters on far away regions," including the expedition team's final destination "three hundred miles further north in the Japanese Empire than a foreign woman had ever before penetrated, in the land of the hairy Ainu, the aborigines of Japan." The blurb also celebrated Mabel Todd's "powers of quick and minute description, keen sense of humor, delicate feeling for nature, and her knowledge of music, botany, astronomy, and other subjects."[11] She would undoubtedly go on to use anecdotes from *Corona and Coronet* to add local color to the scores of talks she gave on her hectic lecture schedule.

In addition to *Corona and Coronet*, Mabel Todd scored two national publications out of the second expedition to Japan. The first ran in the September 1897 issue of *The Atlantic* entitled "In Quest of a Shadow: An Astronomical Experience in Japan," which provided both Japanese travelogue and details about the wispy-clouded totality. Setting up equipment on the northern island of Hokkaido in the town of Esashi, Mabel relayed how "members of the Board of Education and government officials" came to watch the eclipse and the American eclipse team. Before they left the archipelago nation, David Todd was awarded a ceremonial sake cup from the emperor in gratitude for his work promoting science education.

The second piece came a year later in July 1898 in *The Century Magazine*. Unlike "In Quest of a Shadow," this new article, "In Aino-Land," was much more anthropological in scope, describing a remote aboriginal people most of the general Japanese population on the southern islands didn't even know well. Known as "the foreign lady" in all the villages her guides took her, she wrote of classic Aino customs "stunted by the Japanese government," like ritual bear hunts and the tattooing and brutal treatment of women. Still, she observed, "the situation is not without parallel in our own relation to Indians. Yet the Japanese government makes wise laws for the protection of the Ainos, and acts toward them in an altogether civilized manner. A society exists in Sapporo for their assistance."[12]

Before she headed back to America, Mabel Todd collected what cultural artifacts local people were willing to part with. Such a task was not without its sensitive difficulties. She wrote, "To buy any of the utensils, ornaments, or treasures from an Aino house requires tact and diplomacy even more than that necessary in purchasing old mahogany or blue china from some unwilling but hesitating elderly woman on a New England road." By the time her collecting was complete, she had secured Aino robes of elm fiber, bows and poisoned arrows, carved mustache lifters, tobacco boxes, knife sheaths and handles, and a few pieces of Japanese lacquer.[13] What she collected was later gifted to the Peabody Museum of Salem, Massachusetts.

The year following his second and last eclipse expedition to Japan, David Todd released *A New Astronomy*, a text dedicated to two crew mates "in grateful memory of *Coronet* days."[14] His primary purpose for this book was to offer a refined perspective to the common understanding that science education should be offered exclusively in laboratory courses. David promoted the concept of observation as key to all science by citing the just deceased English biologist and evolutionist Thomas Henry Huxley: "The attempt to convey scientific conceptions, without the appeal to observation, which can alone give such conceptions firmness and reality, appears to me to be in direct antagonism to the fundamental principles of scientific education."[15] David compounded that thought by adding, "Earth, air, and water (merely material things) are always with us. We touch them, handle them, ascertain their properties, and experiment upon their relations. Plainly, in their study, laboratory courses are possible. So, too, is a laboratory in astronomy, without actually journeying to the heavenly bodies."[16] Professor Todd's popular handbook on the workings of the universe would be translated into Hungarian and Japanese and go through twenty-five English editions.[17]

The five years following the death of Austin Dickinson were professionally fertile yet emotionally difficult ones for both David and Mabel Todd. David may have lost a best friend, but Mabel lost the love of her life. Despite the drama of the ensuing legal hassle over property promised, Mabel's career as a lecturer, editor, and distinguished author was in high gear. The same could be said for David. Reported to be an easy-going, humorous teacher who went to the aid of students, David was a popular and entertaining lecturer in his own right. In 1899, he increased his writing and editing production with *Stars and Telescopes*, another astronomical handbook. Topics included famous astronomers and the history they made, the sun, planets, stars and nebulae, comets, and the procedure required to measure the distance between the sun and the earth, which by 1903 would be known as an astronomical unit.

David Peck Todd cut his professional teeth as an undergraduate on observations of the satellites at Jupiter, going on to photograph the second-in-a-lifetime transit of Venus while making his biggest contributions to solar study. But there was more. Another bright point in the night sky, Mars, was in the news at the time. What were those long, seemingly straight geological features observed across the red planet's face as seen through upgraded optics? Were the distinguishing features too predictable to be natural? Could they have been constructed by some intelligent civilization? Optics weren't good enough to see that kind of detail, but many educated people, including David Todd, thought a closer investigation of Mars was in order.[18]

Successful American businessman, author, and self-taught astronomer, Percival Lowell, the same man who would go on to build the Lowell Observatory in the dry air above Flagstaff, Arizona, shared David Todd's enthusiasm for Mars.[19] Lowell came to Amherst to discuss Mars with Todd where they worked out an agreement for two separate international expeditions. The first would be a return trip to northern Africa for Todd to direct the photography of a solar eclipse in Tripoli in 1900. David would take the pictures while Lowell would retain ownership of the library of glass plate negatives.[20] The second expedition had David leading a crew up into the Andes mountains of Peru in 1907 to photograph Mars on its cyclical closest approach to Earth. While some Mars enthusiasts wanted to signal the red planet via a sophisticated light source, others thought a more logical approach lay in electromagnetic radio waves. Still others thought the "canals" looked a whole lot like riverbeds as found on Earth and didn't mean anything civilized.[21] The Lowell Mars expedition did its work and finely-detailed photography of the planet was generated. Somewhere along the line, too, Todd Crater on the Mars moon Phobos was named after Professor Todd. Both he and Mabel had asteroids named after them, as well.[22]

Aside from his achievements in astronomy, David Todd had a penchant for solving knotty mechanical problems here on his home planet, notably on Hog Island. David's dabbling with ideas to improve dredging machines, electric organs, and track-laying devices surely led to camp fixes that made summers more comfortable. The primary thing Mabel marveled over was David's clearing of large stones from the beach. First, he used a series of log rollers with leveraged power to move the manageable ones. Later he created a tripod system to clear others. Mabel wrote in her diary in 1911, when their summer camp was in its most rudimentary stage, "David is moving gigantic stones in a very remarkable way. He should be the most famous engineer in this country, for he is a positive genius in all mechanized matters."[23]

The year 1915 marked the first summer the Todd's Hog Island camp was in full operation, celebrated by the classic shore photograph taken by a friend. In that black-and-white image, Japan's continued influence on David and Mabel Todd is evident. Central to the photo is a reliable, restored watercraft, *Takusan*, which was David's responsibility. In addition, Japanese colors are seen flying outside their upgraded shore cabin while a *torii* gate spans the path, welcoming visitors, both human and feathered. In the iconic photo, Mabel stands outside the little house as Hog Island's own *dressy adventuress*, replete in a long dress and sunhat.

Mabel's respect and admiration for David's ingenuity were unflinching. "He is so versatile—his brain is so amazingly fertile. His work is so engrossing and his industry so unflagging that I admire him very much." As complicated as their lives grew emotionally under the pall of their relationships with the Dickinsons, Mabel completed her compliment of her husband by adding, "I think it very rare that two persons, especially married persons, work together so well and so helpfully." Despite all the Amherst complications, Dickinson scholar Polly Longsworth agrees. "Together over the years they created a close, enormously productive colleagueship, the reliable underpinning to their otherwise quirky marriage."[24]

Despite David Todd's "amazingly fertile" brain, by 1920 his wife was concerned about his increasingly troubling manic behavior. There was no drug in any apothecary yet to treat the sexually transmitted disease that claimed him.[25] He would spend the rest of his life institutionalized, though he still worked.[26] In 1922, he published his last book, one his daughter reported was written on Hog Island prior to his hospitalization. *Astronomy: The Science of the Heavenly Bodies* celebrated astronomy as "man's golden chain connecting the heavens to the Earth."[27] He hoped this text would make astronomy a bit more accessible to the general public, a hope echoed not too many years later by the Audubon folks up on the north end of Hog Island about a new breakthrough study in earth science, ecology.

Through his solid career applying technology to good science, one can't help but wonder what David Peck Todd would think of the stunning images of interstellar space made by contemporary spacecraft like Spitzer, Hubble, and the James Webb Space Telescope. He would eventually get improved images of the night sky with his New Amherst College Observatory by 1905 and use it until his retirement over a decade later. In his endless pursuit to photograph the sun's corona with as little diffusion from the atmosphere as possible, he tried his hand at airborne photography from both balloons and aircraft. But for an astronomer who built a career on discoveries found only by way of breakthrough technology, one can only wonder what he would think about the marvels of the universe we are just seeing for the first time today.

Walter Van Dyke Bingham

Walter Van Dyke Bingham is one of two men of Camp Mavooshen who came on the scene around 1920, just about the time David Todd vacated his position as chief handyman in charge. Bingham came that summer, writes Millicent, as "our guest," but before he left he had proposed marriage to forty-year-old Millicent, an age-mate of his, while the two were out on an around-the-island row. She said yes. They were married the following December.

Truth was, she had known Walter Bingham for about seven years, having made his acquaintance at an event at Dartmouth College, where he served as head of the department of psychology. He had fallen in love; Millicent, not so much. On that row around Hog Island, Millicent confessed she felt emotionally dead, a condition that didn't seem to bother Walter.[28] They would go on to be married for over thirty years until his death in 1952, enjoying many summers at their inherited Hog Island haunts while spending hours at the Audubon Nature Camp as distinguished guests, both mixing with campers and offering bits to regular group presentations.

Walter Van Dyke Bingham was born in rural Iowa in 1880 to parents who came in a covered wagon to break and farm new ground. Walter reported memories of Native Americans "bringing skins of wild creatures to sell for a few cents apiece" to his father's door.[29] Agriculture was not to be in Walter's future, however, as he completed his undergraduate work at Beloit College and, following that, taught secondary school for four years, saving money for graduate work. He acquired both his masters and doctorate at Harvard and was awarded a second doctorate at the University of Chicago.

Bingham was a great lover of music, and according to Millicent, had the gift of perfect pitch. He used to say if he hadn't gotten into psychology, he would have liked to have conducted a symphony orchestra. But psychology it was, and during his career, he made important contributions to what would be known in the field as industrial psychology.

Walter had a self-professed penchant for helping people achieve their best. He admitted he didn't get into psychology to fix the broken. "I have preferred to give a hand to the promising rather than the weak, the unhappy, the unadjusted, whom we psychologists may wisely leave... to the ministration of our friends, the psychiatrists and social workers."[30] Walter's focus was assisting clients and students to reach their full potential. In so doing, he made close observations and ran experiments to determine what specific qualities successful people exhibited under what conditions.

An author of a dozen books on personnel and employment psychology, Walter Bingham's primary claim to fame as a pioneer in American psychology came in his work with the US Army. As it became apparent the United States would be drawn into World War I, Bingham and a couple of colleagues developed and revised a series of tests to determine, for the first time, appropriate rank and assignment for enlisted men and recruits. These testing methods were later adapted for use in business and are also credited as being forerunners of the Scholastic Aptitude Tests.[31] Bingham was pressed into service again during World War II when he served as the chief psychologist to the adjutant general's office. His research and results in testing were the beginning of implementing psychology in the real-world workplace as opposed to mind study relegated to the realm of academic scholarship.

Through his teaching appointments at the University of Chicago, Teachers' College of Columbia University, Dartmouth College, and the Carnegie Institute of Technology, Walter Bingham continued to develop his gift of helping others reach professional success.[32] Millicent wrote, "Nothing rejoiced him like seeing a man attain his objective when he himself had been instrumental in making it possible. He found only satisfaction in the knowledge that yet another man had been helped to reach his niche where he belonged." When those who had found success failed to thank Walter adequately for his guidance, Millicent grew indignant. Not Walter. "His sunny temperament, his bright smile, his kindness, his humor and his courtesy, his perceptions of another's need and his prompt effort to help toward its fulfillment were combined with an awareness of self and an indifference to self-interest so genuine that it identified his own happiness with the accomplishments of others."[33]

Walter Bingham came to Hog Island as a psychologist in love with Millicent, not a born-and-bred lover of nature as his wife had. But as one curious about all matters of things, when he found himself immersed in a new family interested in the world of nature, he was drawn into the mystery and beauty of the coast of Maine they so loved. One of his primary interests became the succession of living things, or how the decay of one being provided sustenance for the success of another. Also, the sheer number of saplings sprouting in recent forest openings amazed him. "Seedings by the thousands," he wrote, "send up candidates for maturity. Hundreds reach a youthful height of ten or twenty feet before succumbing to the stresses of competition. Only the fitted grasp the sunlight, keep flexible, and climb on."[34] Hog Island provided him ample opportunities to employ his power of observation that served him so well in his chosen field of psychology.

Little is written in Mabel Todd's diaries about day-to-day improvements at Camp Mavooshen, though she addressed major construction and upgrades. In fall 1932, just weeks before she died, she referred to a second building being constructed behind the little kitchen hut on the shore. The plan for her new building, as mentioned earlier, was to create a camp dining room. After her passing, however, that building was repurposed to be a workshop for Walter. It was on the roof of that building that he made his best jury-rigged camp improvement by creating a rain-catching chamber that fed water by gravity through a hose to the kitchen sink next door.

Millicent observed, "Living in a wilderness camp without running water is a challenge to ingenuity." Walter proved capable of solving at least part of that dilemma, impressing Millicent in the process. She further observed, "Mechanical devices were as familiar to him as the songs of birds to me." In the short time Walter shared island chores with David, they both rigged up a scaffolding concept placed under beach boulders that at high tide would permit the offending stone to be floated off the sand to broaden the beach. Walter also was notorious for clearing dead trees near camp buildings. Using a block and tackle setup, he strategically dropped trunks in a safe spot to then be cut up, split, stacked, and stoked to warm camp buildings on cool nights. "When the tree cooperated as planned, his smile of satisfaction would have graced the successful launching of a formula for a new test of aptitude," Millicent remembered.[35]

More than anything else at Hog Island, Walter loved skippering the *Takusan* around the bay, making various stops and finding occasional adventure. A story he relished telling was the time he took the *Takusan* out with Camp Mavooshen visitors in search of whales reported in the area days prior. Sure enough, they found the pod and at one time there were "no less than three pairs moving around our boat, like elephantine folk dancers doing an infinitely slow and gracefully ponderous waltz. The climax came when one of the pairs appeared beside the boat less than two rods from our gunwales."[36] Not all passengers were comfortable with the proximity of the behemoths, but Walter wasn't worried. Field glasses were raised and lots of pictures were taken. By the time Walter turned the *Takusan* back to camp, his guests were exhausted but exhilarated by the excitement.

Walter Bingham was a psychologist who loved watching people and hearing their stories, and in so doing on Hog Island, created two pieces of unique literature that have been prized at the Audubon Camp for decades. Many visitors hiking the island to the Todd Bingham camp compound are impressed with the "spiral nebula" irons still hanging on the buildings and over the hearth in Mrs. Todd's living room. Walter was impressed as well, seeing them as an illustration of the beauty of function. Not satisfied with his own thoughts, however, Walter made a bit of sport out of asking "Auduboners" what they thought the crude metal hangings represented. He kept a notebook of responses, which in time included "a fern crozier," "cross-section of a conch shell," "the tail of Hog," and "a vortex—keep away or you might get sucked in." Though Walter's good-natured list was never published, Mrs. Bingham kept the story and his process alive by retelling it many times when she came to camp and gave her talk on the history of Hog Island.

Millicent Bingham memorialized important people in her life by publishing books of their remembrance.[37] Upon Walter's passing in 1952, amid her own final push to achieve her mother's wish to make public the remainder of the sequestered Emily Dickinson material, Millicent set in print, with the help of John Baker and Carl Buchheister at Audubon, a published remembrance of her husband entitled *Homo Sapiens Auduboniensis: A Tribute to Walter Van Dyke Bingham*. At the heart of the text was the light-hearted talk Walter gave at an annual Audubon meeting in New York City in fall 1937.

In the introduction to that memorial, Millicent reported how she was a bird watcher, but Walter a *birder* watcher. Those gentle readers here who know birders, know that sometimes their attire and enthusiastic attitudes are easy to parody. Walter's good nature and personal wit made his "Preliminary Notes on Behavior and Ethology of *Homo Sapiens Auduboniensis* in the Muscongus Bay Region" an address to remember. Up to that time, no one could recall the practices of birders or nature lovers being diagnosed through psychological analysis. Surely written to entertain those gathered, some Audubon management wished Walter would have taken his study further into a more serious vein since they were actively trying to find both kids who had the knack for excelling in natural sciences and ways to help the adults who were trying to reach those kids.[38] The entirety of Walter's tongue-in-cheek address cataloging characteristics of birders is happily included as an appendix in this book.

In the dark days following her mother's death, Walter was a comfort to Millicent as she tried to figure out what would happen to her family's beloved island. She wrote, "Walter was there beside me to take my hand as we walked through the moss-carpeted forests or sat on our pier beneath the stars on magic summer evenings." On some nights they talked over plans while they rowed the bay, each stroke of the oars leaving a luminescent "cloud of light deep in the water" that gave them the sense of a "reflected universe of stars."[39] Millicent and Walter knew how special their island was, and though times were hard during the Great Depression, they were dedicated to finding some viable scientific use for Hog Island that would outlast them and the camp Millicent had inherited. That part of the Hog Island story, featuring the National Audubon Society, will be picked up in the next chapter.

G. Howard Hilder

George Howard Hilder was the second to become a male contributor to Mavooshen around 1920. It is unclear how he first connected with the Todds, but as a member of the artist community in the Miami, Florida, area, it appears they met not long after Mabel and David vacated Amherst and relocated to the much friendlier confines of Coconut Grove in 1918. Soon after their arrival, it also appears Mabel Todd became a Hilder patron. For a time, the garage at the Todd Florida estate was transformed into a Howard Hilder studio. In September 1919, when he came to Hog Island for the first time to stay at the Point Breeze in order to visit the Todds' camp, Mabel reported he "greatly enjoyed the sail" down from Waldoboro and was "absolutely enthusiastic over my dear island."[40] Mabel did not host Hilder at her Camp Mavooshen that summer, perhaps because she wanted to stay out of the way of the construction of the new camp house that would become her "living room." In addition, she herself was boarding at the Point Breeze while David was off to Brazil on his last, and horribly failed, solar expedition.[41]

Born in London, England, in 1866, Howard Hilder was a capable artist who studied with masters in Paris and Amsterdam before coming to America in 1905.[42] He is known in the annals of art as a noted painter of scenic murals, illustrations, stage settings, figures, and landscapes in both oil and watercolor.[43] His illustrations made the cover of *Vogue* magazine twice in his early years in the States. In time he would set his artistic roots in Newport, Rhode Island; Charleston, South Carolina; Hog Island; and Coconut Grove. In February 1922, the *Miami Herald* described him as "the leading interpreter of the scenic beauty of Florida."

Hilder's first visit to Hog Island proved consequential like none other. Over the following winter, he and Mabel negotiated an agreement whereby he would be permitted a ten-acre tract of Hog Island on which to build a studio. When Walter and Millicent arrived at Hog Island in 1921, they were tasked with checking out the ten acres Hilder had selected for construction. The tract Hilder liked was located south of the Todd camp on the pitched western shore along the trail that leads to Sand Cove. All seemed in order and the artist's cottage, known on the island as the Osprey, was built that summer. Five years later, Hilder *did*, in fact, return Osprey to Mrs. Todd. Regardless of the reason, relations with Mabel Todd remained warm and friendly and "Hilder of Hog," as she affectionately called him, was a most frequent and welcome visitor at Camp Mavooshen.

Post-Hilder life at the Osprey proved full of summer adventure for other Todd-Bingham guests, as will be documented in the next chapter.

The Hilder family had yet another important impact on Hog Island as real property owners. Somewhere along the way Etta Glidden sold her one-quarter share of Hog Island to Howard Hilder's son, John C. Hilder of Connecticut, a publisher of periodicals. Mabel's diary mentions Jack's visiting from time to time, but there was never mention of any plan to build new structures on his deeded, yet still undivided, seventy acres. Problems arose from both this Hilder tract and the Point Breeze peninsula when John Baker of Audubon required all of Hog Island, not just the three-quarter share owned by Millicent Bingham, to be under Audubon jurisdiction before he would commit to opening his Nature Camp. The "island ownership" problem provided a major headache for Millicent to resolve.

After David Todd's hospitalization, Mabel Todd carried on and created an active winter life for herself as a prominent resident of Coconut Grove, where among other things she worked for the Everglades to become a national park and was active in the local Audubon chapter. Some winters she rented out *Matsuba* and stayed in a smaller local dwelling to save money. Howard Hilder's influence on her life grew in those non-David years, but as frank as she was in chronicling details about her sex life in Amherst as a younger woman, there is no indication in her continued writing that Howard Hilder was any more to her than a dear friend.

In 1923, Hilder began a painting project in Coconut Grove for St. Steven's Episcopal Church, the same church Mabel and David attended. His "Life of Christ" series took over a decade to complete and included twelve unique canvases. When Mabel Todd died in 1932, the "Easter Morning" piece in the series was dedicated in her honor. Though she was a Hilder patron, it is not known how many pieces of his art she owned other than the two murals on Hog Island for which she had bartered. She reported at least one portrait he did of her sitting at Osprey, though the disposition of that piece is unknown.

It is worth noting that Millicent Bingham was not a Howard Hilder fan. Quite unlike her mother, Millicent didn't see the "great painter" qualities in his work. She was disgusted by Mabel's lavish praise, perhaps a bit jealous, and appalled that her mother had loaned him money. Millicent was not happy about the permission given to build an artist's studio on the island, and was especially irritated by Howard and his son Jack's "love of whiskey and painted women," offenses echoed in Charlie and Myra Nash's reasoning to cut off mainland shore access to Hog Island.[44]

Nevertheless, Mabel Todd came to know Howard Hilder, ten years her junior, as "my old pal." For years she took the train to get to her summer getaway, but late in years she took the plunge and bought a car, a Buick. Because she was uncomfortable piloting the vehicle all the way to Maine, it was Howard Hilder who provided that service. In addition, as negotiating the trails at her camp on Hog Island became more difficult for her in her later years, it was Howard Hilder who kept track of her, serving as a caregiver. She wrote in October 1929, "I have never been 'scared' enough here by night as to blow my little whistle for him, always ready beside my bed for such an emergency." But he was nearby.[45]

Both Howard Hilder and the next man of Mavooshen remembered, Frank Lailer, were on the island when Mabel Todd fell on her camp house veranda in autumn 1932. Little detail of that day is recorded, but it was those two gentlemen who tried to make her comfortable in the last few hours of her life. Still, besides heroically tending a dying woman and authoring the last triumphant entry in her diary, as mentioned, Howard Hilder's final impact on Hog Island, according to Millicent Bingham, was anything but positive.

Frank Lailer

The last but certainly not least of Mavooshen's men was Frank Lailer, a local handyman who did countless tasks in Mrs. Todd's and then Mrs. Bingham's camps. Mabel wrote his name in her diary, misspelling it at first, summer after summer from the Todd's earliest days of improving their little piece of Hog Island. One of David's biographical sketches highlights his ability to successfully incorporate local people on his expeditions to complete the more difficult chores of hauling heavy equipment, setting up camp and keeping it in order, and cooking and cleaning. If David Todd had a hand in the hiring of Frank Lailer, it came as one of the better examples of his judge of character.

About five years younger than Millicent, Lailer was born in Massachusetts but had resettled in the Bremen area. Data from the 1940 US Census reports he completed three years of high school, lived on a farm in a house that he owned, and held the occupation as a self-employed "smack captain."[46] In those early days on the island, Mabel reports his help with bay transportation of people and camp materials in his boat, *Romany Girl.* She wrote, as well, of Lailer's having brought his wife and children by the island from time to time, a sign the families may also have had a shared social life.

With the loss of most of the Camp Mavooshen buildings over time due to poor foundations, it is fair to report Frank Lailer had a major role in assuring the durability of the two still standing. With David in Brazil in 1919, the main camp house was framed by a team of local carpenters while Lailer installed the siding. In a July 29 diary entry, Mabel complimented him by writing he was a quick worker in having the house "half boarded in at noon." In late September, she wrote of Lailer installing "my beautiful front door."[47]

Whereas stone masons dismantled an agricultural stone wall back on the island, transforming rocks into the magnificent stone hearth that still graces the living room, Frank Lailer took on key tasks of finishing the family float as well as the construction of the building Audubon refers to as "the writer's cottage." Built in 1920 to be "Millicent's room," perhaps as a reward for the young woman finishing her doctorate that spring, the little cottage on the granite rise south above the living room was placed among fine, large trees that Millicent loved so much. Though the trees would not withstand hurricane winds in the future, Lailer's construction did just fine.

A final mention of Frank Lailer came in an essay in *Down East* magazine in 1992.[48] The narrative tells of one of the first post-Mabel Todd summers just as Audubon began camp operations on the northern peninsula with Mrs. Bingham serving as "grand dame" among the campers. In a casual conversation with the spouse of one of the avid bird-watching attendees, she announced, "Do you see that island over there?" Mrs. Bingham pointed west over Muscongus Sound through a lifting fog. "You are going to buy that island, Professor Holmes." The professor protested, saying, "I am only a college professor. If islands cost a nickel a foot, I could not afford to buy a yard." But as the daughter of a college professor, Millicent thought otherwise. She said she knew the family who owned Ram Island and she would see what she could do.

Sure enough, before too long the Holmes family received an offer even they could afford. The key factor they needed to know before signing papers was knowledge of an on-island water source. Reports there were, but since Ram Island had been in an estate settlement and unvisited for years, nobody knew for sure. It would take a Holmes family winter trek from Cambridge to Maine to find out.

On the day after Christmas 1939, Professor Holmes met Frank Lailer in his white lobster boat at the mainland dock, then the Charlie Nash place, for the short trip across the narrows in cold and rain to Ram Island. Navigating close to the shore due to poor visibility, Lailer got the excited Holmes family safely to their destination. "Here you are," Frank said as he eased the boat against a ledge and threw an anchor ashore. "This is Ram Island. The shack there is the only building I know of. The well's supposed to be near the tallest pine somewhere in the center. I'll wait here." And sure enough, the well was found, and because of Frank Lailer's intrepid sailing in a Maine December squall, Millicent Bingham's intuition turned out to be spot on.

All the fellows enumerated in this chapter helped make Mrs. Todd's Camp Mavooshen, and thereafter Mrs. Bingham's cottages, a viable, comfortable, and welcoming summer destination on the rugged Muscongus Bay coast. From David Todd's fumigating the little clammer's house on the shore and transforming it into the camp kitchen to Frank Lailer's countless island odd jobs and major construction projects. From Howard Hilder's practiced craft that manifested itself into watercolor murals celebrating island birdlife to Walter Bingham's own labor-saving odd jobs and his penchant for recording behaviors observed by birding islanders.

So many of the women and men of the *homo sapiens* class of nature's people who came to Mrs. Todd's Camp Mavooshen and Mrs. Bingham's cottages fell in love with the place and were subsequently changed by Hog Island. They would not be the last.

Chapter 4 Notes

[1] Mabel Todd wrote many articles for *The Century Magazine* and *The Atlantic* and quite a few book reviews for *The Nation*. Through her anthropological studies surrounding solar eclipses, she also wrote at least two publications related to the impact of celestial signs on superstition and witchcraft.

[2] The casual reader of Hog Island history is not interested in a recap of all the works written and published by Mabel Loomis Todd and David Peck Todd, yet the full canon is engaging on a variety of levels. One Mabel Todd title already quoted in this book is *A Cycle of Sunsets*. Another "cycle" title in her repertoire is *A Cycle of Sonnets*, a mysterious collection of fourteen-line poems that were "bequeathed to me by one the tragedy of whose life it has been mine to know, were written in mature years, and in the splendor of his first great love for the fair girl who died during the second year of their engagement." Mysterious, in part, because this collection of poems from Roberts Brothers came out the year after Austin Dickinson died.

[3] Much thanks to Polly Longsworth's careful work in *Austin and Mabel* for David Todd's expedition details included here. Longsworth, *Austin and Mabel*, 258.

[4] David Peck Todd, *American Eclipse Expedition to Japan, 1887: Preliminary Report of the Total Solar Eclipse of 1887* (Amherst College Observatory, 1888; Kessinger Publishing's Legacy Reprint series, 2011), 2.

[5] The naturalist selected was Dr. W. J. Holland from Pittsburgh. David Todd, *American Eclipse Expedition*, 2.

[6] "An Ascent of Fuji the Peerless" appeared in *The Century Magazine* two years after John Muir's essays on the geographical wonders of Yosemite Valley in California in the hope of winning National Park status. Like Muir, "Fuji the Peerless" describes remarkable landscape and botany in close detail. From the Fuji piece: "Airy white birches shook the fluttering leaves in the soft breeze, the Japanese maples, beeches, and ash joined the evergreens in making a shady canopy above, while maidenhair ferns, belated wild roses, yellow lilies, dwarf sunflowers, tall

white serpent aria, and purple monk's-hood combine to hide the delicious wild strawberries lurking in the grass." Mabel Loomis Todd and David Peck Todd, "An Ascent of Mount Fuji the Peerless" (*The Century Magazine,* August 1892), 487.

[7] Austin Dickinson assisted in the design of The Dell by suggesting a private entrance be included away from public view, in addition to a private room in the house reserved for the couple's use. The entrance assisted in his clandestine comings and goings the last seven years of his and Mabel's relationship.

[8] Mabel Loomis Todd, *Total Eclipses of the Sun,* The Columbian Knowledge Series. David P. Todd, ed. (Roberts Brothers, 1894), ix.

[9] This detail regarding David Todd inventions from the *Guide to the David Peck Todd Papers,* Yale University, 2.

[10] The American expedition to the 1896 solar eclipse to Japan departed Boston in December 1895. *Coronet* was a new craft christened that year, owned by Arthur Curtiss James, an Amherst class of 1889 alum, and railroad baron who became the largest private holder of railroad stock in the United States. James was a benefactor for other David Todd celestial observation projects. Mabel Loomis Todd, *Corona and Coronet: Being a Narrative of the Amherst Eclipse Expedition to Japan, in Mr. James Schooner-yacht Coronet, to Observe the Sun's Total Obscuration, 9th August, 1896* (Houghton Mifflin, 1898; General Books, 2009), various pages.

[11] Houghton Mifflin brochure for *Corona and Coronet.*

[12] Mabel Loomis Todd, "In Aino-Land" (*The Century Magazine,* July 1898), 350.

[13] Mabel Todd, "In Aino-Land," 348–350.

[14] In this era, titles printed and embossed on the cover of a book were not necessarily official title page nomenclature. This book was entitled simply *A New Astronomy* on the title page, but the cover reads *Professor Todd's New Astronomy.*

[15] Thomas Henry Huxley quoted on the dedication page. David Todd, *A New Astronomy.*

[16] David Todd, *A New Astronomy,* 3.

[17] Both David and Mabel Todd wrote prolifically and not all can be

cited here. In June 1897, Mabel hit the national big time again with another article in *The Century Magazine,* this one entitled "A Great Modern Observatory: Harvard's Astronomical Work." In it she celebrated the contemporary astronomical photography of Harvard's observatory director, Edward C. Pickering. From a family steeped in the stars and planets, she wrote boldly, "The history of astronomy in the United States is coeval with the origin and development of the Harvard Observatory." Mabel Loomis Todd, "A Great Modern Observatory: Harvard's Astronomical Work" (*The Century Magazine,* June 1897), 290.

[18] The Todds traveled to Peru in 1907 to photograph Mars, but the planet was surely on their minds earlier. In 1899, Mabel Todd authored "The Great Red Planet of the West" for *St. Nicholas,* a children's magazine. That same year she "revised and brought down to date" Joel Dorman Steele's 1884 text, *Popular Astronomy: Being the New Descriptive Astronomy.*

[19] Percival Lowell is described in the *Guide to the David Peck Todd Papers* at Yale University as "the most influential popularizer of planetary science in America before Carl Sagan," which, along with building the Lowell Observatory, surely certifies his astronomical credentials. Another planetary issue Todd and Lowell discussed was a celestial body beyond Neptune. When that last "non-planet" was discovered, it was named after Percival Lowell. PL worked its way into Pluto.

[20] Mabel Todd was not able to tag along with David Todd on his first solar eclipse expedition to Africa in December 1889. That trip to Angola was funded by the US Navy, which also provided transportation for the eclipse team and their equipment. At the time, no women, not even a dressy adventuress, were allowed to sail on naval vessels. The Lowell expedition to Tripoli in 1900 had no such restriction. Mabel Todd would go on to publish *Tripoli the Mysterious* in 1912, a book that offered an anthropological study of another distant place few of her readers would ever visit.

[21] As a Mars aside, note that Edgar Rice Burroughs, the popular American author who wrote the Tarzan series, books Mabel Todd noted in her daily journal that she enjoyed reading, published *The Princess of Mars,* the first of his John Carter of Mars series, in 1912.

[22] Asteroids 511, *davida,* and 510, *mabella,* were named for the Todds.

[23] Mabel Todd diary, August 15, 1911.

[24] Longsworth, *Austin and Mabel,* 46.

[25] It is believed David Peck Todd was hospitalized for consequences of syphilis, paralytic dementia. The couple's permanent separation pained them both. An excerpt from David's handwritten letter dated summer 1926 speaks to their shared tragedy. "Dearest—Lightning is striking all about.... If the next hits me, the last word I ever wrote here on Earth will be this loving word to you, Darling.... I have always hoped and fervently prayed that I should pass on first, for I never could think of seeing your spirit leave me here alone.... So I sit at the open window and invite God's thunderbolt now. I'm as ready and willing to go as I ever shall be." He goes on to address a storm's impact on Camp Mavooshen. David "prayed it might not wreck your Camp—and longed to be there to protect you." Chagrined, he added, "But you say 'the boy' is doing finely—so if you are happier with him—and me here—why, I'm happier, too. I have to be.... [signed] L.H.D" L.H.D. was David's affectionate name for himself: *Lover. Husband. David.* Mabel Todd diary, July 24, 1926.

[26] Arthur Curtiss James, wealthy industrialist and owner and captain of the *Coronet,* set up a fund for David's confined care. Dobrow, *After Emily,* 232.

[27] David Todd, *Astronomy,* 3. Ironically, the 1922 David Todd text was revised by John E. Merrill and released in 1939, the year of Todd's death. Merrill's revision took its place in the Popular Science Library series: *The Story of the Starry Universe: The Science of Astronomy: The Size, Motions, Relative Positions and other Phenomena of the Heavenly Bodies.*

[28] Though Walter Bingham was smitten with Millicent, she could not reciprocate. Perhaps her reported "feeling dead" emotionally was because of her painful encounter with Joe Thomas, a recuperating American soldier she met in France while volunteering in World War I. Not unlike her mother's fervor for Austin Dickinson, Millicent fell head over heels for Joe. Seemed Joe felt the same way, but parts of his illustrious biography didn't sit right at home when his story was retold. The Todd family friend and benefactor, Arthur Curtiss James, hired a private

investigator who discovered Mr. Thomas's stories were fabricated. After his anonymous return to the United States, Millicent pursued him to Colorado for clarification of his feelings. She returned home broken-hearted in 1918. Walter Bingham proposed marriage summer of 1919. Dobrow, *After Emily*, 218.

[29] Introduction to *Homo Sapiens Auduboniensis: A Tribute to Walter Van Dyke Bingham*. Millicent Todd Bingham, ed. (National Audubon Society, 1953), 5.

[30] Quoted in Carl W. Buchheister's epilogue to *Homo Sapiens Auduboniensis*.

[31] Carnegie Mellow University unpublished resource.

[32] Carnegie Mellon University honored Walter Bingham by instituting a professorship in his name: The Walter Van Dyke Bingham Professor of Cognitive Development and Education Science.

[33] Bingham, *Homo Sapiens Auduboniensis*, 15.

[34] Bingham, *Homo Sapiens Auduboniensis*, 18.

[35] Bingham, *Homo Sapiens Auduboniensis*, various.

[36] Bingham, *Homo Sapiens Auduboniensis*, 22.

[37] Millicent Bingham wrote lengthy memorial essays for a handful of people she loved and appreciated. Besides *Homo Sapiens Auduboniensis: A Tribute to Walter Van Dyke Bingham*, other memorial publications included *Mary E. Stearns* (1909), a remembrance of a favorite teacher and mentor in Amherst; *Eben Jenks Loomis* (1913), her beloved grand-father; and two for her mother, *Mabel Loomis Todd: Her Contributions to the Town of Amherst* (1935) and *The Thoreau Family Two Generations Ago* (1958). The "contributions to Amherst" piece was an address given to the local chapter of The Daughters of the American Revolution her mother was active in, while the Thoreau family history was prefaced by Millicent but written earlier by her mother.

[38] In a letter to Carl Buchheister in 1948, Walter Bingham restated Audubon's goal for their Hog Island program eloquently in a statement he made earlier at a science talent search. Walter wrote, "I wound up reminding them of the central purpose of the Audubon Nature Camp: to equip teachers and youth leaders with the *determination* and the *skills*

with which to focus the interests of youngsters on some aspect of our natural resources before they have outgrown this crucially decisive phase of mental development." Emphasis Walter's. Bingham, *Homo Sapiens Auduboniensis,* 38–39.

[39] Bingham, *Homo Sapiens Auduboniensis,* 23–24.

[40] Mabel Todd diary, September 16 and 18, 1919.

[41] David Todd's solar eclipse expedition to Brazil in 1919 was a bigger failure than any other at no fault of his own. Weather was bad and equipment did not ship in a timely manner and arrived about a month after the eclipse.

[42] *The Benezit Dictionary of British Graphic Artists and Illustrators* reports Howard Hilder studied under William Bouguereau, Emile Jacque, and Arthur Perrier in Paris; and Theophile de Bock in Amsterdam.

[43] A variety of Howard Hilder works are available to view at art auction sites via internet search. His 20x14 watercolor on board, "Catedral de San Cristobal de la Havana," was purchased in 2010 for an unknown price. One of his Florida landscape paintings was estimated to sell in the $700–900 range in 2015.

[44] Dobrow, *After Emily,* 235.

[45] Mabel Todd diary, October 1, 1929.

[46] A smack is a traditional masted fishing boat used off the coasts of Britain and America for most of the nineteenth century. They have morphed over time and now are called by other names with various masts and sail shapes and sizes.

[47] Mabel Todd diary, September 29, 1919.

[48] Wyman Holmes, "Mrs. Bingham's Island" (*Down East,* April 1992).

CHAPTER 5

Mother Church

When I walk the woods, listen to the thrushes, spy the osprey circling overhead, or hear the boom of the Great-horned Owl at night, I can never feel that I own such a place. It seems rather the property of all who cherish this and wish to preserve it.

—Millicent Todd Bingham
"Rescuing an Island" / 1936

In mid-autumn 1932, Millicent Todd Bingham assessed how her life would be different in the absence of her recently deceased mother. Surely many issues clouded the task of closing out the always vibrant Mabel Loomis Todd's estate for fifty-two-year-old Millicent, like what *would* happen if she tried to publish the Emily Dickinson poetry and correspondence her mother had sequestered following her humbling loss in court? It was Mabel's late-life wish that Millicent carry forth in the family name to "set things right" and bring more Emily Dickinson to a still-growing audience. Further, what would become of her mother's trove of diaries, journals, and other personal paraphernalia, let alone the island she owned off the coast of Maine?

While the Dickinson complication and ultimate destination of the family archive would take decades to work out, the Hog Island property presented a more immediate problem. Because Millicent had no children as heirs to take on the family summer haven when the time came, what would she do? This problem went well beyond any solution a friendly publisher or willing university library could provide. How *could* she ensure a purposeful future for the island born of her mother's joyful legacy of loving the natural world?

Disposition and future use of Hog Island became a primary concern for Millicent Bingham.

Whatever she could come up with to clarify Hog Island's future, a few other landholders would have to be appeased. The Point Breeze Inn and Bungalows on the northern peninsula had deteriorated through a dozen shuttered summers and was still on the real estate block.[1] Owners Joseph and Nellie Ambrose, finding no takers for reopening a summer retreat in the early years of the Great Depression, were becoming desperate to sell if only to get out from under the island's tax burden. The quarter share of the undivided southern part not held by Mabel Todd, once owned by her partner Etta Glidden, was now property of Howard Hilder's son, John Chapman Hilder, a well-published contemporary author and magazine editor who had brought his family by the island occasionally to visit with both his father and the Binghams.[2]

Howard and Jack Hilder, as it turned out, would have significant absentee input into the resolution of Mrs. Bingham's Hog Island hurdle. The Hilder issues, as well as other island concerns, are articulated in a series of letters between Nellie Ambrose and Millicent Bingham. Summarized by Bingham and saved to the family archive at Yale, the Ambrose letters show two women sharing stories amid the serious business of finding a buyer for the Point Breeze. Contained in that correspondence, too, are traces of the thought process Bingham went through that would lead her to believe Earth science was at the heart of a long-term Hog Island solution.

The Ambrose Letters

Millicent Bingham records the first of Nellie Ambrose's letters in April 1933, six months after she became proprietor of her mother's island property.[3] Nellie begins with a recurring idea proposed by her husband that Millicent herself would be well served by adding the Point Breeze facility to her Hog Island holdings. Joseph was sure that both properties merged would be much more attractive to the type of long-term island use the Binghams hoped for.

Interspersed in the summarized correspondence, Millicent inserted additional details of the father/son Hilder issues that made her Hog Island problem more difficult. When Howard Hilder gave his island studio back to Mabel Todd in the mid-1920s, he took out a loan to purchase the lot and cabin on the Point Breeze peninsula owned by the Slade family from New York.[4] Turned out not only was Howard in arrears on that loan, he had also rifled through other Ambrose buildings for "furniture, linen, dishes, etc."[5] Joseph Ambrose had expressed his displeasure with the larceny in writing, threatening to enter the Hilder's property to retrieve stolen items, but Howard Hilder was characteristically unresponsive to that threat as well as to other written communication.

Son Jack Hilder was indeed a one-quarter owner of Millicent Bingham's island, but he was in no condition to offer any resolution assistance, whether on his share of the property or the problematic issues regarding his father's bungalow. When contacted by Millicent, Jack's family reported that he was very ill and would not recover for many months. Discussion of the charitable donation of his share of Hog Island was beyond family capability at that time.[6]

Another ongoing Hog Island concern the women discussed frequently was convenient mainland access. Back in the day when the Keene family had owned both the northern peninsula of the island and the hillside fish drying business, commerce was brisk and access to water transportation was easy. The road to the shore, however, was not a public right-of-way, and over time, slights, misunderstandings, and a general change of heart led Myra and Charlie Nash to restrict traffic down their hill from the end of the Keene Neck road.[7] This restriction, of course, was a concern for all connected to Hog Island. The only alternative was to bring in supplies and guests from the public docks at Medomak, Bremen, or Round Pond. Joseph Ambrose had consulted a lawyer about the access issue to learn that the Nashes were fully within their rights. The Hog Island peninsula deed signed over "way back" had included no mention of mainland right-of-way.

By late summer 1933, the two women discussed the option of the island's Long Cove, the tidal mud flat separating the northern peninsula from the main island, being converted into a lobster pound. Local entrepreneur and lobster broker Bernard "Bunny" Zahn didn't want all of Hog Island but was interested in working out a business arrangement where the Ambroses could keep their cottages while he could store lobster stock in "the creek." Since the cove's shoreline bordered on the south with the Bingham's property, Millicent would become a financial partner, as well. The women understood that a lobster pound would be a low-odor operation with work noise restricted to daylight hours. And if Bunny Zahn operated a lobster pound in Long Cove, surely he could apply pressure in the town to create public access down the Nash hill. Both women concluded the idea worthy of further consideration.

Two weeks later, however, "After thinking it over from every angle," Millicent reported that she and Walter had decided against the lobster pound.[8] She wanted to know, as well, for another potential island client, the Ambroses' bottom line to part with their peninsula and buildings. "Did I understand you to say that you would take $2000 cash for it? And would that be exclusive of Mr. Hilder's bungalow?" Millicent records no further bidding after the Ambroses countered that $2,500 cash was their best offer.

As negotiations continued unsuccessfully on several fronts, Hilder's issues persisted. In January 1934, Millicent, in Florida, having rented her mother's winter home, updated Nellie on what she knew about Howard. She reported that he "has rented a house in Coconut Grove and appears to be well content with life.... I know nothing of his financial situation except that he made no offer to repay me the $200 which I paid the Augusta Trust Company for him last summer." With a final bite of vitriol she added, "He did not mention it, in fact."

Millicent admitted knowing nothing more about Jack, other than he was still very ill. "I am so sorry for Jack Hilder and hope he will be better soon," was all she knew to write. But returning to concerns about the senior Hilder, Millicent concluded that he "said nothing about returning to the island." It had been October 1932 since Howard Hilder was last on Hog Island, apparently for the prime purpose of tending an aging Mabel Loomis Todd. After attending to her in her dying moments, island artist Howard Hilder lost interest in returning. Whatever financial and other messes he had left behind would have to be worked out by others.

By that spring, the Ambroses grew more insistent on finding a buyer for their island property. In a letter dated April 1, 1934, Nellie wrote that they "must dispose of it this year, as we do not wish to have the care of it." But the specter of Howard Hilder's bad debt continued to cloud the possibility of a transfer of ownership. "We have not done anything about Mr. Hilder's mortgage," Nellie wrote, "as we have more money tied up in the place now than we wish to have." She mentioned, as well, that the elder Hilder owed money to Frank Lailer for work performed upgrading his Waban-aki cottage. As bleak as a Hog Island resolution must have seemed at times, Millicent pushed forward pitching her idea of a science research station or bird sanctuary to whomever in whatever institution would listen.[9]

In their correspondence over the following months, Millicent Bingham continued to sound hopeful that a science institution could be found to solve their shared island dilemma. Millicent was encouraged because it seemed every scholar and college president she took to the island liked her idea of a marine/forest ecosystem field station. Her main obstacle, of course, was a national economy mired in the Great Depression where capital and philanthropic dollars were scarce. Institutions were few and far between that could take on a Point Breeze facility upgrade plus management of a regenerating wilderness island, and Millicent Bingham was having a hard time finding any of them.

Mrs. Bingham began her search locally with Maine colleges, bird clubs, and natural history organizations. Finding no takers, her approach widened to include the regional likes of the National Association of Audubon Societies, The Massachusetts Audubon Society, and the Boy Scouts of America. The Federation of Bird Clubs of New England was ready to put money down, in fact, until their attorney advised they were not chartered to buy land outside of Massachusetts. Other organizations were positive but unable to step up.[10]

With a doctorate in geography, an astronomer for a father, and a psychologist for a husband, Millicent Bingham's greatest wish for Hog Island was that it would become some kind of residential school for science. The Point Breeze could provide the facilities needed from student accommodations to the dining hall to workshop space, while wild Hog Island and the waters of Muscongus Bay could provide the curriculum.

By summer 1934 Millicent carried along with her a brochure from the Allegany School of Natural History when she went to talk to potential island stakeholders. The Allegany School, founded just a few years prior in western New York state, took a unique approach to nature study by immersing university-age students in observation of natural subjects for extended periods during one long summer session. The school's progressive curriculum called for students to spend time in the field or in a laboratory learning, watching subjects carefully, then after consulting notes, making individual observations. "On a third day," as Allegany School registration material reported, "you have a class conference with the instructor." From there more field work might be warranted, more study, or additional time with staff to enable the student "to develop powers of observation, thought, and judgement."[11]

Beyond the curriculum and methodology, another reason Millicent Bingham liked the Allegany School was because it was a cooperative venture among the Buffalo Society of Natural Sciences, the University of Buffalo, and the Allegany State Park Commission. She wrote, "There is no center comparable in Maine." Then added, "It certainly would be a great thing for nature students as well as the state of Maine if such a school or bird camp could be established permanently on Hog Island. Question is, just how to bring it about."[12]

A most important part of that question was answered that November during a chat with a Bingham family friend who offered to remove one big stumbling block in Millicent's Hog Island problem. Dr. James M. Todd, a physician turned New York City developer who summered in nearby Boothbay Harbor, offered to buy the Point Breeze peninsula, including settling Howard Hilder's delinquent mortgage, and give the facility to any organization Millicent could find that would use it.[13] The words were music to her ears. She wrote, "It is impossible to describe the effect that his offer had on me. It was a turning point. I was walking on air."[14] In addition, Dr. Todd, no relation to Millicent's father, offered to send his Boothbay Harbor estate superintendent to the island to review the condition of the Point Breeze buildings in order to determine what it would cost to get them back into summer operating condition. Now that the facilities issue seemed on its way to resolution, all Millicent had left to do was find that unique organization that could bring the science and the students for a very special hands-on summer nature experience.

Once again, Millicent Bingham headed out to talk with colleges, bird clubs, and natural history organizations, only to get continued rejections. Truth was that the Point Breeze buildings needed expensive upgrades. Mrs. Bingham lamented, "After months of endeavor I realized that it would cost so much to fit up the buildings that nobody could afford to accept Doctor Todd's generous offer." The Ambroses, unconvinced the "bird people" would come through after years of unfulfilled promises, began talking seriously about cutting the timber off the peninsula. With no serious offers in hand, Millicent wrote, "It was at this point that proposals from a lumber company and lobster pound filled me with dismay."[15]

John Baker's Audubon

Nevertheless, a resolute Millicent Todd Bingham traveled to New York City in late winter/early spring 1935, where she had an appointment with one of the heaviest hitters in the birding world, Robert Cushman Murphy, ornithology curator at the American Museum of Natural History. After having made her Hog Island pitch countless times to so many organizations, she frankly wasn't optimistic about funding from the museum for her island school but hoped to at least find understanding with one of the most important bird people in the country. As she expected, Murphy offered no help from the museum. However, her idea of a nature study summer school for adults brought a colleague of his to mind, and before Millicent left Murphy's office, she had an appointment set up two days hence with John H. Baker, the newly installed executive director of the National Association of Audubon Societies.

Millicent had sent letters to a variety of Audubon entities regarding plans for Hog Island, but without her personal visit, they hadn't gotten very far. At the time, the Audubon movement was composed mostly of local groups, or "societies," organized around the idea of the conservation of birds. Since the turn of the twentieth century, birding societies from Massachusetts to California had formed to educate the public about the impact of massive bird culling for feathers used in contemporary millinery fashion. In addition, the observation and recording of bird species and their local populations by these Audubon societies through regular bird counts fit nicely into "hands on" science education reforms promoted at the time by progressive educators.[16]

As an organization to coordinate the energies generated by those local societies and to work to arrest bird abuse in America's fashion center New York City, the National Association of Audubon Societies was established there in 1905. The purpose of the NAAS was for "the protection of wild birds and animals" and welcomed membership from bird societies, their members, and interested others. The association's first president was William Dutcher, who received support from T. Gilbert Pearson as secretary and financial agent. Today, both men are considered giants in the history of bird protection in America.

The print voice and "official organ of the Audubon Societies" was not, in fact, published by the National Association. That periodical, *Bird-Lore*, first appeared in 1899, published and funded by another giant in the contemporary birding world, Frank Chapman of the American Museum of Natural History.[17] The bi-monthly periodical "bound the Audubon movement together with a mix of articles, illustrations, and editorials that attracted a readership among people interested in birds and the outdoors."[18] Chapman continued publishing *Bird-Lore* until 1935, when a change of guard came to Audubon that would turn out to have a most important impact on Millicent Bingham's Hog Island dreams.

John Hopkinson Baker was the guard change at Audubon.[19] With skills honed in the banking industry and an ardent birder, Baker saw the National Association of Audubon Societies through a purge of leadership and a redefinition of purpose. First serving as a member, then as president of the board, Baker was elevated to executive director in late 1934 following a boardroom coup over a scandal and declining membership. Baker's new post made him responsible for the Association's day-to-day operations. To help re-burnish the Audubon brand and buck-up membership, Kermit Roosevelt, son of former President Theodore Roosevelt, was named the organization's president of the board in a move designed to bring renewed trust to the newly reorganized non-profit.

As Frank Graham, Jr. reports in his history of the Audubon movement, *The Audubon Ark*, "From the very first day of his administration, John Baker worked to build an elite staff at headquarters, strengthening the Audubon Association's hand in avian research, nature education, and the protection of nesting colonies." The talent Baker brought on board weren't well-established professionals in their fields, but young, energized newcomers with special talents to offer. One of those hires, Roger Tory Peterson, would later admit that the new staff were "literally missionaries who worked for almost nothing because they loved it." Graham concluded that before long, John Baker had under contract "the most extraordinary and idiosyncratic group of bird-conscious young men ever assembled under one roof."[20]

And so it was into that suite of Audubon Society offices that Millicent Bingham strode with her photographs and ideas for a summer nature school. In perhaps the most repeated part of the Hog Island narrative she crafted, Millicent wrote in her first published island history, "Clasping the familiar little packet of snapshots under my arm—young herons in the nest of their tree-top rookery, a squirrel perched on the corner of our table as we sat at luncheon, a seal balancing on a rocky ledge—I went to Mr. Baker's office. I shall never forget that interview. I began in the usual way: 'I have a beautiful island on the coast of Maine. It has been protected from shooting and other depredations for the past quarter century. On the one end of it there is a group of buildings owned—.' At that point he jumped in. 'Just what I want,' he said."

She remembered listening "speechless" as Baker articulated his vision for such a camp, something he had obviously thought much about, and based on the reaction of Robert Cushman Murphy, had shared with colleagues. The amazed Millicent continued, "Within five minutes he had developed the idea of a camp for teachers of nature study. Mr. Baker had not only caught my idea before I had uttered it, he ran away with it."[21] Upon leaving Baker's office, Bingham "dived into a subway" and made for Dr. James Todd to immediately relay that she had at long last found a taker for her island. "He rejoiced," she remembered, pleased that her dream was finally coming to fruition.[22]

Millicent Bingham had, indeed, finally found the organization with the concept and the resources to facilitate the summer school she considered to be Hog Island at best practice. To further honor her mother, the island would be designated by Audubon as the Todd Wild Life Sanctuary. Still, all hurdles were not *quite* overcome. During further negotiations with John Baker, Millicent learned that the Audubon camp would require unrestricted use of the whole three-hundred-plus acre island. With one-quarter ownership still in Jack Hilder's portfolio, something would need to be done, and quickly.

Sensing the Audubon Nature Camp a sure thing, Millicent Bingham dipped into her mother's life savings to settle once and for all Hog Island's Hilder complications. After buying Jack Hilder's parcel, she wrote that the financial sacrifice was made "solely because I want to see the beautiful island preserved for use of nature lovers of the future."[23] To close the book on the "Hilders of Hog," it should be noted that Howard died that upcoming summer in Florida while son Jack passed less than one year later in May 1936.[24]

Roger Tory Peterson and Allan D. Cruickshank, both John Baker hires, brought a strong ornithological presence to the first-year staff of the Audubon Nature Camp for Adult Leaders.[25] Before the rest of the staff could be selected, however, Baker needed a camp director. Bill Vogt, a birding buddy of Peterson who had encouraged Roger to publish his bird drawings into the successful field guide it had just recently become, related that he knew of a Long Island teacher who regularly brought his Lawrence School nature club to Jones Beach State Park, a facility where Vogt served as bird sanctuary director.[26] That teacher, Carl W. Buchheister, was invited to Baker's office where the executive director "interviewed him in his typical direct and searching fashion." In promoting his credentials, Buchheister explained that he and wife Harriet had "practically built" and successfully operated Camp Moccasin, a summer camp for boys in New Hampshire.[27]

When all was said and done, Buchheister passed muster, was hired, and even arranged for Harriet to be named camp dietitian. Over upcoming summers Mrs. Buchheister would not only make all the dining room decisions but become good-naturedly known as camp etiquette consultant. As Frank Graham reflects, John Baker's hiring decision not only proved him correct with Buchheister serving as an effective camp director for twenty years but fortuitous in that Buchheister would become a prime mover in the national Audubon movement over the next three decades.[28]

Besides Carl Buchheister and the celebrated bird guys, Peterson and Cruickshank, other first-year staffers included Dorothy Treat from the Cleveland Museum of Natural History, whose specialty was exciting kids about nature study. Treat would help the teacher campers develop effective ideas they could take back to their classrooms. Gerald Pomerat, a Harvard man from the Woods Hole Marine Biological Laboratory, became the marine and freshwater specialist. The plant life instructor, Vernon A. Young, held a doctorate in forest botany, taught at Syracuse University, and in earlier summers served as a ranger naturalist at Yellowstone National Park. Filling out the staff was Fred Fletcher, the insect life instructor who had trained at Miami University of Ohio and, like Pomerat, was on the faculty at Syracuse.[29]

By late spring 1935, still a full year before campers and just weeks after John Baker had accepted Millicent Bingham's offer, the first mention of Hog Island ran in *Bird-Lore* magazine. The article directed the serious birder on a tour of Midcoast Maine with tips on where specific species had been spotted.[30] When osprey came up, Hog Island was mentioned along with Sheep, North Haven, and Oak islands as locations of "fine nests." No further directions were included, though an "Ornithological map of the Maine coast" confirmed it was the Hog Island at Bremen, just northeast of Wiscasset, and not another island in the region bearing the same name.

In June 1935, Baker dispatched Roger Tory Peterson and his "antique Bell and Howell" 35mm black and white motion picture camera to Maine for site analysis and recording of what specifics on which a camp curriculum could be built.[31] Peterson wrote that he was charged to scout "Hog Island as well as the woods, lakes, and fields on the nearby mainland" and nesting sites on seabird islands in the bay. He found that filming the local birds was a mixed bag. He had no trouble with nesting osprey, but the single pair of bald eagles on Allen Island proved challenging. He wrote that he hid in a spruce-bough-covered blind "for four hours before one of the parents dropped in with a large fish to feed the two half-grown young." Great blue herons likewise gave Peterson problems. Though great blues nested on Hog Island, the heronry was high in the canopy, which made getting a camera close to them nearly impossible. He opted for filming another heronry on an island near Boothbay Harbor where he was told the nests "were fairly low." After setting up his blind, he opted to move what he thought was a birch sapling out of his line of sight. The plan was to shinny up the tree in order to bend it over to tie it off. When Peterson ascended the tree, however, he found it was no pliable birch. Instead of bending, the young tree "snapped off with a loud crack. Down I went, flat on my shoulders on the granite. For the next several days I was in great pain.... That ended my wildlife photography in Maine for that season."[32]

The first full-fledged article introducing *Bird-Lore* readers to Hog Island appeared in the September–October 1935 issue and was appropriately authored by Millicent Todd Bingham. In the essay she writes only of her family's story and the natural wonders of Hog Island and its environs, nothing about an upcoming camp for adult leaders. Entitled "The Todd Wild Life Sanctuary," the article evoked "sweet smelling balsam" and the wash of the bay on the rocks in a travelogue piece surely intended to whet the appetites of potential campers. Millicent tempted her readers with images of "deep mosses and beds of ferns" and "multi-colored mushrooms and the spectral Indian pipe." She added that her mother, the sanctuary's namesake, "is best remembered as the first editor of the poems and letters of Emily Dickinson."[33]

Millicent quoted Roger Peterson in the article as having said Hog Island's dense forests afforded "the best warbler country south of the Matapedia," a region of Quebec on the Gaspe Peninsula. After explaining that the island had been left "to the wild inhabitants" after the "inn and bungalows" had closed, she concluded, "Ospreys have built their nests in the tall tree-tops along the water's edge undisturbed, the Great Blue Herons have reared their young in a solitude as remote as if the Indians were still their only neighbors, while ringing notes of the Hermit Thrush, or the high, clear medley of the Winter Wren, echo and re-echo across the quiet waters of the bay." Aside from the lush language calculated to intrigue potential campers, such eloquent imagery makes one wonder if Millicent's work with Emily Dickinson sharpened her own sense of observation.

The next Hog Island essay Millicent Bingham published appeared in *Natural History*, the magazine of the American Museum of Natural History. Running in the May 1937 issue, publication of the article shows again the strong bond between the Museum and Audubon. In "Rescuing an Island," Mrs. Bingham not only retold her family's story as before but added details of the activities at the Audubon Nature Camp, which she witnessed in full bloom in its first summer of operation. Millicent arrived at camp in the middle of the first session to find that it "exhaled an atmosphere of wonder." Furthermore, she discovered her island had become "a laboratory of eager students." Very pleased with what she found, Millicent observed, "And yet with it all, the wilderness remained a wilderness. The solitude was as untouched as ever."[34]

As Mrs. Bingham wrote about that first summer's nature study education experiment on Hog Island, she referred to "the complex interdependence of all forms of life" as conservation. During that era, however, the study of natural science was a specializing focus on the relationships between organisms and their environment in the newly defined field of ecology. Buchheister had learned of that clarification only recently himself. John Baker had asked him if he knew what "ecology" was, and if not, he'd better "learn it damn quick."[35] Buchheister remembers using ecology as a mantra as the camp's curriculum was developed, and in so doing, broke out specialties into bird life, marine life, plant life, and insect life while scheduling daily workshops in which all that amazing diversity was blended.

In those early years, *Bird-Lore* was the primary print vehicle used to promote attendance at the Audubon Nature Camp.[36] Still published by Frank Chapman when John Baker took Audubon's helm, *Bird-Lore* was about to see major changes as well. In years past on a few occasions, former Audubon president William Dutcher had tried to negotiate control of the magazine away from Chapman but was never successful. Now at the age of seventy and busy with many projects, Chapman succumbed to a persistent John Baker. William Vogt, one and the same who found Carl Buchheister for Audubon, was named the new editor of *Bird-Lore* and was tasked by Baker to work with Roger Tory Peterson to give the magazine a new look.[37] Some of that new look featured front covers with an updated font and images of birds drawn by Peterson himself.

In January 1936, a few issues into Bill Vogt's tenure as editor, *Bird-Lore* ran the first of a series of articles hoping to engage its readership enough to fill five sessions of camp beds. Entitled simply "The Audubon Nature Camp," the article sought to establish the curriculum and the staff's bona fides while describing what attendees could expect. A definition of the camp's scientific purpose was followed by a brief introduction of camp director Carl Buchheister; transportation, accommodation, and dining room details; as well as dates of operation and cost. Two pictures graced the article, one of a still fuzzy chick sitting on a pair of binoculars, the other of a moose grazing in a wild meadow that visually located the camp squarely in Maine. The piece further tempted readers with an impressive list of birdlife they might see, including terns, eiders, guillemots, and puffins. The unnamed author concluded, "First hand acquaintance with these sea-birds will provide interesting contrast to the study of wild life on the island, where Warblers abound, and where there is a rich and interesting flora and fauna." Cost of each two-week session that opening season was $40, which included a $5 deposit.[38]

The summer and fall issues of *Bird-Lore* continued to promote camp attendance with articles and full-page ads, but in addition now carried firsthand reporting and satisfied camper testimonials. In the July–August 1936 issue, Bill Vogt wrote, "From food to quarters, from starfish to birds, from the boatman to the camp director, everything 'clicked.' If there is a harder-working group of campers in the United States, we have not heard of them."[39] By fall, statistics confirmed that 223 campers from two Canadian provinces and twenty-four states "from as far west as California and as far south as Florida" had made the trek to Hog Island. A Roger Tory Peterson photograph of Allan Cruickshank working with campers in the intertidal zone sported the caption, "Many found the camp a revelation." To emphasize that point, the article offered, "No longer will these leaders, responsible for forming juvenile attitudes towards our outdoor resources, think in terms of birds and mammals divorced from their environment." Hoping the next season would bring enhanced enthusiasm to the camp, and maybe even a waiting list, one of the article titles said it all: "'We're coming back!' Participants vote Audubon Nature Camp unqualified success."[40]

The Buchheister era at the Audubon Camp on Hog Island will forever be known as its golden age. Though the staff changed from time to time, stalwarts in their specialty returned summer after summer to continue to work their island magic. Roger Peterson would have qualified as one of those legendary staff members, but he was reassigned by Baker for the camp's second summer. Carl Buchheister ran a tight ship as he expected staff and campers to arrive at programs and meals on time. He also expected everyone to get moving responsibly in the morning and retire after the evening program. One evening during the first session, on the very night that John Baker visited to see if all was going well, Peterson and three female campers were found out on the property after the informal curfew. To complicate the situation, one of the women had fallen into a newly dug well that had not been clearly marked and was injured. After she was extracted and received medical attention, she and her badly sprained ankle were sent home to New York City. Peterson would wonder years later if it was that event that forfeited him a spot on the Hog Island staff.[41]

The primary bird specialist on Buchheister's legendary staff was Allan Cruickshank, the Audubon employee who spent his winters on Long Island working with school programs. Cruickshank was an innovative nature photographer as well, with many of his fine images still hanging at the Hog Island Audubon Camp. He was noted as an energized field group leader with "overflowing good humor." It was Cruickshank who walked through camp early mornings making loud bird calls to rouse campers, and it was he who, upon returning from a field trip on the bay, performed a headstand on the wheelhouse of the *Puffin I* for all ashore to see that a new species for the summer had been spotted on that particular trip. A good-looking fellow, he also became known as the "dean of women" since so many of the female campers found his playing the concertina below their dormitory windows quite charming. Cruickshank's spouse, Helen, was also popular at camp as one of the "Ladies of the Institute," which included all staff wives. She understood her husband's special gifts and rather enjoyed the notoriety herself, and all who knew them spoke of how devoted they were to each other.

Between them, Allan and Helen Cruickshank published nearly two dozen books ranging in interest from birding field guides to regional bird studies to photo picture books.[42] Helen was a noted author and photographer in her own right who can be found selling Bausch & Lomb binoculars in the spring 1954 issue of *The Auk* over the signature "Mrs. Allan D. Cruickshank." Though Allan served as a bird life instructor on Hog Island for over thirty summers, in that time he and Helen relocated their winter home from New York to Florida. From their new home base, Allan continued to travel extensively on the

Audubon Screen Tour circuit where he often met up with Hog Island alumni. On one such occasion, the chapter program chair was absent so one of the members was needed to introduce Cruickshank. A young woman who had attended the Maine camp the previous summer and had only seen him in his Audubon khaki attire reluctantly agreed. For this event, as was his practice on the tour, Allan wore a more formal outfit with a dress shirt and tie. As an icebreaker on many occasions thereafter, Cruickshank enjoyed repeating what the nervous woman said. "It is my pleasure to introduce Allan Cruickshank, our speaker tonight. I spent last summer on an island with him, and this is the first time I've ever seen him dressed."

Another favorite Allan Cruickshank story goes back to the late 1950s, when the United States and the Soviet Union were ramping up the space race. A local Florida resident by then, Allan was familiar with the unprotected wetlands surrounding the new Cape Canaveral spaceport because he birded and photographed there frequently. Seeing a way to protect the massive wetland, Cruickshank approached NASA about wildlife and ecosystem awareness as they developed launch facilities. He encouraged the federal government to create a wildlife refuge from the expanse not utilized by NASA. And because of Allan Cruickshank, the Merritt Island National Wildlife Refuge was established in 1963. To this day, when I watch a launch from the Kennedy Space Center and I see a bird fly by a waiting rocket ship, Allan Cruickshank comes to mind.[43]

For the camp's second summer, Peterson's place as a bird life instructor was taken by Joe Cadbury, a fine birder and a "keen, all-round naturalist" who attended the first session of the camp's premier season and had impressed Buchheister with his enthusiasm and bird knowledge. Joe and his wife, Lucille, were so pumped about coming to Hog Island that first summer that they showed up two days early and asked Charlie Nash if they could camp on his property. Carl Buchheister discouraged the practice. An elementary school science teacher from Pennsylvania, Cadbury was known at camp for not only his birding skills but his fine singing voice at evening programs and for his being a naturally likable guy.

His brother, Bart Cadbury, would join the legendary staff in 1948 as a marine life instructor and go on to become the camp's second director a decade later when Carl Buchheister was named president of National Audubon. Bart was a teacher from Miss Porter's School in Farmington, Connecticut, who brought not only a wife but kids who enhanced the family atmosphere at camp. Ginny Cadbury, Bart's wife, served as John Baker's secretary when he came to camp, and by 1951, took on that same job for Carl Buchheister. When Ginny and the kids came up for their first summer, Buchheister had just acquired title to the Nash property on the mainland where Ginny would tend the two young Cadbury daughters in the old Nash house. As the prime mover in the "Ladies of the Institute," there were many summers when Ginny coordinated the end-of-season camp "birthday party" where Mrs. Bingham was feted and the completed summer season celebrated. When Joe and Bart retired, both moved to Maine—Joe to Waldoboro, Bart to Cushing. It didn't take long for both to become favorite trip leaders for Midcoast Audubon Society birding trips.

Donald Borror from Ohio State became the insect specialist on the legendary staff. Growing from his specialty in dragonflies and damselflies, he developed equipment to record natural sounds, especially those of birds and insects. He realized with his early recordings on magnetic tape that a collection of invisible natural sounds could be cataloged using similar practice as other more concrete natural history collections. Borror is recognized as a pioneer in such recordings with The Borror Laboratory of Bioacoustics at Ohio State University named in his honor.[44] Don Borror brought family, too, including his son Arthur who would grow up, earn a handful of graduate degrees in zoology-based subjects, and join the camp staff in 1961 as a marine life instructor.

Farida Wiley, the camp plant specialist, was another staffer with roots in Ohio and one could say the last of a dying breed. She was not a university-trained specialist with graduate degrees and extensive field research but a self-taught naturalist who found her way onto the staff of the American Museum of Natural History.[45] There she was popular with younger visitors and in 1940 began a regular weekly bird walk in Central

Park. She was "wiry, freckled, and partial to tweed suits." So when you conjure the stereotypical urban bird walk led by an authoritarian older woman with binoculars strung around her neck, you're thinking of Miss Wiley who became a bit of an icon in the city. She led those Central Park bird walks for forty years, going out "rain or shine" and was written about frequently in the New York papers. She was closely connected to the John Burroughs Society and published a popular fern identification field guide.[46] Her popularity at the museum and the awareness of her position on the Hog Island staff surely promoted attendance among potential campers from the New York City region.

Filling out the legendary staff were two individuals, one an elementary school principal from North Carolina and the other a Maine lobsterman who lived just down the shore. The school principal was Margaret Wall, who had received an Audubon chapter scholarship to attend camp in 1947, and like Joe Cadbury, impressed the staff enough to be invited to join them the following summer. Wall earned her legendary status by serving as the nature activities specialist at the camp for fourteen years.

The lobsterman, Elmer Osier, signed on as head boatman and facility handyman in 1940. Before electricity came to the island, Osier fired up the generators every morning to charge the cells that kept the refrigeration and lights running. Bart Cadbury remembered Elmer's story about how he and his father rowed eighteen-foot dories from New Harbor all the way out to Monhegan Island just to set fishing lines. Elmer was a local sailor the camp director could trust. Even if a fog rolled in over an all-day excursion out in the bay, trip leaders were confident all would be well even without a ship-to-shore radio because Osier "knew Muscongus Bay like the back of his hand." Elmer Osier served the camp for over twenty years as the first boatman and the first guy everyone called when a piece of island infrastructure quit working.

The keystone of the legendary staff, of course, was Carl Buchheister, and in a lesser sense, even John Baker.[47] While Buchheister took the wheel and navigated the camp safely through twenty summers, Baker kept his influence visible all the way from his office at Audubon House in New York City. From the beginning of his term, one of Baker's goals had been for Audubon to expand and amplify its function as an educational institution. Even before Baker, *Bird-Lore* ran regular features suggesting how teachers could apply conservation concepts in a classroom curriculum. To further engage the malleable young, local Junior Audubon classes enrolled tens of thousands of children, offering each a Junior Audubon member button and "bird cards" with images and observational data. But John Baker wanted to take ecosystem education a step further to include teacher training. Intense two-week summer sessions where teachers were immersed in the field coupled with hands-on workshops with skilled instructors seemed to Baker the best way to bring the gospel of ecology to the public.[48] With Hog Island programming, John Baker did indeed get what he wanted. And to show his support for the Nature Camp, Baker did all in his power to clear his schedule so he could be in Maine for every session's final program.[49]

Carl Buchheister's developing relationship with John Baker was a life-changer for him. When he came to Audubon, Buchheister was teaching Latin at the Lawrence School, but all of that changed with his appointment as Audubon Camp director. Baker had encouraged the independent Massachusetts Audubon Society to make a financial gift to get the Hog Island camp going. During the first summer of operation, a handful of Massachusetts Audubon board members came up for a visit and the camp staff was advised by Baker to "roll out the red carpet." Carl Buchheister proved the affable host, and before the season was over, he was invited to come to Boston to interview for executive director of the state society. He did, and like John Baker, the Massachusetts Audubon brass was impressed. For the next three years, Buchheister led the Massachusetts Audubon Society, a career diversion that led him into a social- and science-based arena he dearly loved and in which he clearly excelled.

John Baker would say to organization historians that he groomed Carl Buchheister from the beginning to take his place as Audubon's president.[50] Baker brought Buchheister on board the newly renamed National Audubon Society full-time in 1940 as his assistant. Buchheister went on to serve in various positions with Audubon, culminating in a transformational ten-year term as president that saw the society grow beyond involvement in regional concerns to truly national ones. Audubon nature centers popped up in various communities across the country, as did local chapters. Three other summer camps continued successful operation.[51] During that time, too, Audubon became more involved in national issues by promoting the benefits of The Wilderness Act and educating members about the evils of DDT. Through it all Carl Buchheister remained committed to education and especially to the Hog Island program. In the midst of his presidency, he would write unapologetically, "Whatever I am today, the Camp is responsible."[52] He is remembered today as one of the foremost American conservation educators of the twentieth century. Roger Tory Peterson wrote that Buchheister's "influence in America can be observed wherever we find a naturalist working with people in the out-of-doors."[53] High praise, indeed.

When John Baker retired and Carl Buchheister's office moved down the hall, the Buchheister era on Hog Island ended. Though Carl and Harriet still came for visits, his busy New York schedule would not let them continue to spend summers in Maine. Still, many of the camp traditions begun by the Buchheisters continued under the directorship of Bart Cadbury. Mint juleps remained the island drink of choice with glasses raised many evenings in a toast. When Mrs. Bingham came over for her regular visits, a warm welcome was rolled out again and again. Harriet's influence in the dining room carried over with place settings arranged just so for every meal. Lobster bakes on the shore continued to top off each camp session while the end-of-summer birthday party finished off the season. In addition, when Bart was named camp director, Ginny Cadbury stepped easily into the shoes created by Harriet Buchheister as the "faithful partner" of the faithful leader. Dur and Peggy Morton and Mike and Margie Shannon were other "director couples" who would carry on the traditions and decorum institutionalized by "the gentleman from Maryland" and his steadfast spouse.[54]

A related activity the Buchheisters had treasured on the Maine coast was annual week-long treks they and a select few would take out to Matinicus Rock during the mid-summer week the staff had off. Conditions on the rock were primitive, but that didn't deter the Buchheisters. With a navigational lighthouse still in operation, they got to know the keeper and his family.[55] Carl reported that even after retiring from Audubon, he and Harriet returned to Matinicus Rock, "Harriet studying the plants and I the birds."[56] While still serving as National Audubon's president, Carl and his wife became concerned about the growing boatloads of visitors coming out to the rock to see nesting seabirds, including Atlantic puffins. Some visitors heeded the Buchheisters' warnings and avoided walking into sensitive nesting areas; others did not. Not long after, the Audubon Society president happily convinced the Coast Guard and the US Fish and Wildlife Service to further protect nesting seabirds on Matinicus Rock by authorizing an Audubon warden there.

Carl Buchheister came to say that the "happiest days of my adult life were spent on Hog Island." He also went so far as to unofficially christen the camp Audubon's "Mother Church." As a devout Roman Catholic, he did not take that naming lightly. Through the natural and cooperative energies witnessed every summer on the island, Buchheister felt the camp was the best of what Audubon stood for: Wildlife. Citizens. Education. Conservation. Sanctuary. Ecosystems. Science. Fun. Devotion to a cause. It was all there. For Carl Buchheister, the Audubon Camp on Hog Island embodied the breadth of the holy tenets of conservation and ecology and would provide him the rudder he would need to direct the Audubon movement through the turbulent 1960s.

Mrs. Bingham's Legacy

From the time the Audubon Camp opened, Millicent and Walter Bingham continued to call Hog Island their summer home except for the World War II years. During that six-year hiatus, Walter was busy at the war department while Millicent was intent on fulfilling her family destiny of updating the Emily Dickinson canon. In 1929, Mabel Todd reopened the sequestered collection of letters and poems and conferenced with her daughter about how the publication could proceed. Consequences of her mother's death and Hog Island concerns kept Millicent from diving right in, but by 1945 two new Dickinson titles were published by Harper & Brothers. One was a collection of six hundred fifty "new poems of Emily Dickinson" entitled *Bolts of Melody*, credited to the editing of Millicent and her mother. Millicent claimed in the introduction that nearly half of Emily's poetry "remained unpublished to this day."[57]

The other title, *Ancestor's Brocades: The Literary Debut of Emily Dickinson*, was the story only a Todd could tell. This book was Millicent's solo effort to spin the uneasy details of her mother's efforts getting the first Dickinson poetry and letters into publication, and when all was said and done, the lack of appreciation shown to her by Emily's family. The battle lines of the "war between the houses" were laid out in detail. The book ends with the painful reality of the lost lawsuit, but nowhere does Millicent mention the love affair between Austin Dickinson and her mother.[58] Perhaps she and her editors thought full disclosure would somehow sully Emily's reputation. Surely it wouldn't bring the Todd Bingham clan any accolades.

The final two Dickinson-related titles the Todd Binghams published brought with them a battle that Millicent would lament took her Walter away from her. Martha Dickinson Bianchi, Austin's daughter, had taken up the publishing gauntlet for the family after Mabel was forcibly removed and brought a variety of Dickinson poetry to the public.[59] When Millicent Bingham published *Bolts of Melody* and *Ancestor's Brocades* in 1945, even though Martha had died in 1943, the Dickinson family heirs attacked Bingham with a vengeance.[60] The Dickinson family granted Harvard Emily's archive and the university was intent on making it complete. A power struggle of major proportions ensued that was only finalized when the university granted Millicent the right to publish her books if she handed over the Dickinson originals. Walter warned Millicent of the cutthroat negotiations and advised her to stay as clear of the fray as possible and let the lawyers handle it.

By summer 1952, Walter had taken ill and was having a difficult time getting better at home. Millicent was advised by a doctor that her "aura of frustration" was hindering her husband's recovery. Needing to get these final Dickinson materials ready for the publisher, the couple decided she should head off to Hog Island to work while he stayed home in Washington, DC, to recuperate. "Against my deepest feelings," she wrote, "I was persuaded to leave him and go to Maine."[61] Much to her great sadness, Walter died while she was away.

Millicent Todd Bingham's *Emily Dickinson's Home: Letters of Edward Dickinson and His Family* and *Emily Dickinson: A Revelation* finally made publication in 1954. Despite the great personal and professional success, in her heart she felt the bickering caused by the Dickinson negotiations had hastened her husband's death. She knew he fretted much over the difficult discussions she had with Harvard, and so in keeping with the family feud, Millicent placed the blame for Walter's passing squarely on the backs of the unreasonable Dickinsons. In any case, Millicent had finally done all she could to both promote Emily Dickinson the poet and tell her mother's story and "set the record straight" as clearly as her scruples would allow. In a very real sense, the woman was finally set free.[62]

Summer 1948 turned out to be a significant one for both the Audubon Camp and the Binghams. Not only had Carl Buchheister acquired the coveted water access on the mainland by finagling the purchase of the Nash farm, but the Binghams returned to their cottages following a respite brought on by world war.[63] As was their regular practice, the Binghams brought along extra help. Some summers it was a male graduate student proficient at cooking and commanding a dory. That summer Millicent invited her personal secretary, a woman known only in her writing as Willow, to come help get things in order following their multi-summer absence. In wonderful secretary fashion, Willow typed up a dozen pages of stories she witnessed first-hand that offer a unique insight into life at the Bingham cottages.[64] The informal narratives show a side of Mrs. Bingham most people never saw.

When the Bingham crew arrived at their camp that summer, Willow reported they not only found six years of dust but that the buildings had been ransacked. In the "living room of the big house," chairs were over-turned and drawers emptied onto the floor. Nothing appeared to have been taken, even paraffin candles that Willow advised were worth something during the war years. Closets were emptied and a mirror broken, but the thing that really peeved Millicent were the two empty whiskey bottles stashed in the corner. Two days of hard work put the living room right again and comfortable fires once more warmed cool camp nights.

Millicent always said she kept things at camp much like her mother left them. Willow and Walter might have gently disagreed. After the fog cleared one morning, Millicent took Willow out to work on an island path, perhaps one she had blazed as a younger woman. Willow clipped away as directed, though she was warned by Mrs. Bingham not to cut back as far as the trunk. Willow could see that the "clip line" was above Mrs. Bingham's head but right in the face of those a bit taller. She questioned if perhaps the limbs should be cut back farther so Walter wouldn't walk into one in the middle of the night. Following a short debate, Mrs. Bingham deferred to her taller companion and drifted off to another task.

Not long after, Walter happened by and in his gracious way approved of Willow's work. She shared the discussion she had just had with his wife. "You know," she said, "I think Millicent would rather not cut anything at all." Walter agreed and then added, "Her mother didn't feel that way. She was forever fixing the woods to be prettier. You've seen all the benches. She would never have allowed the woods to engulf her." As a way of affirming Willow's path paring and her questioning Millicent, Walter invited her to clear the path from the workshop down to the dock. Willow responded with a smile, "I know. I've seen it. I'm coming there next."

Mrs. Bingham had the reputation of a woman who knew her mind and didn't mind sharing. Her strong, sometimes brusque personality frequently put people off, even her island guests. Not many invited her wrath by questioning her directions or intent. One day that same summer, the plan was for all to head into town for supplies, including checking on the delivery of a load of shingles. Walter rowed the dory over to the Audubon dock, but not before being scolded by Millicent for bad form. Not long after, he was barked at for the car bouncing uncomfortably over uneven roads. Willow noted the criticism and thought to herself it was uncalled for, but of course, said nothing.

The first stop in town was to check on the shingles. Walter left the women in the car as he went in to confirm the island delivery. When he returned, he looked chagrined and advised his wife that the shingles were not there. Though they had been ordered and paid for two months prior, the shop owner let another customer have them knowing he had time to reorder the Bingham squares before the delivery date. The explanation did not sit well with Millicent. She stormed at Walter for his lack of assertiveness and the dishonesty of the merchant for selling her shingles. She herself then went into the shop to berate the staff, all the while assured her delivery would still be on time.

A little later, with Walter running another short errand, the women found themselves alone in the car again. In a bit of introspection, Millicent asked Willow if she thought she had made too much fuss about the shingles. Willow realized she had no option but to be truthful. She wrote, "I knew I was blushing, but I said, 'Yes.' Perhaps I was too vehement, for her eyes widened a little." The ensuing conversation was frank, with the personal assistant telling her employer how the adrenaline just spent was a waste of energy. The shingles were promised on time and no one need be scolded. Millicent responded with her repeated tirade against "outright dishonesty."

Willow realized she had come so far; she couldn't stop now. She then accused Millicent of upbraiding Walter. Millicent countered that when Walter first came to Maine, he knew nothing of island life and she had "taught him everything he knows," including how to row a dory, which he had not done to her standards that morning. Surely she could direct Walter in island ways. Willow then countered that she felt Walter was bullied. Mrs. Bingham responded, "Do I really jump at him? Is it as bad as all that?" Before Willow could answer, Walter appeared at the driver's side window and asked where they were going for lunch.

Willow recognized Mrs. Bingham as a formidable character but still felt warm toward her. During another island work session, Willow began to wonder how the older woman felt about being addressed by her given name instead of Mrs. Walter Bingham as was practice in cultured circles. Thinking out loud, she asked if "anyone of my tender years" had ever called her by her first name. Mrs. Bingham responded, "It's not a custom I grew up with, but one likes to feel that one has an existence apart from one's spouse." Willow was intrigued by her response. On that day, she remembers, she began addressing Mrs. Bingham as Millicent. In the many years she knew her, Willow was "hard-pressed to remember anyone of my generation who called her Millicent." When Willow did, however, "she always seemed to like it."

Summers of island memories were made not just at the Audubon camp and the Bingham cottages but at Howard Hilder's old cabin down the western shore. During Mabel Todd's last years on the island, after Hilder had moved his summer digs over to the Slade cottage, she housed invited friends at the Osprey, as Millicent would later do as well. While there was no guestbook recording the various names of those who stayed at the old artist's cottage, one family stands out. Paul Sorel ran a seminary bookstore in Washington, DC, where he had gotten to know Millicent Bingham. The two became good friends, and in 1952, Millicent invited Paul and his wife Gertrude to summer at the Osprey. The couple had a wonderful time and for 1953, Gert invited her sister and her two boys to join them. One of those boys, Chris Speh, is still a Hog Island fanatic and has collected memorabilia of his youthful summers over the years, including the Willow narrative. In a memoir written in 2005, some forty years after his last summer at the artist's cottage, Speh described what it was like to be a teenage boy with full run of a forested island on the coast of Maine.[65]

Freedom to explore the island on their own didn't happen right away, but Chris and his older brother Tony earned the trust of the adults over time. Uncle Paul told the boys not to panic if they ever got lost while bushwhacking on the island.[66] Just keep moving downhill until the shore trail is reached, then keep walking in either direction until they get to the Osprey. The boys never had to use that advice, but it was good to have it tucked in the back of their minds as they explored Mrs. Bingham's island.

As is the case with any coastal island, fresh water is always a premium. A spring did run some summers just outside the Osprey along the shore trail that was helpful in keeping food cold, but the most important component of the camp water system was the rain barrels. When it rained, water channeled off the roof into these reservoirs. When it rained hard enough, Gert passed out shampoo and heads were washed in the porch roof overflow. Since showers didn't exist, most bathing took place in cold bay water using saltwater soap that Speh admits never really worked very well. One day while investigating the contents of a rain barrel, he noticed little red bugs squirming in the water. From then on he was curious about what else was in his food, knowing that rain barrel water was used to prepare camp meals and do the dishes.

Swimming, boating, fishing, and marketing starfish to a local gift shop kept Tony and Chris pretty much out of trouble. They looked forward to getting weather reports on Mrs. Bingham's "old blue battery radio," and in August 1954, they heard warnings for Hurricane Carol that was about to lash the Maine coast. As the wind and rain picked up, both adults and kids traversed to the east side of the island to witness the intense surf. Impressed as they were, someone eventually suggested family safety as a better pursuit. Chris remembers on the way back across the island trees were coming up by their roots with one nearly injuring his mother. A large pine growing just three feet from the Osprey cabin was rocking so hard that the base of the tree was seen coming up out of the ground. It didn't crash into the Osprey roof, thankfully. The following summer Chris has a good memory of horses rafted over to the island to haul the many downed trees to the shore before the timber was floated over to the mainland for processing.

The most colorful tale of life in the artist's cottage dealt with the outhouse. With the cabin perched on a rocky hillside, a stairway led up a flight to the main level whose porch extended over the shore trail. Due to site limitations, the outhouse was located on the lower level, right along that narrow trail. The facility had a door, but because of odor and general practice, it was rarely closed. The family installed a red arrow to be raised or lowered on the front of the outhouse to alert others of occupancy. On the rare occasion when the facility was in use and an "Audubon" came along on an island hike, embarrassed apologies were offered but no practices changed.[67]

By the late 1950s, Millicent Todd Bingham was approaching her eighties and she knew her era on Hog Island was coming to an end. While most of her island final wishes were realized with the deal with John Baker, one of the unresolved issues was what would happen to the Bingham cottages. She pressed Audubon to plumb utilities down from the camp so the science field station she dreamed of fifty years prior might still come to pass. Now at Audubon's helm, Carl Buchheister explained that good science was already in practice on the island and the cost of extending services was astronomical.[68] In the end, Millicent Bingham packed up her books and effects and spent her last few summers in New Harbor, just across the sound and south of Hog Island. Still, she found leaving the island very painful. In a letter to Gert Sorel during her first summer off the island, Millicent wrote, "In Paul's words, 'It is better to cut the umbilical cord' and depart. Although for me it feels more like pulling me up by the tap root, which goes down to the very source of life itself."

The final matter of Audubon's one-dollar annual lease for the use of the southern part of the island was resolved on August 9, 1960, when Millicent Bingham deeded all of Hog Island to Audubon. One of her guests that day was Rachel Carson, a fellow resident of the nation's capital and a summer person with a place near Boothbay Harbor on Southport Island. Carson was working on *Silent Spring* at the time and even mentioned her visit to Hog Island in the book. On the drive to the event, Carson was disappointed to see roadside vegetation destroyed by herbicide. Cognizant that the state of Maine was promoting itself among tourists as Vacationland, she questioned how those visitors would respond to natural beauty dead on the roadside.[69]

Dedication day on the island was festive as speeches were given and professional photographs were taken. John Baker and Carl Buchheister joined Carson as dignitaries as a large stone selected by Millicent herself was unveiled on the isthmus at the head of Long Cove. Installed on the stone was a commemorative plaque naming both women but memorializing Mabel Loomis Todd as the person who "saved this island wilderness and thus shaped its destiny as a perpetual preserve."[70] It turned out to be a good day that Chris Speh remembers well.

In the official dedication document to the National Audubon Society, Millicent Bingham waxed nostalgic and remembered her mother and father and grandfather on the island and how much they all loved it. In so doing, Millicent restated a date that confirms she knew better when she continually repeated to campers and in publications how her mother saved the island. The well-told story, of course, is that David and Mabel Todd were sailing along the Maine coast summer 1908 when they came by Hog Island to witness a large clear-cut. According to Millicent, Mabel was so impressed with the island's forest that she got in touch with Etta Glidden and the two worked together to secure the title from the various owners and thus save the island from further destruction.

But it didn't happen that way and Millicent knew it. First off, if Mabel and David sailed by in 1908 and then committed family funds to the purchase, how was all the paperwork and sale completed by July 1? In her letter to Audubon's board of directors in 1960, she stated clearly, "Mrs. Todd first saw the island on July 10, 1909." But if that was so, what about the oft-repeated drama about summer 1908? In fact, Millicent Bingham *was* aware her mother had only traveled to Wiscasset in 1908 to sign papers. Mabel Todd didn't see the island that summer and there certainly wasn't any sailing with David, all of which is confirmed in her diary.

One is left to wonder why the daughter who professed accuracy "to the seventh decimal" as a watchword in her professional and personal life felt it necessary to fabricate elements of a story that was already very complimentary to her mother's commitment to the natural world.[71] Perhaps for the same reasons a daughter professing to "set the record straight" could not bring herself to tell the world of the illicit relationship with her mother and settled instead for colorful half-truths. When all was said and done, it would seem, good work performed just wasn't enough.

Chapter 5 Notes

[1] In correspondence to Millicent, Nellie Ambrose lamented some potential buyers of the Point Breeze expected repairs to be made to buildings before the change of ownership. That expense, of course, was beyond their intention of unloading the place "as is."

[2] John Chapman Hilder published articles in a variety of magazines, including *Popular Science Monthly, Harper's, Ladies Home Journal,* and *The Elks Magazine,* which he also edited for a time.

[3] The unpublished, unpaged "Letters from Mrs. J. A. Ambrose" reside in the Millicent Todd Bingham Papers, Manuscripts and Archives, Yale University Library.

[4] After the Point Breeze closed post–World War I and the Slades moved on to Cape Rozier, they sold their cottage to Howard Hilder. Mabel Todd's diaries indicate Hilder spent his days at her camp, sometimes painting, sometimes doing necessary chores. Nothing is recorded about sleeping arrangements, but in one diary entry already cited, Mabel noted her keeping a whistle at her bedside to use at night to rouse a sleeping Howard Hilder to come to her aid if needed.

[5] Besides theft, Nellie Ambrose reported, "The Hilders abused and tore the [Point Breeze resort] to pieces and sold and gave away three-fourths of the contents of the buildings." Ambrose letters, November 30, 1934.

[6] When Millicent Bingham tried to ask Jack Hilder about donating his quarter of Hog Island for Audubon use, his wife reported he was "flat on his back" and would "not be cured for more than a year." Jack Hilder died in May 1936 at age 43, just weeks before the Audubon Nature Camp opened. There is no indication he had any interest in the Audubon operation.

[7] It would seem Howard Hilder can take some responsibility over the Nashes closing access to their dock on the shore. Nellie wrote, "We are trying to sell to someone the Nashes will like as it makes quite a difference. We would never have had this fuss about the right of way if the Hilders had not drank so bad." Ambrose letters, August 5, 1934.

[8] Millicent Bingham goes into narrative detail about Bunny Zahn's

lobster pound proposal. She had just walked back from the Bremen post office when "Mr. Zahn invited me to go rowing. When we were a ways out from shore, he announced his intention of building the lobster pound by building a wall across the head of the cove from the Ambrose property to mine. He had their permission. I told him I had other ideas for the use of Hog Island." Ambrose letters, August 17, 1933.

[9] As hopeful as Nellie Ambrose was that Millicent would find a potential taker for Hog Island among the "nature" crowd, she had her doubts. "I hope you succeed in making someone think the place is suited for a sanctuary. Personally, I do not think it is, as there are too many evergreen trees and no maples or other trees that a large variety of birds need." Well aware that Millicent was trying to find a buyer for the Point Breeze at the same time she sought a science solution for her own holdings, Nellie replied, "However, we thank you just the same for trying." Ambrose letters, April 7, 1934.

[10] A taste of Millicent Bingham's contacts: "The Augusta Nature Club, the Bangor Bird Conservation Club, the Portland Society of Natural History, and the Federated Bird Clubs of New England, as well as the National Audubon Society and the Massachusetts Audubon Society. All agreed that the island would be an ideal location for such a sanctuary and that it ought to be owned by a club or group of clubs, but they were not in a position to purchase." Ambrose letters, June 20, 1934.

[11] Information on the Allegany School was drawn from an article in the *Vassar Miscellany News* (March 14, 1934) and an online registration document for the 1940 season found on a Cornell University website.

[12] More of Mrs. Bingham's thoughts that day about a Maine version of the Allegany School: "I think it would be a public benefaction, one which would increase in interest and importance as a center for students as the years go on. Being an island, it is much better for their purposes than a place on the mainland where they would constantly have to be trying to keep mobilists (sic) and picnic parties from disturbing the birds." Ambrose letters, June 20, 1934.

[13] James M. Todd was a native of Illinois with a medical degree from Northwestern University. After practicing for a few years, he transformed

himself into a New York City developer working in various partnerships over time. His companies built "many hotels, apartment houses, and office buildings, including the Graybar Building where he had his office." This same report continued, "His firm managed many of these buildings including the rebuilding and managing of Rockefeller Center." Recognized as a "great benefactor of Boothbay Harbor," a statue of Dr. Todd resides in the town's Oak Lawn Cemetery. (Tupper, *Boothbay Register.* Unpaged.) A separate report credits a James Todd firm with restoration of parts of Williamsburg, Virginia.

[14] Millicent Todd Bingham, "Rescuing an Island" (*Natural History,* May 1937), 320.

[15] Bingham, "Rescuing," 320.

[16] Nature study, a hands-on concept of understanding the natural world promoted by Anna Comstock at Cornell University, was in its heyday between 1890 and 1920 and is surely a springboard for the curriculum developed for the Audubon Nature Camp. Nature study techniques are evident in the Allegany School of Natural History curriculum.

[17] Frank Graham, Jr. advises in *The Audubon Ark* that Frank Chapman was to bird illustration in his time as Roger Tory Peterson was in the twentieth century.

[18] Frank Graham, Jr., *The Audubon Ark: A History of the National Audubon Society* (University of Texas Press, 1990), 129.

[19] In fall 1934, the National Association of Audubon Society's operating officer was T. Gilbert Pearson, the former secretary/treasurer of the organization under first president William Dutcher. By 1934, a scandal rocked the membership over money raised in association sanctuaries. When Baker took over Audubon that fall, he didn't remove Pearson completely but relegated him to a small space in Audubon's Broadway Avenue offices. For more on Audubon history, see Frank Graham, Jr.'s *Audubon Ark.*

[20] Graham, *Ark,* 129.

[21] Bingham, "Rescuing," 320.

[22] With Audubon taking up Mrs. Bingham's offer and Dr. James Todd purchasing the Point Breeze lock, stock, and barrel, Joseph and Nellie

Ambrose were finally out from under their island burden. The Ambroses were invited to an Audubon Camp open house in July 1936 where they heard both James Todd and Millicent Bingham tell their version of how the camp came to be. In the last of the Ambrose letters dated July 26, 1936, Nellie responded regarding that island visit: "Thought we might see you again after the morning but did not. Was sorry to hear from Dr. Todd's speech that we caused you so much unhappiness because we wanted to sell, but he did not mention that we turned down more than half a dozen sales with a larger money offer than we got, because we did not wish to displease you." Ambrose letters, July 26, 1936.

[23] Ambrose letters, undated June 1935.

[24] One last Howard Hilder mystery remains that may never be answered. In communication with Nellie Ambrose, Millicent Bingham reported that the senior Hilder had committed suicide in Florida on July 17, 1935. While Bingham does not reveal her sources, she surely knew people in Coconut Grove who would know such details. On the other hand, *The Palm Beach Post* reported Howard Hilder's death by heart attack on June 30 and posted in their July 1, 1935, issue. John C. Hilder's death on May 20, 1936, at the age of 43, shares no such mystery. Turns out neither Hilder would be alive for the opening of the Audubon Nature Camp in June 1936.

[25] It is unclear if Allan Cruickshank was a "first day hire," though Roger Peterson reported he himself was. "I joined the staff on November 1, the very day that Baker assumed the presidency." Roger Tory Peterson, "The Maine Story" (*Bird Watcher's Digest,* November-December 1986), 76.

[26] For posterity's sake, this author adds that in our personal interview, Carl Buchheister offered that Ernest Thompson Seton books were a "real influence" on him as a boy, as they were for Roger Tory Peterson. Graham, *Ark,*133.

[27] Buchheister's daughter Mary Carol Massonneau remembers Camp Moccasin "quite fondly." She reports her parents developed the summer operation on the suggestion of Lawrence School parents who saw value in Carl's after-hours nature club there. Massonneau is unclear why the Laconia, New Hampshire, location was selected. She believes her

parents ran the camp for kids through 1935. Carl W. Buchheister and Mary Carol Massonneau interviews.

[28] Over time, John Baker would say that Carl Buchheister was his personal choice to succeed him at Audubon. In December 1939, Carl was named assistant to the executive director. When Baker's title reverted to president in 1941, the year after the National Association of Audubon Societies officially became the National Audubon Society, Buchheister became assistant to the president and upon Baker's retirement in 1959, president. Carl Buchheister retired from Audubon in February 1967. Graham, *Ark*, 139.

[29] First-year staff as reported in "The Puffins Await You!" (*Bird-Lore* May–June 1936), 204.

[30] "Along Maine's Coast: Where and How to See Some of Our Most Striking Bird Colonies" (*Bird-Lore*, May–June 1935), 186.

[31] June 1935 was not the first time Roger Peterson had seen Hog Island. He reports, "Actually, I first laid eyes on Hog Island...when I was scarcely out of my teens. At the time I was acting as nature counselor at a boys' camp—Camp Chewonki—at nearby Wiscasset. On one of my days off I was invited by a local resident, Mrs. Sortwell, to sail among the islands in her yacht and point out the birds. I clearly remember that after we had cruised past the ship chandlery on Hog Island I spotted an osprey nest." Peterson, "Maine Story," 76.

[32] Peterson, "Maine Story," 78.

[33] Millicent Todd Bingham, "The Todd Wildlife Sanctuary" (*Bird-Lore*, September–October 1935), 349–51.

[34] Bingham, "Rescuing," various.

[35] In my 1982 interview with him, Carl Buchheister advised it was Bill Vogt who provided him with the literature to understand the science of ecology, which is defined as "the careful study of interactions between organisms and their environment."

[36] Naming the summer Hog Island operation the Audubon Nature Camp did mislead some potential campers who were seeking a destination where clothes would be optional. The naturist movement was alive and well in New England. In fact, Nellie Ambrose reported to Millicent

Bingham the possibility of the Point Breeze becoming a nudist colony. Nellie wrote, "They already have one in Maine and you know Edna Vincent Millay is much interested and is one of them. I do not believe they would trouble anyone, as they keep much to themselves. And we must sell the place..." Ambrose letters, November 30, 1934.

Carl Buchheister liked to tell the story of a registered camper who assumed she could sunbathe in the buff. Frank Graham reports Carl responded to her, deadpan, "We don't have enough people here to make it an aesthetic experience." Graham, *Ark,*139.

[37] Graham, *Ark*, 142.

[38] "The Audubon Nature Camp" (*Bird-Lore,* January–February 1936), 37.

[39] "We're coming back!" (*Bird-Lore,* July–August 1936), 288.

[40] "The Audubon Nature Camp" (*Bird-Lore,* September–October 1936), 349.

[41] Frank Graham, Jr. tells one version of the curfew story, Roger Peterson another. Graham implies this was not the first time Peterson had taken "the comeliest lass in camp" out "owling" after hours. Peterson claims it was Allan Cruickshank who popped off to a camper about Roger taking her out for night birds. Peterson blew it off as a joke until the woman asked if that night hike might be possible. Peterson thought it would be okay, and off they went. Two other women in the dorm were curious about what they were up to and followed them. One of the women fell into the well. All was innocent that evening, according to Peterson. For Graham's version, see *The Audubon Ark,* p. 141. For Peterson's take, see "The Maine Story" in *Bird Watchers Digest,* October 1986.

And yet a third version of that infamous night's events exists in print from none other than the woman who actually fell in the hole, Gunni Manson. Manson reported her version in the Clearwater (FL) Audubon Society newsletter in fall 2008. She explained that as a twenty-four-year-old, she and a camper friend went out after dark and she fell into a deep hole. Manson supposed it was "a basement structure which had not been covered," but in any case, she was hurt. She reported, "I have a big scar right here." Ms. Manson told her friend to go back to their room so she wouldn't be punished for being out after curfew.

Eventually Peterson, who had heard what he thought was "an animal making a crying sound," and Carl Buchheister arrived together to pull her out. Assessed for injuries, Manson says the following day she was "transported back to her home in New York City." Manson makes no mention of John Baker.

[42] Some Cruickshank titles include *Hunting with a Camera, Birds around New York City, Bird Islands Down East, The Pocket Guide to Birds,* and *The Birds of Brevard County, Florida.*

[43] US Fish and Wildlife, the agency that operates the Merritt Island NWR, maintains the Allan D. Cruickshank Memorial Trail that traverses miles of wetland in an opportunity to get out of the car and look more carefully at what Allan loved so much. Also of note is the Helen and Allan Cruickshank Sanctuary operated by Brevard County Parks and Recreation in their old winter hometown of Rockledge, Florida.

[44] Don Borror founded the Borror Laboratory of Bioacoustics at Ohio State University, which houses one of the largest collections of recorded animal sounds in the world, including over 30,000 recordings of over 1,400 species of animals.

[45] As a young girl, Farida Wiley developed a deep love for nature and taught herself much. Her parents died when she was still a teenager, and so she moved to New York with her newly married sister. There Miss Wiley took a job at the museum teaching botany to blind students. She worked at the American Museum of Natural History for sixty-two years.

[46] Farida A. Wiley's fern guide, first published in 1936, is titled *Ferns of Northeastern United States: Illustrations and Descriptions of all Known Species in the New England and Middle Atlantic States.*

[47] The first nature activities specialist on staff at the Audubon Nature Camp was Dorothy Treat, who would later become the director of the Aullwood Audubon Center in Dayton, Ohio. In an unpublished letter sent to Baker in December 1963, she remembers staff training that first summer. "I remember you talking to us so earnestly about using no technical nor scientific terms but expressing ourselves in simple, every day language; urging us to do as much of our teaching as possible in the field so the campers would learn at first hand and be led on by

our own great enthusiasm for the out of doors.... And there was one thing more—you were always telling us that we must avoid the words 'study,' 'classes,' 'courses,' anything which would remind our campers of school." Treat copied her letter to Dur Morton, then camp director, and Paul Knoop, education director at Aullwood, in order to put Audubon education priorities under John Baker in print for posterity. Interestingly, in his response, the five-year-retired Baker had no memory of having behaved so. He did say, "But I must admit that it so well represents my point of view, it almost follows that I must have said it." Dorothy Treat, personal correspondence, December 16 and 26, 1963.

[48] The early conservation movement was populated by energized citizens, some zealots, who held the concept of "wise use" of nature as a spiritual tenet. As the movement matured, conservation clarified itself by those professing the "gospel of beauty"—save a tree or landform because of its inherent worth—and those motivated by the "gospel of efficiency"—save that tree or landform because industry can use it later. Recognizing John Baker as one who professed the "gospel of ecology" speaks to his passion for awareness of natural diversity.

[49] In our July 2004 interview, Bart Cadbury noted to the best of his recollection John Baker "came to every final program."

[50] Graham, *Ark*, 141.

[51] Frank Graham, Jr.'s composite list of Audubon Camps includes Maine, Connecticut, California, Texas, and Wisconsin. Upon closure of the California camp, operations moved to Wyoming.

[52] Unpublished letter from Carl Buchheister to Millicent Bingham, August 17, 1962. Millicent Todd Bingham Papers, Manuscripts and Archives, Yale University Library.

[53] Quoted from *Biographical Dictionary of American and Canadian Naturalists and Environmentalists*. Google books image capture.

[54] Carl Buchheister and Mabel Loomis Todd would have been fine together because both expected common courtesies even on a wilderness island. Mrs. Todd entertained in long linen dresses wearing a hat. Carl Buchheister and John Baker both were seldom seen without wearing a tie. Celebrating regional differences in a joyful manner, Mr. Buchheister

would address a male guest, staff member, or workman as "the gentleman from Ohio" or whatever state he was from. Thus, Carl Buchheister gladly embraced the honorific title "gentleman from Maryland."

[55] The only location close enough to Hog Island to see puffins during the Buchheister era was Matinicus Rock which was why it was on the itinerary for an all-day boat trip in the early years. Mary Carol Massonneau reports that it was often difficult to make landings there. Upon Audubon's approach, coast guard staff would throw down a rope and winch dories up onto "the rock." On the way out, dories were loaded then pushed down the sluiceway, splashing into the water. On one occasion, Carl confidently stood in a dory on the way out to sea to address those aboard. When the boat hit the water, Buchheister was thrown overboard. A good swimmer, drowning was not a problem but he reported the water was "damned cold." Upon return to camp and Harriet Buchheister's hearing that news, her main concern was if Carl's fashionable watch would dry out. Because of difficulty and distance, Matinicus Rock was eventually dropped from camp field trips. Still, because of these and other visits, the Buchheisters developed a life-long love for Matinicus Rock and the people of the coast guard operation there.

[56] In 1905, Matinicus Rock was the first Audubon wildlife sanctuary established in Maine. The Matinicus Rock light, run by the US Coast Guard, was automated in 1982. Details of Carl Buchheister's Matinicus Rock story are taken from an unpublished anniversary address he made at the Matinicus Rock sanctuary on August 16, 1984. Mary Carol Massonneau further reported that her mother, in her love of botany, identified "all the plants on Matinicus" in her weeks over many summers there.

[57] Millicent Todd Bingham and Mabel Loomis Todd. *Bolts of Melody: New Poems of Emily Dickinson* (Harper, 1945), vii.

[58] Austin Dickinson and Mabel Loomis Todd's affair was well documented by 1974 in Richard B. Sewall's authoritative biography *The Life of Emily Dickinson.* Dickinson aficionados would have to wait another ten years for Polly Longsworth's *Austin and Mabel: The Amherst Affair & Love Letters of Austin Dickinson and Mabel Loomis Todd.*

[59] The poetry in the collections Martha Dickinson Bianchi edited were those titles sent by Emily to Susan Gilbert Dickinson, Martha's mother. Poems and letters that Lavinia Dickinson held after the lawsuit were added to that collection. Some of Martha Bianchi's best-known Dickinson titles are *The Single Hound: Poems of a Lifetime* (1914), *The Life and Letters of Emily Dickinson* (1924), *The Complete Poems of Emily Dickinson* (1929), and *Emily Dickinson Face to Face* (1932). The complete collection of Dickinson poetry would not reach publication until the Thomas H. Johnson edition in 1955.

[60] In Millicent's dispute with Harvard, her doctoral alma mater, a Dickinson family opponent of the Todds called Mabel "a thief" who had been "convicted of misrepresentation and fraud in two courts" and, of course, had no right to any Emily Dickinson material still in her possession. Lyndall Gordon, *Lives Like Loaded Guns: Emily Dickinson and Her Family Feuds* (Viking, 2010), 372.

[61] Julie Dobrow, *After Emily: Two Remarkable Women and the Legacy of America's Greatest Poet* (W. W. Norton, 2018), 293.

[62] Author of the definitive Emily Dickinson biography, Richard B. Sewall, interacted with Millicent in his writing process. She came to trust the Yale professor, and when it became obvious the Amherst College archive was not equipped to accept the expansive Todd Bingham family papers, she selected Yale University. She may have preferred Harvard, her graduate alma mater, but the negotiations over the Dickinson papers soured her on that option. In the end, Millicent Bingham selected Richard B. Sewall to serve as her estate's executor. Dobrow, *After Emily,* 328 and 335.

[63] The Bingham return to Hog Island in 1948 is calculated, not confirmed. Willow clearly stated it had been six years away but did not date her narrative. Your humble author is assuming 1942 was the first summer the Binghams stayed in Washington, DC.

[64] A special thank you to Chris Speh for providing the unpublished "Willow's remembrance" unearthed from the Sorel/Speh family archive. The narrative comes in three sections, all assumed written over the same summer, though none are dated. In the first section, Willow refers to the time of her writing as "twenty years later." If so, then perhaps the

Willow narrative was written ca. 1968 as memoir of Millicent Bingham, who died that December.

[65] Chris Speh, "The Hog Island Experience" (Personal reflection, unpublished, July 2005).

[66] Paul Sorel was a bit of a character and storyteller. Chris advised that Uncle Paul could maneuver two friends into a contentious conversation, then leave them to their own devices. He also told a tale about the origins of the Osprey cabin. Apparently unaware of its root with Howard Hilder, Paul Sorel's yarn was that Mabel Todd built it for her secret lover, Austin Dickinson. When Chris Speh learned Austin Dickinson died a dozen years before Mrs. Todd bought the island, Speh responded in an email, "Oh, no! You've ruined one of my most favorite family stories!"

[67] Paul and Gert Sorel would summer at the Osprey until the late 1960s when they bought property on the mainland in Medomak. Carl Buchheister recognized the Sorels as good friends of both Mrs. Bingham and Hog Island and on one occasion told them they "belonged" there. When Chris Speh's mother and brother died, Catherine T. Speh in 2001 and John A. "Tony" Speh in 2000, their ashes were scattered at the Osprey site.

[68] Another option for the Bingham cottages Millicent hoped for was that Carl Buchheister's family would put it to use after she vacated. "Regarding my camp buildings at the time I made the deed of gift [to Audubon in 1960], I thought that in appreciation of Mr. Buchheister's devoted service he should have the use of them for himself and his family for as long as he wished. This did not turn out to be what he wished at all." Millicent Todd Bingham, "History and Possible Future Use of the Todd Wildlife Sanctuary" (Millicent Todd Bingham Papers, Manuscripts and Archives, Yale University Library, 1965), unpublished.

[69] Rachel Carson's reference to Hog Island appears in "Earth's Green Mantle," chapter 6 of *Silent Spring:* "In the summer of 1960 conservationists from many states converged on a peaceful Maine island to witness its presentation to the National Audubon Society by its owner, Millicent Todd Bingham. The focus that day was on the preservation of the natural landscape and of the intricate web of life whose interwoven

strands lead from microbes to man. But in the background of all the conversations among the visitors to the island was indignation at the despoiling of the roads they had traveled." Rachel Carson, *Silent Spring* (Fawcett, 1962), 69.

The day following the dedication, Ms. Carson wrote the following note to Millicent: "Ever since I left you yesterday I have been thinking of how full your heart must be, and of the thoughts that must fill your mind— thoughts of the past, and of the future as your dreams for the Island are fulfilled. There should be for you a deep satisfaction in having been able to make such an abiding contribution to preserving not only the tangible beauty of the island, but the things that are 'eternal.'" Quoted in Dobrow, *After Emily,* 331.

[70] The entire message on the plaque reads, "The Todd Wildlife Sanctuary presented to The National Audubon Society by Millicent Todd Bingham in memory of her mother Mabel Loomis Todd (1856–1932) Who fifty years ago saved this island - wilderness and thus shaped its destiny as a perpetual preserve. August 1960."

[71] Polly Longsworth personal email to Tom Schaefer, October 21, 2014.

CHAPTER 6

Legacy

If a child is to keep alive his inborn sense of wonder...he needs the companionship of at least one adult who can share it, rediscovering with him the joy, excitement, and mystery of the world we live in.

—Rachel Carson
from *The Sense of Wonder* / 1956

Summer 1957 marked the last season of the Buchheister era on Hog Island. For the twenty-one years since the Audubon Nature Camp's opening in 1936, except for two World War II summers when the facility was shuttered, the camp's program had been developed and successfully directed by Carl Buchheister, and as many others would add without hesitation, his splendidly capable wife Harriet.[1] During that time, summers in Maine were almost sacred for the Buchheister family. Carl and Harriet, and for as long as they could with their three daughters, religiously returned annually to provide a season of hospitality and instruction for an enthusiastic clientele while continuing to develop a sense of family among the staff.[2] The end of the Buchheister years on the island, however, did not mark the end of "Mother Church's" influence on the evolving National Audubon Society.

By summer 1958, Carl had been elevated at Audubon to replace John Baker as national president and Midcoast summers, even those special weeks between sessions on Matinicus Rock with the puffins, had to be amended due to his increased workload. The camp would soldier on under a new director, though deciding who among the established staff would fill that top leadership post was a tough call for both Carl and Harriet Buchheister. One of their daughters, Mary Carol Massonneau, recalls overhearing many of her parents' deliberations, whether in their New York City apartment or in their cabin on Hog Island. In this case she remembers what her father would recall as one of the hardest things he ever had to do when he took the train to Philadelphia to personally inform Joe Cadbury that the new camp director would be his younger brother, Bart. Joe, of course, had been on staff since the camp's second year while Bart hadn't come aboard until over ten years later. Not knowing how Joe would react to his brother getting the prestigious job, Buchheister made the trip to deliver the uncomfortable news himself. Carl would tell his family later how a normally quiet Joe Cadbury took the news stoically, while his wife and Lady of the Institute, Lucille, crossed the room to Carl, put her arms around his neck and said, "We understand."

One of the reasons the Buchheisters settled on Bart and Ginny Cadbury to take on the next chapter of the Hog Island operation was because they felt that under the skill sets of this very capable couple team, oversight of both program and social life would continue as modeled. The Cadburys' four years' experience working summers with older boys at Camp Keewaydin in Vermont helped in the decision as well.[3] The legacy staff would still be in place, so with Allan Cruickshank, Joe Cadbury, Don Borror, and Farida Wiley all returning, Carl and Harriet Buchheister felt Bart and Ginny Cadbury could best sustain the camp atmosphere so carefully nurtured under the elder couple's leadership.

Before this narrative veers off into the Cadbury years, however, it might be beneficial to take a step back to see how the Audubon Nature Camp operation had matured under the Buchheisters and to determine just what it was the legacy staff was charged to carry on. First-year nature activities staffer Dorothy Treat, who had moved on by summer 1941, was on Hog Island for the opening of that season's first session. Her observations published in *Audubon* magazine provide a snapshot of what the camp had grown into by its sixth season.[4]

Along with offering the compulsory litany of sensory details from glistening "gneisses, schists, [and] chunks of quartz" to the description of a comfortable fire warming a foggy and wet island afternoon, Treat reported the big news of the summer was the construction and occupancy of the Fish House, the only major structure Audubon has ever added to the Point Breeze complex. Until then, camper gatherings were held in either the dining room or the first floor of the old casino building on the waterfront. Campers from the previous summer started the fund to construct a larger and more appropriate meeting hall which found donors over the winter among "interested alumni and friends." The building provided such a different island landscape that returning campers "rubbed their eyes and wondered if this was really the same place they had camped in before."

Designed to blend into a Maine coastal setting, the long-proportioned Fish House smelled of "spicy fresh pine lumber." Plenty of books and "drop-leaf reading tables" encouraged campers to engage in topics essential to the camp curriculum. Perhaps the most arresting feature of the new building was the Camp Mavooshen–like hearth that was "a truly magnificent affair, massive with high mantel and towering chimney all made of native rocks." With "great logs blazing," coffee steaming, and a light lunch waiting for arriving campers, the Fish House was deemed "warm and friendly," just as it still is today.

Dorothy Treat reminds us, too, that access to Hog Island in those early years wasn't as easy as driving down Keene Neck Road and dropping gear at the boat house at the bottom of the hill on the shore. Back then Charlie Nash still owned the mainland tract and refused access to Audubon. Instead, campers met staff and a boat at the public dock in Medomak and were transported downriver to the island. Treat writes of that June afternoon: "Most of the staff are on the grass in front of the office looking out across the bay ... watching for the boats to round Oar Island with the season's first campers."

The article is punctuated by sixteen Allan Cruickshank photographs, ranging in subject from campers at work to native butterflies, starfish, and, of course, birds. Camp staff are described along with their credentials, as are some programming notes, like the still-popular first-day shake-down cruise. Treat mentions, too, "the camp log" that all could access where lists of birds found in what locations over multiple summers were recorded. She writes, "Over 200 species of birds have now been seen in the vicinity of the Audubon Nature Camp. From 50 to 60 may be seen and heard on a single trip to the near-by mainland." How could any potential birding camper resist numbers like those?

It is worth noting that though Treat describes the camp's all-important, though novel to some, hands-on approach to science education, she never gives name to the prime element of the camp curriculum, ecology. She describes that "campers learn at first hand the many interrelated factors—soil, water, light, weather, as well as the mutual dependence of plants and animals upon each other.... Such information builds intelligent appreciation of the out-of-doors and provides a sound basis for its conservation."

Surely what is written is an adequate explanation of ecology, but she never articulates the word. Conservation is instead the key term connected to appreciating and understanding the "out-of-doors." As a museum educator steeped in the good work out of Cornell, Treat was very comfortable using the expression nature study. In the article's summary, after offering that at the end of that sixth season, over 1,200 different adults had spent over 1,400 two-week sessions at the camp, Treat reflected, "The influence of the camp in teaching nature study. appreciation is indeed far-reaching." And to punctuate another priority inherent to every Carl Buchheister summer, she would have been remiss if she hadn't added that island living also "generates a contagious kind of enthusiasm, too."

Another *Audubon* magazine article from that era clarifies from a different perspective what made the legacy camp program unique. Biologist and National Audubon Society board member Dr. Paul Sears wrote that he had tried "no fewer than three times in my life" to develop a program for "intelligent laity" for the teaching of nature appreciation that sidestepped the trap of "intense professionalism." His ideal program would be set in "rich and beautiful natural surroundings" with first-class management and staffing. Cost "must be inexpensive" and enrollment "open to those who seem most likely to get something out of it and carry the inspiration back to others." He further stressed the staff must be "without a trace of intellectual snobbery." Sears seemed to echo John Baker who stressed camp programming avoid the use of complicated terms and a feeling of being too school-like. Learning about nature should be hands-on, interactive, and fun. Sears was pleased to report that he had found what he had dreamed of on Hog Island. Such an articulation of the camp's success affirms the Baker and Buchheister "legacy" status that would remain the operational template for years to come.[5]

The Bart Cadbury Era

The first of the Bartram Cadbury and family summers at the Audubon Camp was 1948, as mentioned prior, a fortuitous year for Hog Island. For the first time in six summers Buchheister's staff removed the shutters at the Bingham cottages in preparation for Millicent and Walter's arrival. In addition, the aforementioned Charlie Nash had recently died in a tragic accident in which a tree he was trying to fall had, in fact, fallen on him. His widow, Myra, was not interested in living by herself at the end of Keene Neck Road, nor was her family prepared to take the homestead over, which meant the property was available for sale in order to settle the estate. Negotiations between the Nashes and Audubon had not always gone well over the years, so Carl Buchheister opted to engage a local advocate from Camden to serve as his agent. After the sale went through, members of the Nash family cried foul, finding the property steeped in Keene family history was not remaining with a local owner but instead going to National Audubon. All proved legal, however, and by summer 1948, Hog Island finally secured the all-important water access that Baker and Buchheister had sought from the beginning.[6] And as a bonus, the camp picked up structures on the mainland that would serve adequately as staff housing and office and utility space.

Life for the Nashes in their farmhouse at the top of the hill hadn't been easy, or at least not all that comfortable by modern standards. They were of a breed of Maine countryfolk who worked the land and sea however they could to make a living, which was in fact, how Charlie

Nash died. Their dwelling was simple with no electricity and no running water, though there was a pump at the kitchen sink. The bathroom was a little building out back with a crescent moon on the door.[7] Apparently comfort was not a prime concern in the Nash household. Nevertheless, while Bart rowed over to the relative conveniences at camp every day, the old Nash house, in all its rustic charm, was the summer setting for wife and mother Ginny Cadbury to tend her two little girls, Betsy, age three, and Peggy, just a baby at five months.

Carl Buchheister, his staff, and their wives, were very aware that life in the Nash house would be a challenge for a young family. Harriet Buchheister and Helen Cruickshank worked hard preparing the place best they could. When Ginny and the girls arrived, the women met them with a warm welcome and a vase of lilacs on the kitchen table. Following was a quick primer on how to get the water running through the iron pump at the sink and how to operate the two-burner kerosene stove. No diaper service in the area meant Ginny would be doing that washing by hand and on rainy days, hanging laundry inside the house. Girls were bathed in a galvanized tub when needed and pre-bedtime evenings were lit by oil lamps. Since the family wasn't officially part of the camp staff, Ginny was responsible for procuring and making meals on Bart's summer pay. And since Bart rowed over to the island around 7:00 a.m. for the morning staff meeting and didn't get back across until late due to his busy field trip schedule and staff responsibilities, Ginny was pretty much on her own with the little ones. The Nash house proved to be the only Audubon Camp location with a telephone, as well, which meant the shore contingent was tasked to send messages over to the island by way of student assistants rowing over for mail.

Meanwhile, Joe and Lucille Cadbury and family made a home in the lightly remodeled barn next door, known today as the Puffin House. Back then the main living space was one large room with a sink and water pump at one end and a big table in front of large, screened windows that overlooked the bay. On rainy days, those windows were closed by old exterior barn doors, which could turn conditions inside dark and stuffy in a hurry. Double beds and cots were up in the loft while three stalls remained below, one designated for bikes and toys. Lu Cadbury had two boys of their own, Joel and David, to tend and was assigned other responsibilities to aid in running the camp from the mainland. Between sessions, staff came over for fun-filled parties and on occasion, Uncle Joe brought his car up close and turned up the radio. One staff party included installing linoleum on the Nash house kitchen floor. But as difficult as most of that must have been, Ginny remembers, "We had a good time, though."

Still, Bart's four-hundred-dollar salary didn't get it done financially for his family. Ginny kept careful books and found they had actually *lost* money over that first summer. At the end of the season when Carl queried staff on who would be returning, Ginny made it clear they could not. "We can't afford to come to camp," she remembers saying. "We just can't." Not wanting to replace his marine life instructor so quickly and in the interest of doing what he could to help, Buchheister offered Bart another one hundred dollars in salary plus island kitchen assistance in providing some daily meals for his family. Bart and Ginny talked it over and considered the changes enough, so they decided to give the camp another try.

Another factor that made life in the old Nash house somewhat ticklish for Ginny and the kids was the upstairs bedroom situation. Recognizing how hectic life on the island could be through years of experience, Harriet Buchheister requested space on the mainland where she could escape, relax, and when the spirit moved, create. Betsy Cadbury remembers very clearly that kids were not allowed upstairs unless beckoned by Mrs. Buchheister to bring something or run an errand. The hallway outside the bedroom stored paints, block printing materials, and other art projects, all things the kids knew never to touch. It should be noted that Harriet's upstairs retreat bedroom also boasted the best view of the bay from the Nash house.

As staff children got older, exciting and adventurous opportunities arose on Hog Island. Carl Buchheister's revised feeding plan was for all families to take breakfast on their own, then gather at the dining room on the island for the mid-day and evening meals, where the kids would finish before the campers were called in. Swimming in Porthole Cove followed on afternoons when conditions permitted, and if a kid were really lucky, they got to spend the afternoon on the island, whereas the other kids returned to the mainland until supper. The lucky child got to hang around staff and their nature activities and thus picked up lots of specific knowledge at a tender age. It's not surprising those kids became fine birders. One camper story has a "tiny child" announcing the breed of an unusual gull that flew by. When asked by an incredulous camper how such a small child knew what kind of bird that was, the youngster responded, "I don't know, it just is."

Living on the waterfront, of course, provided special concerns for parents. Before kids were allowed to take a boat out on their own, each had to show Uncle Joe proficient swimming skills. The first hurdle was to jump off a dock and swim one hundred feet without touching the bottom, but not until a kid could swim all the way from the mainland to the island would he or she gain permission to row a boat solo on open water. Betsy Cadbury remembers she and her cousin David were both ten years old when they managed the feat. "It was a big deal," she remembers. Taking a boat out on their own meant "total freedom." The time after their lunch when staff and campers were engaged in eating and then prepping for afternoon activities proved a prime opportunity to sign out a boat. "We went all over the bay," Betsy recalls wistfully, landing on places like Crow and Oar islands where they tied up and explored.[8]

The four Cadbury kids kept busy at the old mainland farm with fun projects from fort and treehouse building to more creative endeavors. Auntie Lu taught them to sew, which resulted in their making small balsam pillows sold to campers from the front porch step of the old Nash house. Profits were minimal but afforded them enough for treks through the woods to the Medomak country store where popsicles and cold soda made the trip worthwhile. Little Peggy might tire on the walk back home, so older cousin Joel would pick her up, which made the trip more tolerable.

Turnaround time between sessions was a whirlwind with little time off, which is why the annual unscheduled week between sessions three and four was so important to staff and their families. Monhegan Island was a destination for some, while other staff took off to all points of the compass to take advantage of the time and place. Joe and Lucille Cadbury took their boys camping and canoeing. The Buchheisters and Bart and Ginny Cadbury usually snagged a student assistant or two to help band petrels on Matinicus Rock. Betsy Cadbury remembers while other kids got away, she and Peggy stayed at a babysitter's house, which was usually a Keene or an Osier in the Bremen area. At Alice Osier's place one summer, the girls were exposed to Maine farm living. Betsy remembers a particularly traumatic experience for her five-year-old sister when after a chicken was beheaded for Sunday dinner, the body ran around the farmyard "spurting blood." Betsy offered, "Wonder Peggy ever ate chicken again."

As staff kids grew into their teens, many were signed up by parents to work off-site in service to others. Art Borror, following in the steps of Roger Tory Peterson, worked as a counselor at Camp Chewonki while years prior some of the kids shipped off to counsel at Pine Tree Camp, an outdoor experience designed for handicapped children.[9] The summer prior to her first year as a Pine Tree Camp counselor, Betsy Cadbury remembers working diligently through all aspects of the Hog Island curriculum so she could be proficient as a nature study instructor herself. She got so good at it, in fact, that she intimidated her life science teacher back at school, where she could recite Latin names for insects that she had learned from the many hikes where she assisted her favorite Hog Island instructor, insect life specialist Don Borror.

Running a residential summer camp on an island off the coast of Maine provided myriad management obstacles. Providing electricity and potable water for essentially a small village of people to gathering all the supplies needed to keep that village fed and comfortable presented perpetual logistical hurdles. Harriet Buchheister shouldered many of the supply problems in the early years by spending hours on the phone ordering camp necessities while coordinating road trips through the region for staff to pick up needed groceries and supplies.

Some products could be delivered to the boathouse on the mainland, but not until 1948. In any case, everything on the island still must be hauled by boat then transported over a gangplank, which, depending on the tide, can be less or more of a challenge. In addition to providing utilities and meals, just setting up camper rooms, sweeping floors, cleaning toilets, and providing fresh linen for everybody every two weeks, five times a summer, was a monumental undertaking that required more labor than the camp staff could provide.

Just as Frank Lailer was an unsung and forgotten hero at Mabel Todd's Camp Mavooshen, Regina and Tom Carter deserve special recognition as essential energy sources for the successful operation of the Audubon Nature Camp during the Cadbury years. Living year-round just down the shore in New Harbor, the Carters served as camp custodians, which included both watching over facilities in the off-season as well as providing prime elbow grease to keep the camp running. Like Lailer, Tom was a fisherman-handyman who, along with Elmer Osier, made necessary repairs to camp infrastructure and stepped in to help more when needed. The Carters also hired and supervised local work crews that came in between sessions to reset camper accommodations. And as if that weren't involved enough, Regina also took on the immense job of doing camp laundry in her home ringer washing machine. Betsy Cadbury remembers driving by the Carter place with her babysitter and "seeing all the sheets billowing out in the wind." The sweet folks that they were, the Carters would also get a fire going in the Nash house wood stove for the Cadburys on cool arrival days. To round out their service on the island, the Carters were also caretakers for Mrs. Bingham at her family camp for a time in the 1950s when Regina cooked and rowed Millicent to shore while Tom ran errands, and as expected, performed camp maintenance and odd jobs.[10]

As helpful as the Carters and so many others were, the operation of the Audubon Nature Camp would have been impossible on Hog Island if not for substantial infrastructure improvements made to the old Point Breeze facility. From the time camp opened in 1936 through the early 1960s, electrical power was provided by a pair of Wisconsin gasoline engines that were hand-cranked about 4:30 in the morning by Captain Osier to recharge batteries. And since power on the island was exclusively direct current, staff found much equipment useless, and what did work was "always difficult." When an electric cable was dropped across the narrows in 1962 connecting the camp to Central Maine Power, island life not only got easier but quieter. Prior to that, when the camp director called for "lights out" at 10:00 p.m., the time the generators were turned off for the night, he really meant to turn lights off to conserve battery power for overnight consumption by essential appliances.

Water was undoubtedly the most essential utility on the island, and it too provided a world of difficulty in its delivery. Fresh water was not available plentifully anywhere on Hog Island, whether on the Audubon peninsula or on the larger re-wilding section. The Todds and Binghams had always grappled with supply, as did occupants of the Osprey cabin. Audubon dug four wells on the peninsula that proved adequate but running out of water by the end of the season was always a concern. The quality of that water was a concern on occasion, as well. When Harriet Buchheister heard a health inspection was imminent, she was known to climb up onto the wooden water holding tank behind the kitchen and dump in chlorine bleach.[11] Daughter Mary Carol Massonneau chuckled that it took a little while for the smell to dissipate, but it worked. Everyone knew the loss of fresh water on the island would be catastrophic for camp operations.

Late in his tenure as director, Bart Cadbury experienced his "worst equipment emergency," and it, indeed, dealt with the water supply. Maine had suffered near-drought conditions that year and well water levels on-island ran so low he sent a message to Carl Buchheister in New York City that if there was no improvement within forty-eight hours, campers would have to be sent off the island. In his usual convincing style, Buchheister got in touch with his Coast Guard buddies and asked for an enormous favor. Within Cadbury's critical forty-eight-hour window, the head of the Boston office of the Coast Guard ordered the USCGC Laurel be pulled off buoy maintenance duty to transport water to Hog Island. The Laurel's tanks were normally used to refill lighthouse island cisterns, like the one on Matinicus Rock the Buchheisters used during their off-duty week there. On this occasion the Coast Guard saved the day and the season by restoring adequate water levels to the Audubon Camp's wells.[12]

Until a water line from the mainland was installed in the mid-1960s, the only showers available on-island were of the saltwater variety. Showering campers were issued a bar of saltwater soap and one basin of fresh water for a final rinse. Toilets even flushed on salt water, which was hard on not only the plumbing but Muscongus Bay. Inevitably, island septic tanks filled over weeks of operation with overflow going directly into the bay. For some summers the Audubon Camp had the dubious distinction of being the biggest polluter in the bay.[13] Over time and with some experimentation, new sewage systems and leach fields were installed on-island that, though delicate, proved capable of handling the camp's annual wastewater load.

Bart Cadbury said when electricity and water finally made it to the island, "the whole outfit became more efficient." True as that was, he found new degrees of difficulty following Elmer Osier's retirement. As established, Osier was a fine seaman, experienced in Muscongus Bay waters, who adapted well to changing weather conditions. Still, the camp required more than one boat pilot and often under Osier that second boatman was just a college student. To solve that hiring problem, Carl Buchheister suggested both Joe and Bart Cadbury secure commercial boat operator licenses.

They did, which eased that issue, but another snag with the *Puffin I* and the *Osprey I* caused significant concern. In earlier camp seasons, ship-to-shore radio was optional, and with Captain Osier at the helm, the directors saw no problem. Coast Guard regulations had changed, however, which caused Audubon to upgrade both boats with the required radios. Trouble was the equipment didn't pass inspection just days before the first campers arrived.[14] All worked out in time, but with the loss of Elmer Osier, Bart Cadbury found himself not only camp director but first boatman and the first person on the island to hear that something wasn't working as planned. He remembers that summer as a particularly difficult one.

Perhaps the Audubon Camp's nearest disaster took place in 1954 on the island, not on the water, when two hurricanes blew heavy destruction throughout New England all the way into Midcoast Maine. The second storm, Edna, hit the camp after the season closed and caused many tree falls across the thin-soiled island in part due to the heavy rains deposited by the first storm that had hit just two weeks prior. That first northbound tropical cyclone, Hurricane Carol, attacked the island with fury just three days before the end of the last session, causing Carl Buchheister and his staff to reconsider established emergency procedures.[15]

All at the Audubon Camp were aware a big storm was coming, but nobody knew the details. In the early 1950s, weather reports were available primarily through local radio broadcasts, not the extensive network of media sites posting advisories and warnings today. At their morning meeting, the staff decided evacuating campers to the mainland was not necessary. Staff wives could head out shopping for the end-of-season "birthday party" coming up in a couple of days, but everybody else would sit tight.

By 9:00 a.m., Buchheister was already questioning those decisions when the wind picked up and the rain went horizontal. Ginny Cadbury was typing a letter in the camp office "when all hell broke loose." Staff gathered campers into the Fish House when reports came in that the Porthole residence was shaking in the heavy wind. Elmer Osier advised the boats to be put out on anchor to get them away from the rocking docks. So much heavy surf washed up over the Queen Mary deck that there was concern about the building being lost to the storm. Before the day was out, the mainland dock had broken away from its moorings and had to be retrieved.

Over at the old Nash property, the Cadbury children, under the care of Auntie Lu, had a "very, very exciting time." As the eye passed and the winds quieted, the kids walked down to the shore to witness tremendous waves. Helen Cruickshank and Harriet Buchheister, the Ladies of the Institute who had gone shopping, were marooned on the mainland with no access back to the island or down the Keene Neck road, which had been washed out at a low spot by a surging tide. All were safe, but excitement ran high.

By midday on the island, Carl Buchheister grew concerned about Millicent Bingham's welfare and dispatched Joe and Bart Cadbury to hike out into the storm to check on her. Bart recalled that trip across the island was "the most eerie experience in my life." Wind roared in the treetops while it was "perfectly quiet below." Millicent and caretaker Regina Carter were found safe and sound, but on their way back to camp the Cadburys had to work their way around myriad new tree falls. Some trees in Hog Island's shallow-rooted forest rocked so hard by relentless wind that root masses were seen coming out of the ground six inches or more. Art Borror, who was nineteen that summer, remembers so many trees down in the interior of the island that the passage was impenetrable. Visitors to the island today who are impressed with the extensive fields of ferns have hurricanes Carol and Edna to thank. Where fallen trees made an opening, ferns took advantage.[16]

Amid the dangers of weather and the technical troubles of operating a residential summer camp on an island, it should be stressed that enthusiasm and engagement carried most days at the Audubon Nature Camp. And while much of that enthusiasm and engagement were products of campers interacting with the serene setting, enterprising staff, and invigorating curriculum, a fair modicum came by way of the staff spouses who made their own significant contributions. The Ladies of the Institute personified wives supporting their husbands and in so doing added their own dynamic elements to the success and charm of the Hog Island program. Paychecks were made out to the staff member, but in reality they represented income earned by both husband and wife.[17]

Harriet Buchheister, who friends on the island affectionately called Susie, was a prime mover in developing special complementary events. Photographs from pre-Audubon days show Mabel Todd and Millicent Bingham entertaining at their family camp in wide-brimmed hats and full-length dresses while male guests wore ties and jackets. In that spirit of gentility, once a summer Mrs. Buchheister and the Ladies of the Institute put on a "proper tea" complete with sent invitations to campers. Ladies donned hats and gloves as tomato and cucumber sandwiches accented with island-grown herbs were served.

The biggest production by the staff wives was the end-of-season banquet, referred to as the camp's "birthday party." For the day prior, the Fish House was off limits to fifth-session campers as the women decorated the room, transforming it into a themed dinner theater. One year they highlighted Wallace Stegner's novel *The Big Rock Candy Mountain* by fashioning a fountain of red water flowing over collected beach rocks.[18] Maritime themes were common, as expected, with lobster buoys hung and fish netting draped about with cutouts of birds and sea creatures completing the motif. One year a five-foot-tall lighthouse was constructed. Tables were set formally, and the Ladies of the Institute served as wait staff. A blanket was hung at the fireplace end of the building to serve as a kind of curtain for the entertainment to come. Distinguished guests attending the gala event always included Millicent Bingham, John Baker, and often Roger Tory Peterson.[19] Sometimes local authors Henry Beston and Elizabeth Coatsworth came.[20] Following a festive meal there was always a birthday cake. After dinner, however, the fun really began.

Skits, singing, and talent shows completed the evening. The diminutive Helen Cruickshank and Harriet Buchheister crawled into a window behind the curtain to put on bird costumes and paper mâché masks of puffin and guillemot. They then emerged to strut around the room, chirping in "puffin talk," then disappeared. Joe Cadbury and Allan Cruickshank were famous for their comic interpretation of "the fair young maiden and Barnacle Bill the sailor," with Allan as the young maiden dressed in a bathrobe, singing in falsetto, with wood shavings as hair and straw hats placed strategically to "fill out the robe." The two inevitably brought the house down. A rousing campfire singalong filled out the evening.

With the wives and staff addressed as "aunt" and "uncle" by the children who grew up in the Hog Island program, it was surely a natural progression for the student assistants who served summers there to feel like they had been adopted into a larger family. That, especially, was a significant contribution engendered by the Ladies of the Institute headed up first by Harriet Buchheister then Ginny Cadbury. Uncle Don added on by telling one of the children that the dragonfly she had just identified was perhaps the most lovely on the island. Uncle Carl did his part when he gushed over the lapel flower the girls would bring into his office. And regarding the student assistants, young men who not only helped prepare meals and clean dishes but accompanied field trips and assisted in whatever capacity called for, Ginny Cadbury would say, "I loved those guys. They were my kids." Twelve weeks of total immersion in island life could lead a surrogate mother to feel that way.[21]

Though nature study and ecology-based activities dominated life at the Audubon Camp, Millicent Todd Bingham and a coterie of other notable women left impressions on the staff. As mentioned in the last chapter, Rachel Carson was one of them. Carson lived in Mrs. Bingham's hometown of Washington, DC, for a time and worked for the US Fish and Wildlife Service as she developed a penchant for writing about natural history subjects, primarily the sea. In 1953, she began coming to a Maine summer place on Southport Island near Boothbay Harbor, a geographic neighbor of Hog Island. It is not known how Mrs. Bingham and Ms. Carson met or how close they were as friends, but as mentioned earlier, Carson was Millicent Bingham's special guest at the island transfer ceremony in August 1960.

A pair of noteworthy women visitors left an impression on the Audubon camp soon after it reopened following the war years. Story has it that Dr. Miriam Van Waters and Geraldine Thompson came to camp "every year" and were always assigned Porthole #4. Thompson was a social welfare reformer from New Jersey while Van Waters served as superintendent of the Massachusetts Reformatory for Women at Framingham.[22] Not feeling tied to attending all the scheduled field trips year after year, Thompson and Van Waters "wrote their own program," according to Bart Cadbury. Allan Cruickshank liked to tell the story of his passing by Porthole Cove one morning on the way to lead the early bird walk when much to his surprise he encountered Geraldine in the buff, skinny-dipping in cold Muscongus Bay waters. Despite that legendary notoriety, Thompson and Van Waters are remembered in other ways.

Financial solvency for the camp always relied on "filling the beds," so getting the word out in national publications was always a priority. One day Geraldine Thompson approached Carl Buchheister about sending a telegram to "her dear friend" Eleanor Roosevelt, wife of former US President Franklin D. Roosevelt, inviting her to come to camp to experience it first-hand. As Carl's secretary, an excited Ginny Cadbury was responsible for transcribing the message and shipping it over to Lucille Cadbury, mainland secretary, who phoned the telegram into "Pearly Waltz's pharmacy" in Damariscotta. Though Mrs. Roosevelt declined the invitation, she did dispatch her secretary, and in her August 28, 1951, nationally published column, *My Day*, Eleanor Roosevelt sang the praises of the Hog Island camp and Audubon for advancing "public understanding of the value and need of conservation of soil, water, plants, and wildlife and the relation of their intelligent treatment and wise use." Such national exposure was good for the Maine camp and the other three Audubon camps operating that summer, not only to fill beds but to further promote a sound environmental ethic within the general public.[23] Ginny Cadbury reported another significant camp contribution from Miriam Van Waters was her introduction of the concept of composting kitchen scraps.

Shirley Briggs was another camper of some notoriety who made contributions to Hog Island and its history.[24] As a friend of Millicent Bingham and sister Washingtonian, Briggs came to the island regularly where she and her traveling partner Harriet Sutton stayed at the Osprey cabin. At times, the women just appeared on the mainland dock without notice, prompting Carl Buchheister to ask once, "Did anyone know they were coming?" In August 1960, Briggs was present for the transfer ceremony to Audubon. In fact, the best photographs that survive of that important day are black and whites taken by Shirley Briggs. She went on to publish some of those images and text of the guest speakers in the periodical she edited for an East coast audience, *The Atlantic Naturalist.*[25]

But the female guest who made the biggest impact on Audubon Camp daily life was, of course, Millicent Todd Bingham, who made it a point to meet and greet every session of campers and tell her family's story. When word went out that Mrs. Bingham was coming for dinner and her evening presentation later that day, the excitement level rose in camp. Someone on staff, or maybe a family teen, would row over to the Bingham dock for transport. She was always welcomed, often with an evening drink in the director's office with the shades pulled.[26] Breath lozenges to disguise the telltale sign of liquor were distributed before staff and honored guests dismissed into the dining room. According to the Cadburys, nobody was fooled except those who cared to be.

Millicent Bingham is etched in Audubon Camp history as a short firebrand who always came wearing sneakers and perhaps in the vein of Emily Dickinson, the same long white dress. Bart Cadbury remembers her "flashing black eyes. Absolutely piercing." As a teen, Betsy Cadbury thought of Mrs. Bingham as an "iron fist in a velvet glove." Upon stopping by the camp office, the first query to Ginny Cadbury was, "Now, dear, tell me who is important this session. Whom should I know?" Once Ginny was particularly peeved by the question and responded, "*Every one* of the people here is an important person." Mrs. Bingham didn't blush, replying, "Oh, of course. That's not what I meant." Ginny remembers, "It was just so obvious, and it just was awful. Carl was amused by this, too."

Millicent Bingham seemed to thrive on the attention she received when she came to camp. She enjoyed mingling with campers, as did her husband, Walter, though her evening address was the high point of the visit.[27] After a formal introduction by the camp director, Mrs. Bingham would take the Fish House podium and begin her oft-told Hog Island tale. She credited her father with taking her all around the world, encouraging her love of geography. She explained how she often served as interpreter for her father's expeditions because languages were "easy for me." When addressing her mother, she repeated the mantra that Mrs. Todd loved wilderness more than all else.[28] Mention of Pelham Knob led to the first mention of Hog Island, where she then mis-told the family's origin story for reasons we can only speculate. Anecdotes from years of summers at her mother's Camp Mavooshen punctuated her storytelling. Elements of Emily Dickinson were woven in, but never a mention of her mother's affair. At the conclusion of her talk, Bingham always received warm applause and remained for a time to engage with interested campers.

As tough and formidable as Mrs. Bingham could be, she could on occasion turn over a softer and more reflective side as illustrated in the Willow narrative retold in the last chapter. Mary Carol Massonneau was surprised to have Millicent Bingham as a visitor upon giving birth to her first child. Massonneau didn't know Millicent well, except for passing greetings on the island, so a hospital visit from the celebrity of Hog Island was special. An unremembered gift was given and congratulations were passed along. What Massonneau remembers most about that day was when Mrs. Bingham asked, "Dear, tell me what it's like to have a baby." She was interested in the details, including the emotional journey. Bingham, of course, was childless, and this stop to see Carl Buchheister's daughter gave her an opportunity to ask about a life-changing experience she would never have herself. Massonneau said, "I remember thinking what a poignant moment this was because I had always thought of her as a little unapproachable about sentiment."

Summer 1960 was a benchmark for Millicent Bingham. As the day of the transfer to Audubon neared, both Betsy and Ginny Cadbury have tender memories of Mrs. Bingham. As Bart's secretary, Ginny remembered how precise Millicent was in confirming the exact wording Audubon would have printed onto the commemorative plaque. The correct placement of the boulder that would hold that bronze plaque was another issue. Betsy Cadbury was fifteen that summer and busy at camp learning the curriculum she would teach at Pine Tree Camp the following year. Turned out she was the only one available to row Mrs. Bingham when needed. The two rowed around the island more than once to determine if the selected location of the memorial at the head of Long Cove was best. During those voyages, the discussion turned to Emily Dickinson now and then, but her mother's memorial was foremost on Mrs. Bingham's mind, Betsy remembered. As one of the camp kids, Betsy had never spent much time at the Bingham compound, but that summer she got a full tour led by Mrs. Bingham herself. The young woman was particularly surprised when the older woman asked her opinion and seemed to listen sincerely.

The year 1968 marked two significant milestones that would usher in a new epoch of Hog Island and Audubon Camp history. Following twenty-one summers of no family vacations and exhaustive but rewarding work, Bart and Ginny Cadbury retired from camp service where, according to Carl Buchheister, they had directed "'Mother Church' ... to constantly attain greater success." Millicent Bingham, age eighty-eight, was not able to negotiate a trip to Maine that summer, but wrote, "With my repeated gratitude to you both for your dedicated leadership, and sadness that it must come to an end." In appreciative response to those sentiments, Ginny replied, "How we wished you could have been with us at the birthday party—it was a lovely one, and in your absence Harriet cut the cake, which we thought quite appropriate." Ginny continued explaining how difficult the last banquet was for her. "Somehow the lumps in my throat just came, and I was sure I could never get through that one." She agreed with Millicent Bingham's thought that "this *is* the end of an era." Still, she hoped "the camp that so many gave so much to will continue to provide both inspiration and information to the people who will come to it in the future."

The second milestone that year came on December 1, when Millicent Todd Bingham died in Washington, DC. She is buried at Arlington National Cemetery next to her husband, Walter, who earned his place among American heroes working for the army during war years.

The Morton Years

Duryea Morton may have been the first director of the Audubon Camp in Maine to start out as a kitchen boy, but he would not be the last. One could offer further that his initial exposure to the Audubon Nature Camp as a young man encouraged life forces into motion, causing ever-widening ripples that blossomed into a career in science education that would reach into classrooms nationwide.

Morton's interest in all things nature goes back to his first memories as a child when he created homemade bird nests out of grass clippings.

All failed to attract feathered residents, but that didn't dampen the boy's interest that was encouraged by a mother who provided plenty of books on nature, many by Frank Chapman. "That got me started," Morton remembers. His first connections to Audubon came in grade school through membership in a Junior Audubon club and later when Allan Cruickshank came to his Litchfield, Connecticut, boarding school to give a lantern slide presentation on the Kissimmee Prairie in Florida. Interested students at the school also had the opportunity to bird with a notable visitor, Smithsonian Institution's birding specialist, Sidney Dillon Ripley. At sixteen, Morton and a buddy trekked into New York City over spring break to meet and greet two very important bird people to ask questions about how they should pursue their burgeoning interest.[29] Letters requesting interviews were sent to both Museum of Natural History ornithologist, Ernest Mayr, and John Baker at Audubon. Both gentlemen granted meetings with the young men.

The first to meet with them that week was Ernest Mayr, who suggested courses ornithologists should take, including German, before inviting the boys to lunch where they chatted with museum ornithology staff who had just returned from field trips and had exciting stories to tell. Later in the week the youngsters returned to meet with John Baker, who after a short meeting passed them off to Roger Peterson who was at work painting magazine covers. Lunch that day was with Allan Cruickshank. Morton remembers the week as "mind-boggling."

As with so many others, World War II got in the way of Dur Morton's career plans when he was drafted during his first semester in college. Returning from Italy where he had earned a Purple Heart, he found maintenance work at the Audubon Center in Greenwich. Looking for more, Morton met at Audubon House with John Baker's assistant, Carl Buchheister, who could offer only a summer dishwashing job at the Maine camp. Morton took it. That summer, 1946, was the first season the camp reopened following the war and adequate supplies of groceries had not caught up with post-war demand. Campers were asked to bring one half pound of sugar and their ration books to help provide meals for each other. Harriet Buchheister searched the region for available resources and as the only scullery staff who knew how to drive a standard transmission, "senior kitchen boy" Dur Morton drove with Mrs. Buchheister "all over the state to pick up a loaf of bread here, or three heads of lettuce at a vegetable stand" over there. Trips could take all day long as the two scavenged as far as Augusta and Portland. The following summer, the reliable Morton was promoted to second boatman to work with Captain Osier.

The next few years found Dur Morton finishing college and working afield from Audubon, but in 1950 he returned to Hog Island as second boatman, and the summer following added nature activities to his resume as Margaret Wall's substitute for two sessions.[30] In 1951, while still serving as second boatman, he lived down the shore from Millicent and Walter Bingham in the Osprey cottage. Morton hoped for more out of his Audubon employment, but with little luck. The legendary teaching staff on Hog Island was solid during those "golden years" and with nobody creating vacancies, no summer teaching positions opened. In 1952, Morton relocated to Virginia where he taught natural history at the Potomac School and in summers developed and directed his own nature study day camp.

Through those years in Virginia, Carl Buchheister stayed in touch with Morton and in 1959 came calling with a job offer to direct the Audubon Camp in California.[31] Though Morton declined, another opportunity arose soon thereafter that he did accept when the director of the Audubon Center in Connecticut suddenly resigned. From 1959 until 1967, Dur and Peggy Morton lived on property in Greenwich directing the center, and for most of those summers, directed the summer camp there as well. Buchheister liked what he saw and elevated Morton to coordinate operations of all the Audubon camps in 1964, and by 1967, named him director of the Educational Services Department that added centers and printed educational materials to his oversight.[32] Morton finally returned to Hog Island in 1971, this time as director, where he served until 1977 when he was named an Audubon vice president in charge of the Environmental Information and Education Division. Indeed, Dur's innocent beginnings creating grass bird nests as a kid coupled with the influence of a few nature-promoting adults—the very thing Rachel Carson promoted and John Baker hoped to inspire at the Audubon Nature Camp—led him into a meaningful career celebrating science education that reached well beyond his own classroom.[33]

As illustrious a career as Duryea Morton fashioned at Audubon, friends often smile and say his *biggest* contribution to the organization, especially to Hog Island, was hiring Steve Kress. Like Morton, Kress experienced a youth steeped in learning about birds with the help of willing adults that led him into a revolutionary career in ornithology. Steve Kress's prime adult influence was Irving Kassoy, a Columbus, Ohio, transplant who had made his name in the jewelry business in New York City, where he had also become known as an urban authority on owls.[34] Kassoy was an original member of the Bronx County Bird Club that included Allan Cruickshank and Roger Tory Peterson, but after selling his business in 1950, moved to Columbus so his wife could be near family.

Also like Duryea Morton, Steve Kress had a buddy who was avidly interested in all things nature, but mostly birds. When the two heard about a group of local birders willing to take kids out to find hawks and owls, the boys signed up. Kress remembers how much he revered Peterson's field guides, writing, "Peterson was pretty close to God to me." So, when the announcement was made that Audubon artist Roger Tory Peterson would be a part of that season's Audubon Wildlife Film Series in Columbus, Kress made plans to attend. To top off the influential experience, Irving Kassoy brought young Steve forward, introducing him as his friend, to meet his famously published old birding buddy from New York City. Throughout high school, Kress became a regular attendee of the Audubon film tour.

The Columbus Audubon Society held its film series events at the natural history museum on the Ohio State University campus. On one occasion, Kress went looking for interesting announcements posted at the museum and picked up brochures for Audubon camps in Maine, Wisconsin, and Connecticut. Liking what he read but realizing he wasn't old enough to attend, he wrote to each camp, hoping a summer job might be available for a "nature boy." The director of the Audubon

Camp at Greenwich liked what he read and offered sixteen-year-old Steve Kress a job cleaning dishes. That director, Duryea Morton, would years later remind Kress, "All good men start as dishwashers."

But it wasn't just dishes that kept Steve Kress busy all summer. Morton required student assistants to engage in a research project and present the results by summer's end. The Greenwich Audubon Center is located not far from the White Plains, New York, municipal airport and Kress found it curious that when aircraft flew over, bullfrogs would start singing. Every evening after "finishing my enormous pile of dirty dishes," he went down to Mead Lake to make observations. The completed report impressed Morton so much that he forwarded it to Audubon president Carl Buchheister, who passed it along to the *Audubon* staff. To Kress's amazement, the magazine ran the article. Publication success meant so much to the young scientist that the magazine's acceptance letter hung on his bedroom wall at home for years after.

Steve Kress worked at the Audubon Camp in Connecticut for two summers, the second as the campers' lodge housekeeper and maintenance guy. Not able to get to Hog Island as often as he liked, Carl Buchheister instead often took the train out of New York City to visit the Greenwich camp. Kress remembers Buchheister's first regular stop was in the kitchen to encourage student assistants how valuable their work was to camp success. In the evenings, Buchheister's storytelling at the Morton residence intrigued Kress and sharpened his interest in "seabirds, remote island lighthouses, and the coast of Maine." By season's end, Kress asked Morton regarding the availability of a teaching position on Hog Island. Like his boss before him, however, Kress learned that the long-running "legendary" Maine staff provided few openings for Audubon to fill.[35]

Kress finally got his wish to be a bird life instructor at the Maine camp in 1969, one of only two seasons under the directorship of Herbert "Doc" Houston. Unfortunately for Kress, with the passing of Bart Cadbury's leadership, Houston decided landing campers on bird islands was too risky and discontinued the tradition. Identifying and talking about unique birds in the bay on all-day trips had to be done in a boat which was a big disappointment for Kress. Still, it was during Doc Houston's term that the newest bird life instructor began to wonder if it might be possible to repatriate Atlantic puffins to their former nesting range on a windswept island in the wild waters beyond Muscongus Bay.

Steve Kress's brainstorm to return puffins to Eastern Egg Rock entered his awareness by way of a book he came across on Hog Island. Trying to learn even more about the local ecosystem, Kress pulled Ralph Palmer's *Maine Birds* off the Fish House library shelf to learn that out there on the fringe of the bay where weather can be treacherous, the Atlantic puffin (*Fratercula arctica*) had found a rocky island on which to breed. Over time, fishermen seeking bait for their livelihood took them in huge numbers until they were gone. In his book *Project Puffin*, Kress notes the significance of that realization. Just six words, he wrote, "the puffin bred on these rocks," changed his life in ways that would propel him into ornithological rock stardom.

Summer 1971 saw the reunion of mentor and apprentice when Dur Morton added director of the Maine camp to his Audubon resume. Kress was pleased to hear that landings on bird islands would resume and was hopeful his new boss would embrace his idea to repatriate puffins. Kress had written a proposal for moving forward on his enterprise the summer prior and had revised it over the off-season. Morton gave Kress time off from teaching to tinker with his seabird ideas that would become his Project Puffin and furthermore contacted Carl Buchheister for preliminary funding from Audubon. As the nuts and bolts of the expansive project took shape, it became evident to all involved that what Project Puffin would surely need was a skilled boatman who could navigate staff and equipment safely on and off rocky islands miles out near the sometimes stormy north Atlantic. The sailor brought on board for that monumental job was Joe Johansen, another exceptional Duryea Morton hire who, along with his wife, Mary, would add their unique piece to the storied lore of Hog Island.

Like long-time boatman Elmer Osier, Joe Johansen was a capable and skilled old salt who prided himself on knowing the water.[36] He reported with enthusiasm, "I've tied up on every facsimile of a dock on the Maine coast. Over 3,500 miles of coastline, not counting the islands." With Bart Cadbury feeling overwhelmed following Osier's retirement, Bernie Webber had been hired to take on the camp's chief navigational post. Webber was a Coast Guard buddy of Johansen's and when the two bumped into each other in Camden in spring 1974 and began chatting about their retirement, Webber asked Johansen if he still had his "ticket," or operator's license. Webber had heard the Audubon camp was looking for a new boatman and thought Johansen would be a good fit. Bernie Webber had served the Hog Island camp for three summers and his replacement was looking to move on, as well. In part because Johansen revered Webber as "the biggest hero in my time in the Coast Guard," and in part due to his own curiosity, Joe took a drive down Keene Neck Road to see what the Audubon camp was all about.[37] There he met the boatman, Dick McClennon, who gave him the low-down on the operation. Days later McClennon resigned and Johansen was invited to fly to New York City, or as Joe liked to call it, "Skyscraper National Park," to meet with Dur Morton who gave him the job.[38]

Joe Johansen learned his craft on the water by serving twenty years in the Coast Guard in the Gulf of Maine. His career had begun as a keeper of the Ram Island Ledge Light where he and a partner were tasked with keeping the incandescent vapor lamp operational regardless of weather conditions. Through that experience in isolation, Johansen became a historian of life, including raising families on desolate islands where lights and foghorns assist maritime navigation. As Hog Island's head boatman, he took the instructor spotlight when campers went ashore on Franklin Island where he stood over the foundation of the keeper's long-gone house to talk about what life was like there in an era past. He explained how the children got to school and what plants grew best in the island kitchen garden. He went on to explain how automation of these facilities was surely more economical and practical but pulling keepers off those special islands removed human eyes and ears from the horizon while closing the book on a unique chapter of remote maritime life that would never come again. The irony wasn't lost on him that for most of his career in the service his job was laying and maintaining underwater cable that brought electricity to the islands that made automation possible.

About the time Johansen took the Audubon job, Steve Kress received permission to collect the first cohort of puffin chicks for transplant on Eastern Egg Rock. Collected in Newfoundland then flown to Maine, the birds had to pass disease checks in Bangor before being sent on their way to Bremen. Johansen remembers everything that day took longer than expected, so it was in the middle of the night when he was finally rowing a dory freighted with young pufflings ashore at Egg Rock. He offered, as well, with a chuckle, "If the guys I worked with could see me now—rowing puffins ashore at midnight—they'd be laughing their sterns off." Nevertheless, Johansen added with pride he rowed "in excess of 900 puffins out there."

As year-round residents at the old Nash house on the mainland, Mary and Joe Johansen experienced the property, island included, like no other Audubon employees at that time. They retained warm memories of grandkids coming over to slide down an icy hill in winter and the colors and smells of changing seasons not experienced during summer weeks.

As locals, the Johansens further enhanced the camp by putting a friendly face on Audubon. Medomak selectmen didn't like it when Audubon filed for tax-exempt status, which they turned down, and fishermen weren't happy about field trips dredging the bay bottom disturbing scallop beds. Neighbors didn't like all the traffic on Keene Neck Road, either. The Johansens listened, passed along concerns, and changed what they could. They made good friends with mainland neighbor Elizabeth Noyce, of Intel processor fame, who had a tennis court installed on her property specifically so Joe could invite friends over for friendly competition.[39] Neighbors liked Mary and Joe and that was good for Audubon. When all was said and done, Joe concluded, "I don't care who in the hell has been to the Audubon Camp, there is no one—no one—that liked it better than Mary and me. I'm telling ya', nobody's had the times that we had."

Through Joe Johansen's twenty years as a boatman, maintenance guy, warden, prime storyteller, and regional puffin lecturer, he always seemed to leave a memorable impression on campers. Captivating stories of interesting people he met in the Coast Guard and his "bodacious" vocabulary endeared him to most. Still today when I take a shower at home I let my wife know I'm "heading for the rain locker." At the end of his career, affection for Joe was demonstrated in a staff organized "This is your life" skit that highlighted his unique expressions and mannerisms. "Oh, my God," he said. "I never laughed so hard in my life." Love flowed in the Fish House that evening.

Love coursing through the spirit of the island and its visitors was not that unusual, actually. Couples who met on Hog Island and in the process found a life partner number in the dozens with a handful returning to have their weddings performed there. Romantic coupling occurred so often during the Buchheister years that Harriet instituted a good-natured twenty-five dollar "marriage tax," and story has it quite a few contributions were collected.

The broader sense of respect and care for all—staff, campers, and family—was a mantra stressed under Dur and Peggy Morton's leadership.[40] As difficult as some groups might have been, Dur didn't remember any session that didn't "come together" by the end. He has a fond memory of a mildly disabled camper who collapsed on the trail and needed overnight medical attention off-island. In the morning, the doctor suggested the gentleman be sent home. Instead, the camper pleaded he had never been to a place like Hog Island and really wanted to stay. Diagnosis reconsidered, the camper returned and when necessary, staff pitched in with piggyback rides. By session's end the camper asked permission to read an original poem penned that week at the last evening's program, affectionately titled "The Captain and His Lady." Upon departure the next morning, Dur gave the young man a stamped postcard to drop in a mailbox to confirm he got home safely. He did. Tears flowed as Dur remembered that moving story.

Dur Morton made other significant Hog Island hires, like Joe Van Os and Kathy Blanchard.[41] Under his tenure camp buildings were given navigational names, as they are known today, like the Porthole, the Helm, and the Bridge while the island and mainland docks were upgraded into durable stone-filled cribs. As camp registration dipped when recreational and educational dollars found more attractive desti-nations, he and the staff redesigned the program and alternated one-week sessions with the standard two-week version. The change filled a few more beds, but critics lamented the depth of discovery lost in the abbreviated timeframe.

Over the next few years, Dur Morton and other friends of the camp realized that an overhaul in thinking about how the Audubon Camp on Hog Island operated was needed in order for it to thrive in a new century. When the historical dust settles, camp aficionados just might argue that the roots of the camp's successful "new era" were grounded back in 1973 with Steve Kress's first attempt at raising pufflings in his Hog Island cabin.

Chapter 6 Notes

[1] In her 1989 obituary in the *New York Times*, Harriet G. Buchheister was listed as not only a wildlife conservationist but "co-founder, with her husband ... of the Audubon Camp on Hog Island, Maine." Web download.

[2] Carl and Harriet Buchheister had three daughters—Harriet Reggio, Mary Carol Massonneau, and Betsy Shortell—all of whom spent summers in Maine with their mom and dad for as long as they could. The Buchheister nanny, Beatrice Quinn, came to Hog Island for the first few seasons until the girls were old enough to tend themselves. Mary Carol Massonneau interview.

[3] From 1944 through 1947, Bart and Ginny Cadbury spent summers at Keewayden Canoe Camp on Lake Dunmore in Vermont, where his prime responsibility was to take older groups of boys out on the Allagash River for two-week expeditions. In so doing, Bart put his Maine Guide license to appropriate use. Foreshadowing her upcoming responsibilities on Hog Island, Ginny served as secretary to the camp director their last summer in Vermont. By 1947, daughter Betsy was a toddler and Ginny was pregnant with their second child, Peggy. Bart resigned at the end of the season with both he and his wife wondering if a camp for boys was the place for them to spend summers as a family. In May 1948, the marine life instructor position came open at the Audubon Nature Camp, and after talking it over with Carl Buchheister, Joe Cadbury approached Bart about taking the job. An appointment was made for Bart to see Carl in New York, and as Ginny retells the story, Carl "was persuasive." Daughter Betsy would lament in later years that with her father so busy every summer of her youth, she never got her two precious weeks on the Allagash with him. Cadbury/Borror interviews.

[4] Dorothy Treat also reported that the 1941 season was the first to have every bed filled before the start of the first session. Dorothy Treat, "June comes to Hog Island" (*Audubon*, July–August 1941), 355–62.

[5] See Paul B. Sears, "The Audubon Camp Philosophy" (*Audubon*, March–April 1954).

[6] After Charlie Nash died in 1947, his wife Myra planned to move to New Hampshire to be with family. When the sale of the farmhouse went through, Carl Buchheister did not want her or her extended family to know it was Audubon making the purchase. In an interview with this author, Bart Cadbury remembered, "Carl really conned [the family] into that one."

[7] In an interview with the author, Ginny Cadbury giggled when she told the popular family story of her daughter, Peggy, and the outhouse. When Ginny took the girls outside to "do their business," she flippantly called the outhouse the *casbah*. Years later as a senior in boarding school, Peggy was humiliated to learn that *casbah* is not the official name for outhouse.

[8] A mostly complete roster of children who summered on the mainland or on Hog Island with their parents during the Buchheister-Cadbury years: Three Buchheister girls (Harriet, Mary Carol, and Betsy); two sons of Joe and Lucille Cadbury (Joel and David); son of Don and Libby Borror (Art); and two daughters of Bart and Ginny Cadbury (Betsy and Peggy). Other children included Gratia Lau (instructor Joe Lau's daughter) and Elsie Kellogg Morse, daughter of Juliet Kellogg, who not only gets credit as the first camper off the train for the first session in 1936, but also served as first aid officer for a time. Elsie spent summers on the island with her mother and would go on to marry second boatman and up-and-coming academic Doug Morse. Another child during this era was Georgie Pinkham, a local boy whose parents provided maintenance and other operational support. The Pinkhams lived in one of the old Point Breeze cottages where Ann served as a first aid officer. Betsy Cadbury remembers Georgie's father, the camp maintenance man, responsible for building loudspeaker consoles and cupboards in the Fish House.

[9] All three Buchheister girls counseled at Pine Tree Camp in their teens, with Mary Carol influenced sufficiently to become a mental health activist who worked at mainstreaming special students into the classroom. Art Borror and Betsy Cadbury also counseled summers at Pine Tree Camp on Belgrade Lakes near Waterville, Maine, as did Elsie Kellogg Morse, while Peggy Cadbury worked at Camp Med-O-Lark at Lake Washington in Washington, Maine.

[10] Ginny Cadbury has fond memories of another volunteer who came to camp early to help set up: nationally known sculpture artist Joy Buba. Joy and Henry Buba came initially as campers around 1950. Joy returned for preseason set-up assistance because fellow New Yorker Harriet Buchheister was a good friend. Joy continued the tradition for years after Ginny took over. Joy Buba (1904–1998) was a bust specialist, children's book illustrator, and landscape and portrait painter.

[11] Harriet Buchheister was a firm believer in the disinfecting quality of chlorine bleach and instructed staff to apply it freely. Art Borror remembers while a student assistant scrubbing then sloshing bleach as directed inside the lobster cooking kettles, which would then have to pass Mrs. Buchheister's mandatory "sniff test."

[12] Many un-noted stories are included here, like this one of the *USCGC Laurel*, drawn from multiple interviews with Bart and Ginny Cadbury, Betsy Cadbury, and Art Borror.

[13] Another problem for the camp was disposing of dining room garbage. Back in the 1950s, when Art Borror was a student assistant, such refuse was dumped into the narrows. Staff would row a dory out with refuse then arouse hundreds of gulls by "banging the trash cans." Art reported, "Most of the stuff never hit the bottom. It would get gobbled up by the gulls." Large compost piles behind the kitchen tend most of that waste today.

[14] Bart Cadbury reported that Audubon vessels needed to pass three coast guard inspections: navigation, engine, and boat safety. These regular boat inspections not only made boats "more difficult to operate" but also added unexpected expense to camp operations. Bart remembered pleading with the New York office that more resources were needed for watercraft. "I said if we don't get what we needed for the boats, I'm going to have to close the camp." All worked out, but he concluded, "It was that close."

[15] Hurricane Carol made its first landfall striking Long Island, New York, and later coastal Connecticut on August 31, 1954, with wind speeds of 110 mph. Great property damage ensued with sixty-five deaths reported. By the time Carol made landfall on Hog Island, Art Borror estimates wind speeds of 50 to 60 mph. Due to Carol's intensity, that name was

retired from the naming list of storms in the Atlantic basin. Hurricane Edna followed within two weeks, making landfall in Massachusetts on September 11, 1954, accounting for twenty fatalities. No one was on Hog Island at the time to make a wind speed estimate.

[16] Following the 1954 hurricanes, Carl Buchheister arranged for the International Paper Company to harvest the island's tree fall. Horses were rafted over the next summer to drag fallen timber to the shore, as Chris Speh remembered. From there wood was floated across the narrows and processed on the mainland by the boathouse. The most noticeable tree fall on the peninsula was on the east shore trail just south of the Crow's Nest residence. Mrs. Bingham experienced serious tree loss at her compound, as well.

[17] Being a staff wife had its share of stress, as well. Schedules were busy and accommodations meager and tight. Harriet Buchheister tried to remedy some of that by engaging the first boatman to take the women out occasionally on boat trips into the bay for "girl time."

[18] A replica of the Eastern Egg Rock tripod was crafted one year for the birthday party. White paint as bird guano completed the look.

[19] Bart Cadbury could not recall John Baker missing any end-of-season banquets. In Bart's words, Baker's attendance indicated how the Hog Island program was a jeweled "treasure" of the National Audubon Society.

[20] Local residents Henry Beston and Elizabeth Coatsworth "would come to the island often," according to Ginny Cadbury. Beston gave evening programs using his original slide photography themed on the "coming of the light" that valued natural seasonal beauty beyond utilitarian "dollars and cents." Two of Beston's better-known books are *The Outermost House: A Year of Life on the Great Beach of Cape Cod* and *Northern Farm*. Coatsworth won the Newbery Medal in 1931 for *The Cat Who Went to Heaven*. Maine artist Andrew Wyeth came to camp as a visitor to attend Carl Buchheister's presentation of the Audubon Film Series production, "Pastures of the Sea."

[21] Through the Buchheister and Cadbury years, student assistants were essentially unpaid interns. Most often college students working in the natural sciences, the young men were paid in room and board and

experiences on field trips with a world-class staff. Bart Cadbury came to pay his student assistants $25 for lasting all five sessions. Betsy Cadbury remembers one female student assistant annually assigned to help Don Borror's wife, Elizabeth, tend the island gift shop, which she oversaw. It is unclear when the number of female student assistants increased. In later years, student assistants were encouraged to complete field or research projects under the supervision of a staff member, as Dur Morton required in his days as director of the camp in Connecticut.

[22] Wikipedia reports most of the female inmates at the Framingham, Massachusetts, prison were convicted of prostitution, extramarital sex, or alcoholism charges. Van Waters emphasized rehabilitation by developing educational opportunities including an art and crafts course, literary class, drama class, and a prison newspaper. She thought the Hog Island experience important enough that she sent her own staff to camp on scholarship. Thompson was also interested in prison reform and juvenile justice, but in addition is remembered for playing an influential role in preserving Island Beach State Park and promoting the protection of wildlife habitats in New Jersey. Wikipedia further reports Miriam Van Waters was a "closeted lesbian" whose lifelong companion was Geraldine Thompson. Wikipedia, "Miriam Van Waters" (Downloaded February 21, 2017).

[23] Eleanor Roosevelt's column, *My Day*, was published by United Features Syndicate and ran in newspapers across the country. Her August 1951 mention of the Hog Island program was not her first. In summer 1937, she identified "Miss Julia Parker of Hyde Park" meeting with her telling details of her island camping experience. At the end of that column, Roosevelt writes, "To hear about it all made me feel I would like to start off at once and visit Hog Island... Perhaps next summer if I motor that way I may have an opportunity to see the interesting work which is being carried on there." Eleanor Roosevelt, "My Day" (United Features Syndicate, August 14, 1937).

[24] Whenever the name Shirley Briggs came up in interviews with the Cadburys, her friend and camping partner Harriet Sutton was uttered in the same breath. Both women always came together. No known Hog

Island contributions are credited to Sutton.

[25] See Millicent Bingham's "Gift of an Island Wilderness" in the *Atlantic Naturalist* (October–December 1960).

[26] Story retold with a giggle a few times by Ginny Cadbury.

[27] Walter Van Dyke Bingham was remembered by Bart Cadbury as "a delightful man" who stayed in the background when Millicent commanded camper attention.

[28] In a July 10, 1950, cassette tape recording of Mrs. Bingham's presentation to campers archived by Audubon, it appears she once pronounced her mother Mabel's first name as /may-BELLE/, not the traditional /MAY-bl/. This would confirm Ginny Cadbury's recollection of Millicent's pronunciation of her mother's name that no one else can verify, including Emily Dickinson scholar Polly Longsworth. Perhaps the first pronunciation above was a familiarity used only by immediate family.

[29] Dur Morton's Litchfield boarding school birding buddy was Phil Humphrey, who would go on to direct the University of Kansas Natural History Museum from 1967 to 1995.

[30] Dur Morton worked the summer of 1948 at a University of Michigan field station at Douglas Lake with Sewall Pettingill and graduated from Albion College (Michigan) in 1950.

[31] While the Audubon Nature Camp in Maine was the first adult summer camp operated by National Audubon, it was not the last. Other camps included Greenwich, Connecticut; Milwaukee, Wisconsin; and Kerrville, Texas. A fifth camp in California later moved to Wyoming. Only the Maine camp remains in operation today.

[32] During Dur Morton's tenure he supervised operations of Audubon centers in Greenwich, Connecticut; El Monte, California; Dayton, Ohio (Aullwood); Sharon, Connecticut; Princeton, New Jersey (Stoney Ford); and Milwaukee, Wisconsin (Schlitz).

[33] Over his illustrious career, Dur Morton's photography and writings on conservation education appeared in *Audubon, Nature Magazine, Virginia Wildlife,* and *Atlantic Naturalist.* He authored two books, *Who Lives in a Field* (1959) and *Young Naturalist Handbook* (1960), both out of print.

[34] For the rest of Steve Kress's story, see *Project Puffin: The Improbable Quest to Bring a Beloved Seabird Back to Egg Rock* by Stephen W. Kress and Derrick Z. Jackson, Yale University Press, 2015.

[35] Summers between 1965 and 1968 took Steve Kress to the Audubon Camp in Wisconsin as an assistant bird life instructor and New Brunswick, Canada, as a naturalist. From 1968 through 1972, he served full-time as assistant director of Glen Helen Nature Center in Yellow Springs, Ohio, where he is credited with establishing the Raptor Center, a rehabilitation operation for injured and orphaned hawks and owls. See: https://www.glenhelen.org/raptor-center.

[36] For more detail on Joe Johansen's experience in the Coast Guard, see "Splicing the Lights: Interview with Joe Johansen" by Peter Ralston. The Island Institute. *Island Journal.* Volume 6. 1989.

[37] In our interview, Joe excitedly told us why he held Bernie Webber in such high regard. In 1952, a nasty February storm blew into New England where Webber was assigned at the Coast Guard station at Chattam on Cape Cod. Distress calls were received from the collision of two tanker ships, the *SS Pendleton* and the *SS Fort Mercer,* not far offshore. Though Webber didn't like to talk about it, on one occasion he was "half way in the satchel" (intoxicated) when Johansen asked for details. According to Johansen, "I says, 'Okay, give me the scoop on this story. You shouldn't even have gone out.'" What follows is Joe Johansen's version of Bernie Webber and his three crewmate's heroic tale: "So the snow is comin' straight. He's going right into this breeze in a 36-foot double edged-motor lifeboat (MLB)—an old wooden lifeboat. When he goes over the Chatham bar, he loses his compass. He didn't know where in the hell he was goin'. All he was doing was going into the breeze. All of the sudden he runs into the side of the *Pendleton.* Thirty guys aboard. He goes alongside the Jacobs ladder, they come scrambling down. The last one down was the cook. Cook fell. Bernie had the boat in gear to stay alongside. The cook got caught in the screw. But they went back, just heading with the breeze until he saw some lights. Folks wondered the next day how he got all those guys aboard." Bernie Webber and his crew were awarded the Coast Guard's Gold Lifesaving

Medal for their heroic action. If this story sounds familiar, Walt Disney Pictures made a movie of Bernie and his crew's valor in *The Finest Hours* (2016). Actor Chris Pine was featured as Bernie C. Webber, USCG, one-time Hog Island first boatman.

[38] Joe Johansen was famous for his creative sailor's word choice. At one point "Joe's bodacious vocabulary list" was assembled and copied for campers. Terms included *bulldust* (a told story) and *splicing the main brace* (imbibing in an alcoholic beverage). In addition to his colorful vernacular, Johansen also left his mark on campers with his authentic love for the sea and its denizens. A sweet memory of my own is when on an all-day trip, dorsal fins of a pod of minke whales were spotted. Johansen turned off the boat's engine for quiet observation while referring to the whales as "brothers."

[39] Intel Corporation was co-founded by Robert Noyce, Elizabeth's husband. Soon after the couple bought property at the end of the Keene Neck they divorced, with Bob seldom visiting the cottage estate afterward. Betty became a significant benefactor to various Maine charities but never Audubon or the Audubon Camp.

[40] Dur and Peggy Morton continued the staff family tradition by involving their children, Leslie and David, in camp operations.

[41] Kathy Blanchard was camp storekeeper and evolved into the first Puffineer on Eastern Egg Rock. Joe Van Os was fresh out of college, looking very much the hippie when he came for his Audubon interview. Dur Morton remembers him having a hard time getting past the receptionist. When he showed up for work, though, he was shorn and gave a much better public appearance in uniform khakis. Joe would go on to found and operate Joe Van Os Photo Safaris. See https://photosafaris.com.

Audubon Era Gallery

Friends of Hog Island Digital History

Hog Island Audubon Camp (Schaefer)

Audubon trail markers fashioned after tin can lids
originally used by the Todds (Schaefer)

Bird-Lore, July-Aug 1936 (FOHI)

Bird-Lore, March-April 1940 (FOHI)

John H. Baker (FOHI)

Carl W. Buchheister (FOHI)

Audubon Nature Camp ca. 1936 (FOHI)

Open house 1936. Photo by Lindsay Photo Service. (Yale)

Eugene Davis, head boatman (FOHI)

Campers arrive in *Puffin I* ca. 1939 (FOHI)

Day trip on the bay (FOHI)

Day trip with Allan Cruickshank, Alexander Sprunt, Carl Buchheister, and Robert Cushman Murphy of the NY Museum of Natural History (Yale)

Harriet Buchheister (Yale)

The Buchheister family. Left to right: Betsy, Mrs. B, Mr. B, Harriet, Mary Carol (FOHI)

Carl Buchheister studies nesting cormorants.
Note Allan Cruickshank with view camera in background. 1936 (FOHI)

Cruickshank postcard (FOHI)

Allan Cruickshank (Yale)

Allan Cruickshank performing headstand indicating
new bird species sighted on trip (FOHI)

Cruickshank's famous headstand (Yale)

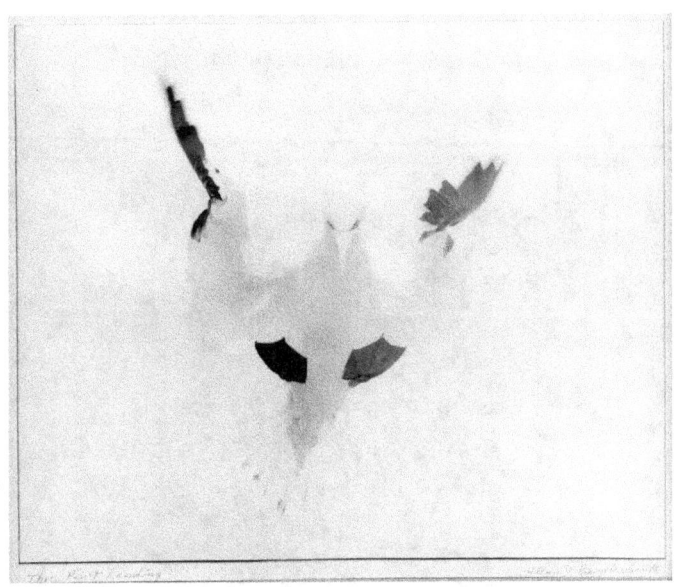

Cruickshank's "Three Point Landing" hangs in the camp dining room (FOHI)

Cruickshank's "Misty Morn" (FOHI)

Cruickshank postcard sent 1947 (FOHI)

Allan & Helen Cruickshank (FOHI)

Joe Cadbury (FOHI)

Don Borror (FOHI)

Farida Wiley (FOHI)

Camp staff on Monhegan, 1938 (FOHI)

Fish House construction ca. 1940 (FOHI)

Camp staff, 1941 (FOHI)

Installation of flag pole (FOHI)

Camp staff, 1946. Front left to right: Marcus Olds (marine life), Carl Buchheister (director), Allan Cruickshank (birds), Art Smith (insects). Back- Joe Cadbury (birds), Farida Wiley (plants), Dorothy Treat (nature) (FOHI)

Carl Buchheister prepares lobster (FOHI)

Camp staff, 1949. Front left to right: Farida Wiley, Don Borror, Margaret Wall. Back-Peter Mott, Joe Cadbury, Frank Roberts, Bart Cadbury (FOHI)

"Ladies of the Institute" (staff wives), 1954 (FOHI)

Annual end-of-season camp birthday party with costumes (FOHI)

John Baker and Millicent Bingham cut the camp birthday cake, 1959

Douglas Morse, boatman, *Osprey II*, 1958 (FOHI)

Bart Cadbury, 1951 (FOHI)

Ginny & Bart Cadbury (FOHI)

Joe Cadbury's boys & Bart Cadbury's girls, 1951 (FOHI)

Joe Cadbury, Bart & Ginny Cadbury (FOHI)

Artist and volunteer Joy Buba's sketch
of kitchen upgrade, 1964 (Ginny Cadbury)

Mainland birding trip (FOHI)

Millicent Bingham with Rachel Carson
at camp presentation to Audubon, 1960.
Photo by Shirley Briggs. (FOHI)

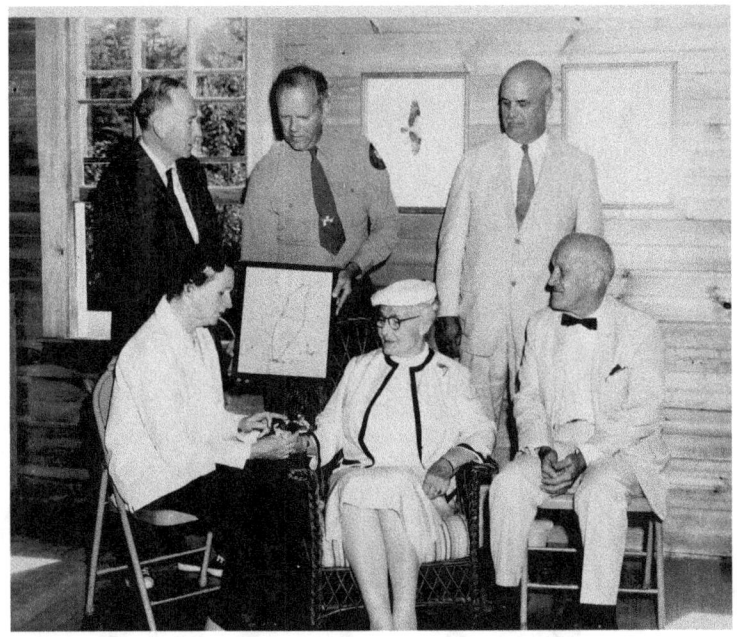

Dedication day guests, 1960. Photo by Shirley Briggs. (FOHI)

Todd Wildlife Sanctuary dedication plaque (Schaefer)

Duryea Morton (FOHI)

Dur Morton sketch of Mrs. Bingham's "lobster house" (Yale)

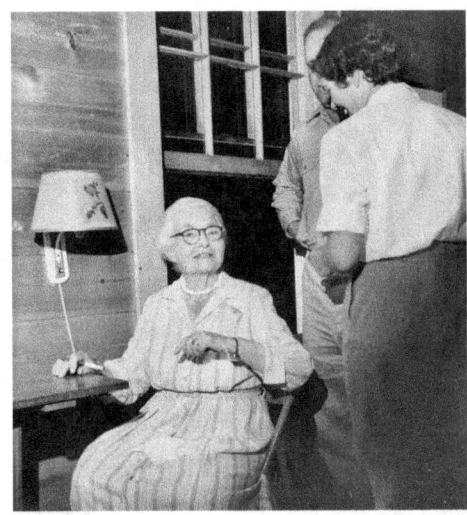

Millicent Bingham visiting with campers (Yale)

Aerial photo of Audubon camp buildings
from unknown source (Yale)

Steve Kress with puffin transport unit (FOHI)

Joe Johansen and crew erect Cruickshank Wildlife Refuge sign, 1976 (FOHI)

Dedication of the Allan D. Cruickshank Wildlife Sanctuary on Eastern Egg Rock, 1976. Elvis Stahr (Audubon president), Lee Shipps (Maine BLM),Carl Buchheister, Helen Cruickshank, Roger Tory Peterson (FOHI)

Bingham camp site, 1981 (Schaefer)

The old lobster house (Schaefer)

Camp cooler (Schaefer)

Workshop behind lobster house since moved
for camp staff housing (Schaefer)

One of Mabel Todd's benches (Schaefer)

Main camp building in 1981, twenty years unoccupied (Schaefer)

Veranda detail, 1981 (Schaefer)

Veranda and front door, 1981 (Schaefer)

Mabel Todd's camp insignia (Schaefer)

"Osprey Point" by G. Howard Hilder (Schaefer)

"Heron Rookery" by G. Howard Hilder (Schaefer)

Joe Van Os with campers (Schaefer)

Wreck Island field trip (Schaefer)

Joe Johansen (Schaefer)

Steve Kress on Wreck Island, 1981 (Schaefer)

Steve Kress with puffin at Eastern Egg Rock (Bill Scholtz)

1981 camp staff (Schaefer)

Last day tradition, 1981 (Schaefer)

All that was left of Howard
Hilder's Osprey cabin in 1981.
Chimney has since fallen. (Schaefer)

Main house showing wind damage, 2004 (Schaefer)

Main house upgrades by Friends of Hog Island, 2011 (Schaefer)

Torii and restored main house, 2014 (Schaefer)

Restoration to original porch rail design, 2016 (Schaefer)

Restored Writer's Cabin, 2012 (Schaefer)

Juanita Roushdy (FOHI)

Friends of Hog Island (Schaefer)

FOHI volunteers, 2006 (FOHI)

Scott Weidensaul (Amy Weidensaul)

Queen Mary raising in process (FOHI)

Queen Mary raising completed fall, 2022 (FOHI)

At the end of Keene Neck Road (Schaefer)

CHAPTER 7

Audubon's "True North"

The history of the National Audubon Society is, ultimately, the story of how one group of people organized to get others looking at the wild world, not with indifference or even with fear, but with *love*.

—Frank Graham, Jr.
The Audubon Ark / 1990

Through the first three-plus decades of the Audubon Camp in Maine's operation, only two men set the course of the National Audubon Society as its president. The first, John H. Baker, was an investment banker turned nature education supporter who envisioned a summer camp for adult leaders as a key component to the society's vision of promoting the conservation of wildlife ecosystems. The second, Carl W. Buchheister, Baker's handpicked protégé, was weaned at Audubon with the understanding that the Hog Island operation was the society's showcase for how nature education could work. As subsequent Audubon administrations moved into place, however, global concerns from population growth to clean water to declining bird numbers forced a reordering of organizational priorities. Such would prove to be a difficult time for Audubon Camp operations.

When Carl Buchheister left Audubon's helm in 1968, he recommended to the board that Charlie Callison, an able and loyal Audubon vice president, should succeed him. Much to Buchheister's and Callison's dismay, the board voted to look outside the organization in a management shake-up. Nevertheless, Callison was appointed interim president and for two years led Audubon in the "Baker-Buchheister continuum" while the board searched high and low for the man with the right name and the right connections to raise Audubon's national standing a notch or two.

The candidate ultimately selected was Elvis J. Stahr, Jr., a Rhodes scholar, college president, and Secretary of the Army under President Lyndon B. Johnson. Many thought Stahr an odd match for the National Audubon Society since he had little background or known interest in nature issues.[1] One thing he did bring, however, was connections in the nation's capital, which were held in highest regard as more and more environmental concerns came into the public consciousness that cried out for legislative fixes that Audubon hoped to influence.

This change in course at Audubon was important for Hog Island operations because it signified a shift in priorities in the New York and nascent regional offices.

With chapter membership growing and sanctuaries and nature centers in operation and development across the country, Elvis Stahr, along with every other National Audubon president since, found alternate priorities to address besides operating a summer camp in Maine.

What would prove even more troubling was the realization that through most of those years, the camp and National Audubon had one significant problem in common: running at an annual financial deficit. By the time Russell Peterson became National Audubon president in 1979, the society was stuck in a trend of accumulating larger annual deficits due to more priorities on the organization's plate than it could afford. Concern for endangered species, Audubon's foray into national television, Peterson's own "Think Globally/Act Locally" campaign, and the operating responsibility of a plethora of Audubon properties around the country taxed the society's income and endowments. When Peter A. A. Berle took over for Peterson in summer 1985, eliminating deficits and reaching a balanced budget was a top priority. Animosity from members was a concern, though the inevitable byproduct of the programming and chapter support reductions required. Somehow the Audubon Camp in Maine survived those cuts, though needed infrastructure upgrades and lagging annual attendance were becoming significant concerns.

Trouble in Paradise

Though worry was growing among staff and camp alumni about the health of the Hog Island operation, those campers who were discovering the wonder of the place for the first time missed that drama. In my own case, it was August 1981 when the Dayton Audubon Society sent me to Maine on a scholarship. I still can't believe my luck to be there at the same time as Carl Buchheister on one of his last visits. Although he and Harriett were in failing health, that didn't stop him from crossing the narrows to retell stories and accompany campers on a walk down to the Bingham cottages. I remember listening to everything Mr. Buchheister said like I was in the presence of a buddha.[2]

To further increase enthusiasm that summer for us island rookies, word came in from Eastern Egg Rock that for the first time transplanted puffins had returned "home" to the Cruickshank Sanctuary to bear offspring. Almost ten years of dedicated effort by Steve Kress and the "puffineers" was not only finding scientific success but also a national audience exposed again to the Audubon cause with a special focus on seabirds and just as importantly, Hog Island.[3]

It is highly likely the attention garnered by Steve Kress's success with restoring seabird habitat and the publicity that came with it saved the camp in Maine from closing while other worthwhile national programs fell to the Audubon budget ax. Some regional offices were dismantled, dozens of staff dismissed, the Wisconsin Camp closed, the Audubon Screen Tour shuttered, and chapters given a leaner dues split while operation at the camp in Maine carried on, subsidized as it was.[4] Deficit spending impacting nature's paradise was nothing I heard about or even remotely considered that summer.

Before delving more deeply into Hog Island's problems that would lead to a series of management changes and subsequent single-season closing, summer 1986 brought an anniversary milestone worthy of mention. The Audubon Camp in Maine's fiftieth-anniversary celebration was held on a July Saturday with a host of alumni invited back by way of a letter signed by Roger Tory Peterson, self-promoted as the camp's "first ornithology instructor." He reminded those aficionados on the mailing list, "The dream to create a living laboratory that inspires people of all ages to appreciate and protect our natural heritage has come true and come of age" at the Maine camp. Later that year Peterson authored an article in *Bird Watcher's Digest* about the anniversary celebration, recalling in the process some Audubon and camp history, the poignant death of Carl Buchheister on the golden anniversary's very weekend, and updates on Steve Kress's success with puffins. Peterson made it clear as well that it wasn't only puffins with a new lease on nesting grounds on Eastern Egg Rock, but common, arctic, and roseate terns "now nesting again by the hundreds" under the watchful eye of puffineers.[5] He concluded that "the art of attracting birds has now gone far beyond the garden, the feeding tray, the birdhouse, and the birdbath." Now it included sound recordings, mirrors, and painted decoys imagined one summer by a former Audubon camp "kitchen boy" who came of age as an instructor on Hog Island.

In all the interviews made for this project, no one could put their finger on a precise reason why by the mid-1980s the fortunes of the Audubon Camp in Maine slipped the minds of both Audubon House and potential campers. Beds filled well enough in early summer, but as July and August sessions commenced, attendance was consistently down. Some contend that vacation dollars were limited and potential campers either found other educational options closer to home or were drawn to more varied offerings, like Road Scholar. Others think Dur Morton's departure from Audubon's employ under Russell Peterson diminished the camp's clear focus in the home office and contributed to subsequent staffing problems. Still others point to Audubon's general budget slashing and its inevitable impact on educational programming and staff morale.[6] For these and surely other reasons, by the early 1990s it became increasingly apparent that traditional two-week sessions were simply not sustainable any longer and that the kind of trouble the camp in Maine found itself in could only be untangled through creative problem-solving.

A seemingly unrelated issue at the time that would come to have a major impact on the Hog Island operation was the problem of branding the

Audubon name. The organization had copyrighted the National Audubon Society moniker but could not claim exclusive use of the more general surname, Audubon.[7] That along with some state Audubon organizations, like Massachusetts and Maine, which were independent conservation groups with no connection to the National Audubon Society, clouded the concept of what Audubon actually was for members, potential members, and potential donors. When John Flicker ascended to the National Society's presidency in 1995, one of his ideas for strengthening Audubon was to solve the marketing complication by unifying various entities through consolidation and then, to keep budgets under control, strategic decentralization.

While Flicker's initiatives would impact Audubon nationally, it was particularly significant in Maine. There, his concept of a "Seamless Audubon" would incorporate all chapters and the independent state office into a restructured Maine Audubon Society under a National Audubon umbrella. A pressing concern was keeping members happy with the new agreement, whether their chapter had incorporated under National Audubon or independent Maine Audubon. From spring 1996 in Rockland, where John Flicker introduced the Seamless Audubon concept at a Midcoast Audubon chapter meeting, and extending over the next three years, dozens of local meetings were held statewide to debate if consolidation was in everyone's best interests. Maine Audubon management came to like the idea for a few strategic reasons, including the influx of National members into its own databank. To sweeten the deal, Flicker promised delegated power to Maine Audubon to manage strategically important sanctuary properties in the state, which until then had been handled out of New York City. In addition, National Audubon would provide financial assistance to help in the transition.

One of the properties turned over to Maine Audubon management was the Borestone Mountain Audubon Sanctuary, a sixteen-hundred-acre upstate pristine forest jewel with trails and nature centers that made it a well-known and popular outdoor destination. Another high-profile property targeted for transfer from National to Maine was the more remote and therefore more problematic Audubon Camp in Maine on Hog Island.

Friends of Hog Island

In that atmosphere of impending change, the concept of a Friends of Hog Island organization first appeared. The earliest dated reference to a Hog Island Friends group came in a development letter authored by Talbert Spence, National Audubon's vice president of education. Dated November 20, 1997, it encouraged "Maine camp alumni" to honor the efforts of "the most gifted and far thinking people in environmental education," then dropped names like Buchheister, Cadbury, Cruickshank, Borror, and Peterson. The purpose of the mailing was to gain support for a projected $1.5 million effort to upgrade the island wastewater treatment system, improve camp buildings and boats, and in John Flicker's plan, "develop a year-round program which will extend to teachers and youth throughout Maine."[8] Donors contributing to that legacy fund would be included in the number of Audubon Camp in Maine Friends.[9] Records do not report how much money was raised in this effort, in part because no follow-up reference to Audubon Camp in Maine Friends is found in subsequent publications, mailings, or emails.

The more far-reaching iteration of a Friends group for Hog Island was documented the next spring following initial meetings with camp director Sam Hands, Bart and Ginny Cadbury, and former staffer Robbie Rubly-Burggraff. As a product of those discussions, Hands published in March a notice in one of the earliest editions of *Across the Narrows*, the irregularly published newsletter of the Maine camp, that a Friends group was forming. Front-page fare that issue was a list of "Workshop Dates for 1998" below the headline story, "And What's the Temperature in Your Snowbank?" On the bottom of the second page, readers found "Audubon Camp Friends Group is Forming." Reading on, they learned, "To guide and steward the Camp through continuing renovations and the expansion and rejuvenation of our conservation mission, we are forming a Camp Friends Group. Your participation will be tangible, rewarding, and very much appreciated! Call or write for details. If we don't hear from you, maybe you'll hear from us!"

Within the next two months, the name of the nascent group morphed into Friends of Hog Island and a vision of what they hoped to contribute to the Audubon Camp's well-being was more carefully defined. In a May 25, 1998, letter sent to a carefully culled list of sixty camp supporters, Bart Cadbury wrote that a Friends of Hog Island group was forming "to ensure the future of the island." In inviting all recipients to FOHI's first annual meeting the following July, Cadbury hit on both concrete realities and heartstring tugs he hoped would catch alumni attention. After opening lines with sensory jogs to "salt breezes and spruce woods," he stated the founders' hope for the new organization. "We believe that a capital fund drive is needed to create an endowment for the Camp" that would fund both renovations and special projects. In addition, input "identifying a vision for the Camp in the coming century" would be an expected contribution the group would make to Audubon management. To make the Friends of Hog Island's vision extra clear, Bart reinforced, "We want to know that no matter what happens to budgets, no matter how much restructuring and restaffing takes place, Hog Island will continue to provide top quality educational programs and preserve its history and tradition."

The founders seemingly didn't know what kind of response to expect from their invitation, but they figured new volunteers would help. "We believe a small group of dedicated individuals, with the assistance of National Audubon staff, can make a difference." Then he encouraged them to become charter members. "That's why we are inviting you in on the ground floor, the very beginning of the organization. We know that you love the Camp and have worked hard for it in the past. We need your help now."

In true camp tradition, the first Friends of Hog Island annual event was planned to be more than just a business meeting. A schedule of proposed classic camp activities was included in the mailing that noted "shakedown" and Harbor Island cruises, early morning bird walks, and various talks and workshops throughout the five-day gathering.[10] Along with the mention of great meals and the always popular lobster feast, Bart Cadbury's letter and the reunion week agenda were crafted to

299

reignite enthusiasm in the Hog Island faithful, required if the changes needed were to be realized.

The Friends of Hog Island's first annual meeting was facilitated by camp director Sam Hands who opened the forum with the pronouncement that "changes from central to local control are being implemented by the National Audubon Society."[11] Though talks promoting a Seamless Audubon in Maine had been taking place for two years, no specific details of Maine Audubon's impact on Hog Island was made clear, except for John Flicker reporting that "the most important issue is getting Maine Audubon and the various chapters of the National Audubon Society in Maine to work together toward a common goal." Achieving that, "the memberships of the different groups could be merged and National Audubon would have a partnership with the resulting organization." Perhaps decisions on Borestone Mountain and Hog Island hadn't been finalized yet, but surely those in attendance realized that a restructured Maine Audubon Society would have a significant role in Hog Island's future.

Other meeting content included significant issues, including John Flicker's clarifying that based on a recently completed strategic plan, Audubon was restructuring to focus on a "grassroots organization structure" with emphasis on birds, wildlife, and habitat. He stressed how important volunteers were in Audubon nature center operation and initiatives taken on by local chapters. He also discussed in detail the plusses and minuses of Audubon "friend" organizations from the home office's point of view, though he was hopeful, as the founding four had been, that FOHI would set a goal of establishing an endowment that would provide a percentage of the cost of the camp's annual operations.

A primary concern of the broader group of founders was the condition of aging camp buildings.[12] Undoubtedly they were pleased to hear that renovations and upgrades to the Queen Mary living quarters were expected to be completed yet that summer and improvements to the Port Hole, the old hotel from Point Breeze days, were in the planning stage. Though replacement wiring in most buildings would have to wait, the sewage treatment system was in the process of being modernized and would come online by that fall. Boat and kitchen upgrades were also needed, so an estimated improvement price tag of $1.3 million didn't seem out of line.

Before the meeting week was over, a "Resolution by the Friends of Hog Island" was approved and published in the first FOHI newsletter the following December. The resolution named a newly formed executive committee before identifying the "compelling concerns" of the charter members. First of all, they stated the need for a full-time camp director. Second, the need to advertise and market the camp "to maximize enrollment." Finally, they resolved the need to "reach out to former staff, alumni, and their communities to create a fund to finance capital improvements and infrastructure renewal."[13] The rest of that premier issue featured various camp stories, including an essay by Frank and Ada Graham, more specific details on the need for fundraising, and a request for "lost" names and addresses to enhance FOHI's growing mailing list. To make it amply clear what the organization hoped to accomplish, the newsletter officially pronounced, "The mission for the Friends of Hog Island is the preservation of the Audubon Camp on Hog Island and the support and enhancement of its educational goals."

By fall 1998, the Friends of Hog Island chalked up their first major organizational victory when National Audubon hired Seth Benz as the camp in Maine's first full-time director. Talbert Spence, Audubon vice president of education, knew of Benz's successful work at Hawk Mountain Sanctuary in Pennsylvania and as a student and then staff member at the Audubon Expedition Institute.[14] Hiring a director full-time put added stress on the camp budget but with friends now in place to help fundraise and Maine Audubon on the cusp of taking over management of the whole Hog Island operation, John Flicker hoped Audubon was finally on its way to a viable solution that would help the camp find secure footing into the twenty-first century.

Like a thick Maine fog, quite a bit of change rolled across Hog Island in the bellwether summer of 1999. The Friends of Hog Island executive team took steps forward on camp advertising, fundraising, and name data collecting while scheduling the group's second multi-day annual meeting on the island in July. Steve Kress and his various seabird endeavors experienced continued success to the point that a donated piece of Zahn property adjacent to the old Nash mainland tract was in serious consideration for the home of a proposed Seabird Center.[15] In addition, National Audubon and Maine Audubon continued deliberations about all things Maine that would culminate in a memorandum of understanding that transferred management of Hog Island to the statewide entity. Still, considering all, one could argue the most significant news for Hog Island that summer was the hiring of Seth Benz as camp director.

After Dur and Peggy Morton's leadership from 1971 to 1977, Audubon Camp in Maine directors didn't last very long.[16] First off, it was a part-time summer job. Staff and director both needed other jobs to keep winter roofs over their heads. Plus, organizing and implementing complicated and ever-changing schedules, providing bedding and three nutritious meals a day for an island village of dozens of people, and doing whatever necessary to keep legacy infrastructure functioning took a toll on all the staff, but especially the director. Steve Kress, himself, served as camp director for five years in the mid-1980s, but juggling directing with family and his Seabird Restoration work proved too much. Mike Shannon served for four years. Don Burgess lasted for three. Manlius and Mary Sargeant only one.

Seth Benz had learned about the need for a director at the camp years prior from one of his former Audubon Expedition Institute students, Rick Ylagen, who came onto the Maine Camp staff in the early 1990s. As intriguing a proposition as directing Hog Island was, Benz would not honestly consider it unless it was full-time. In the interim, Steve Kress hired Benz to join his Seabird Restoration Project team on Stratton Island for summers 1992 and 1993.[17] By summer 1997, Talbert Spence was in negotiation with Benz about the Hog Island job, and by fall 1998, Benz accepted the newly designated full-time assignment. Seth Benz would go on to serve for ten summers as camp director until the operation was shuttered at the end of the 2008 season, one hundred years after Mabel Loomis Todd and Etta Glidden had bought their shares of Hog Island.

The new director had heard through the grapevine that National Audubon interest in Hog Island had waned throughout the 1980s. By the time Benz came on board, though, some infrastructure improvements had been made at camp. Queen Mary renovations were complete and work had started on adding bathrooms to the Port Hole residence by the year-round facility caretakers who lived over at the Nash House, Scott and Lynn Saunders. For their work, those of us who bunked at the Port Hole and were forced to run next door to the wash house to go to the bathroom in the middle of the night will be forever grateful.

Seth Benz had never run a summer camp before, though his work with the traveling Audubon Expedition Institute gave him varied helpful experience.[18] Truth was for that first summer, though Benz was the camp director, Steve Kress offered advice behind the scenes as to what needed to get done next. In their discussions, one of the topics the two agreed on was bolstering camp attendance by enhancing the spring ornithology sessions, in part by adding staff with national birding chops. Benz remembers it was Kress's idea to hire Robert Ridgely and Frank Gill, while in time it was his to hire Kenn Kaufman and Scott Weidensaul. Since the inception of transforming the first-of-season sessions into ornithology workshops, they have proven popular with excited campers learning from the best birders in the business. General sessions later in the summer, as had become almost expected, continued to lag in attendance.

When Maine Audubon took over management of the Audubon Camp in 2000, the facility's official name changed to the Hog Island Audubon Center.[19] Upgrades to mainland and island facilities were implemented with finances supplied by National Audubon that made the Keene Neck Road property more of a nature center destination for birders and those who wanted to walk both forest and shore trails. Island trails were always open, too, but visitors had to find their own transportation over, which is why Hog Island moorings are occupied from time to time by Muscongus Bay sailors who seek a wilderness island hike.[20]

The Maine Audubon management mantra from the beginning was "fill the beds," an expression familiar in island operation for the simple fact that if campers don't come, expenses must be covered out of other funds. To help with long-term financial solutions, Friends of Hog Island stepped in to solicit and collect endowment contributions deposited into a Maine Audubon account. In addition, FOHI helped produce a new camp brochure targeted for wide distribution, especially at local visitor centers along the Maine Turnpike and US Route 1. Like Benz, however, Maine Audubon was unfamiliar with the myriad technicalities of running a summer camp and keeping a burgeoning national alumni association informed and happy. As a result, the learning curve for Maine Audubon management was often uncomfortable for not only them but Seth Benz and Friends of Hog Island volunteers.

While Maine Audubon did everything it knew to attract campers, Benz approached the attendance anomaly from a programming perspective. Since the ornithology specialty sessions did well early in the summer, could the camp entice birders to new offerings to fill sparse July and August weeks? Maine Audubon gave Benz flexibility to create programming that would hopefully fill a minimum of thirty-five of the potential fifty-plus beds available since that was the point that put a session in the black. Over the next few summers, the camp premiered mini sessions on kayaking, yoga, nature literature and journaling, and various art programs, some with a special focus on Girl Scouting. The most successful session conjured at that time was Teen Ornithology, which since its inception in 2002, has proudly boasted one hundred percent attendance in every session offered.

Hog Island Audubon Center management proved to be more problematic for Maine Audubon than the newly acquired Borestone Mountain Sanctuary. Borestone management was, indeed, completely under Maine Audubon's control, while Hog Island still had an active contingent of National Audubon folks around. Project Puffin continued to have its summer headquarters on the mainland property, which funneled all the puffineers and their gear through the Hog Island Center property and out into the bay. The Friends of Hog Island were, likewise, really products of National Audubon's legacy. When Friends attempted negotiations with Maine Audubon about specific tasks they could be responsible for, some staff in the state office in Falmouth thought Friends volunteers were angling to chip away at the agreed-to memorandum of understanding Maine had with the New York office. Seth Benz found, too, that having "legacy people" around camp was sometimes uncomfortable. He heard more than he'd like to remember how contemporary sessions didn't quite stack up to those offered under the leadership of the Buchheister, Cadbury, and Morton administrations.

Publicity seemed to be at the heart of the attendance problem. With a focus on Maine's population, which was, indeed, the purpose of a Seamless Audubon, camp promotion from the state office in Falmouth wasn't getting out to would-be campers around the country. Friends of Hog Island worked to engage writers from national publications to come to camp then write about their experience, but success was limited. Over the term of Seth Benz's leadership, the Audubon Camp broke even financially only three of his ten summers. With an annual camp budget at the time around $700,000, it is easy to see how shortfalls and the necessary deficit spending made Maine Audubon nervous. With the Audubon consolidation came a disbursement of cash from National to Maine to assist the transition, but that money was running out.

By the time the third annual meeting of Friends of Hog Island rolled around in July 2000, the camp was in its first season under Maine Audubon management. The reunion week continued with what would be known as a "Work and Learn" event. Along with evening talks and various outings, building improvement and site upgrades performed by FOHI volunteers were added to the schedule. Enthusiasm was high and all were amazed at the number of tasks completed from painting the Fish House steps to construction of wooden tent platforms down the island in a driving rain to planting colorful annuals in all the flowerpots and beds around camp and on the mainland property. Meeting minutes report continued efforts to build a development program for a sustaining camp endowment. President Art Borror thanked the new newsletter editors who had resurrected the old *Across the Narrows* masthead for FOHI use in two new editions published since the previous summer's meeting.[21] Decisions were also made on the travel brochure and how a new Friends of Hog Island information website would be hosted by Maine Audubon.

Despite the positive tone of meeting minutes, all was not well with the Friends of Hog Island relationship with Maine Audubon.[22] In casual conversations around camp, various FOHI members reported uncomfortable meetings with and messages from the state office over any number of initiatives. When I took over FOHI presidency in summer 2002, an introductory meeting was set up with Maine Audubon's Sue Cilley and Bill Hancock at the Falmouth office. I remember coming out of the meeting a bit shellshocked after having been probed several times with the question, "Yes, but what do you *want?*" It seemed obvious to a cadre of Friends that Maine Audubon was a less-than-welcoming place for out-of-state volunteers.

At the annual meeting in 2002, Friends thought it was appropriate and timely to pursue their own memorandum of understanding with Maine Audubon in order to spell out just what they could do to help the camp prosper. Perhaps, the discussion went, having a plan on paper would ease the tension between the two entities committed to the camp's successful operation.

Ken Spirer, a FOHI and Maine Audubon board member, prepared preliminary work on a potential memorandum that was discussed at a special meeting held that winter on a frigid January Saturday at the Sharon Audubon Center in Sharon, Connecticut, thought to be neutral ground for both Friends of Hog Island and Maine Audubon. Friends made their plea for more responsibility with a dash of autonomy while Maine Audubon held the position that their local control was all that was needed and FOHI's requests were unnecessary complications. By the end of that meeting, Bill Hancock and the Maine Audubon team stated clearly that it would be the camp director's sole prerogative to engage Friends of Hog Island in whatever task deemed necessary. Friends committees could continue to operate, but they would be under the direct guidance of the camp director. Hoping for more concrete tasks they could dedicate their energies to, disappointed FOHI representatives who sat through the meeting felt like they had been shown the door.[23] A cascade of resignations from the Friends of Hog Island board followed, including Betsy Cadbury and not long after, me, as president.

Though Friends of Hog Island was diminished by Maine Audubon's action in Sharon, FOHI vice president David Klinger stepped into the void caused by resignations and in spring 2003 authored a letter to FOHI membership in a newly formatted *Across the Narrows*, this version produced solely by Maine Audubon. Klinger described the disappointment in the Sharon meeting, but stated, "Now is the time to move on and move forward, lest we jeopardize our successes to date and lose sight of our common objective: the betterment of the Audubon Camp in Maine, its program, and its island home." He promised that at the upcoming "Work and Learn" week, now moved earlier on the calendar to coincide with annual camp-opening chores, those gathered would parlay with Seth Benz to see "how a committee system of volunteers will work." And true to their deep affection for Hog Island, most FOHI members adopted the new course easily and their good work continued.

As mentioned, camp financial deficits remained as Maine Audubon, under the direction of property manager Bos Savage, upgraded essential failing island infrastructure as necessary. In addition, a Hog Island Building Committee investigated options for improving current structures and perhaps building new ones to tempt campers with more conveniences than the rustic facilities the camp had always offered. Early on in their discussion, however, the committee learned that new structures were problematic due to a local building code that required wider shoreline setbacks than the island peninsula could accommodate. The only alternative was to plant a new building in the exact footprint of an existing one, which could mean the demise of the Porthole, the Queen Mary, or the Fish House. Before anything like that could happen, a lot of money needed to be raised in endowment fund and capital campaigns.

A Hog Island Audubon Center Capital Campaign meeting handout indicated some successes achieved in those ongoing efforts by spring 2007. The $400,000 gifted to date bought the camp a new program boat, the *Puffin V*, along with a capital fund influx that upgraded electrical systems and improved the emergency exit from the top floor of the Queen Mary.[24] Additional money was allotted to marketing consultation, reportedly an essential expense if the additional $3 million dollar capital campaign goal could be reached.

By that summer, however, an email exchange between two members of the capital campaign committee articulated a troublesome perception of how the development process for Hog Island was going. FOHI volunteer and Hog Island stalwart Betsy Cadbury, present and accounted for during that summer's "Work and Learn" session, emailed Chris Speh, a Maine Audubon board trustee and the same Chris Speh who had spent summers on Hog Island with his aunt Gert and uncle Ted Sorrell at the Osprey cabin back in the 1950s. Cadbury hoped her contact with Speh, another dyed-in-the-wool Hog Island lover, could clear some discomfort between the organizations.

Amid discussions with Friends during the work week, Cadbury had picked up among those gathered questions about how serious Maine Audubon was about keeping Hog Island operating. Continually hearing "fill the beds," Cadbury questioned Speh if Maine Audubon's "sword of Damocles" would drop if "a building is significantly damaged in a storm, or some other factor requiring a major financial outlay" were to occur.

Cadbury had the sense that decision-makers at Maine Audubon were not aware of the unique dynamics of Hog Island. She drew on a childhood memory when she suggested that all the staff and every member of the Maine Audubon board of trustees spend time on Hog Island to get the feel of a very special place. She remembered how Carl Buchheister insisted all directors of the National Audubon Society attend a camp session so each would have the opportunity to experience the island's wonder personally. After that, keeping the camp alive would not come down to just a set of numbers but personal connections to nature.

Speh responded that Maine Audubon did, indeed, have financial concerns, though he felt Hog Island took the brunt of the blame. He felt a commitment to the Hog Island operation from talking with the state staff. And as much as he loved the island and the summers he had spent there as a boy, he made clear that "if the long term prognosis is that there will be many more bad years than good," then shuttering the camp would be necessary. He finished, "I think that it is unrealistic to assume that Maine Audubon will continue to support Hog Island if it becomes apparent that material revenue-expense deficits are going to be the norm going forward."

It was just one year later that the sword of Damocles that Betsy Cadbury so feared finally fell. Registrations for the late summer and fall 2008 sessions were down as usual and it was apparent that the camp was going to lose tens of thousands of dollars yet again. The decision was made mid-summer to cancel the last few sessions as word went out to interested parties from both Maine Audubon and Seth Benz that the camp would close for the 2009 season and that, as of that fall, camp staff, including Benz, were all looking for work.

To further complicate life at the state office in Falmouth, Maine Audubon executive director Kevin Carley had taken a new job and along with the termination of the entire Hog Island staff, interim director Sue Cilley found her hands full. Nevertheless, she indicated that Maine Audubon had not given up on the island operation yet when she distributed a "preparing a business plan" proposal in January 2009 that basically laid out the realities of the Hog Island situation succinctly before concluding the next important step was to hire a consultant to prepare a workable financial plan for the future. In making her case for the $75,000 expenditure, Cilley affirmed Maine Audubon's awareness of Hog Island as "one of the sacred resources of the conservation community: a place that has transformed generations of visitors and motivated them to dedicate their personal and professional lives to bird and habitat conservation." By mid-April, Ted Koffman, Maine's new state executive director, announced that a consulting company had been selected and a plan for Hog Island's "sustainable future" was under way.[25]

The sequence of events developing that plan is not clear, but by early summer 2010 Maine Audubon had sold the *Puffin V* to cut their losses and had no agenda of their own for upcoming island programming.[26] In the meantime they negotiated a deal with nearby Camp Kieve-Wavus in Nobleboro for the island to be made available to their youngsters for overnight outdoor camping. No buildings except the washhouse would be used.

With that in mind, Steve Kress took the initiative under Project Puffin to schedule the always-successful ornithology workshops, held early and late in the season so as not to conflict with the Camp Kieve agreement, yet keeping the legacy of birding alive on Hog Island. Although the absence of the *Puffin V* was a major stumbling block, to solve that problem, Kress employed his own professional mantra, "It's all about partnerships," to contract with Camp Kieve-Wavus to charter their boat, the *Snow Goose III*, when not in use by their own campers. Reports were that all worked according to plan that summer, but by fall, scuttlebutt slipped out that Audubon was preparing to sign an agreement that would put the final nail in the coffin of the venerable old Audubon Camp in Maine.

The Kress Factor

Camp historians will no doubt say that the seeds for the Hog Island Audubon Camp's 2010 renaissance were sown forty years earlier when camp director Dur Morton gave rookie naturalist Steve Kress the time and a little bit of budget to see if Atlantic puffins could be repatriated to Eastern Egg Rock, that little bit of sea-washed stone out on the far reaches of Muscongus Bay. It was the dynamic success Kress and his Seabird Restoration team achieved there and on other Maine bird islands that brought into public awareness the concept of restoring a species' range by way of "social attraction."[27] Following confirmation in scientific journals of successfully luring in wild birds with anchored decoys and audio recordings of successfully breeding populations, features ran in *Down East* and *Smithsonian,* as well as media bites on National Public Radio and YouTube, that informed wider audiences of Kress's innovations while establishing his place in the annals of ornithological history. A delightful consequence of that publicity was a resurgence in the viability of the Audubon Camp in Maine.

As established in the previous chapter, Steve Kress's roots with and affection for Audubon, but especially the camp in Maine, go back to his youth in central Ohio when he shook Roger Tory Peterson's hand at a Screen Tour presentation. His first wildlife research may have been amphibians but grew into birds and bird islands upon his listening to Carl Buchheister's myriad sea stories after having finished his cleaning responsibilities at the camp in Connecticut while still a teenager. Following a two-year gig as an instructor at the Audubon Camp in Wisconsin and another couple of summers working in St. Andrews, New Brunswick, Kress finally got his chance to teach on Hog Island, a place that years prior had captured his imagination and set the course of his career.[28]

The depth of Steve Kress's influence on the Audubon Camp in Maine is extensive, beginning as a bird life instructor, then within a year as a puffin researcher. From 1982 through 1986 he added camp director to his resume, during which tenure he initiated restoration work on the main Bingham cottage, Millicent's mother's "camp house," by having the foundation shored up by a local contractor. He also supervised floating the two Bingham buildings nearest the shore around the island and reestablishing them on the camp peninsula as staff housing.[29] Over the next two decades he continued as a headline camp instructor and home-grown birding rock star, all while developing components of the Audubon Seabird Institute, which came to include both Project Puffin's island work and the Project Puffin Visitor Center in Rockland. It would surprise no one then, when Maine Audubon shuttered the Camp in 2009, that it was Steve Kress's natural reaction to conjure a plan that he hoped would reinvigorate Hog Island's education and birding legacies that were so dear to his heart.

By early 2010, word was out that Project Puffin, under the auspices of the National Audubon Society, not Maine Audubon, was taking reservations for select ornithology workshops to be held that summer on Hog Island. This was not an official reopening of the camp but a stopgap offering to accommodate the always well-attended spring and summer birding sessions with Kenn Kaufman and Scott Weidensaul. DownEast. com reported not long after that "it's not yet certain whether the birding programs are on the verge of a glorious new chapter, or experiencing their last hurrah." The article added that Maine Audubon was engaging partners in conversation regarding their giving up "responsibility for the buildings" and instead finding "a partner organization that would have a strong interest in programs that were within the scope and intentions" of the island donors. Camp Kieve-Wavus was noted as one of the partner organizations in the negotiations.[30]

Nevertheless, Kress's notification under Seabird Restoration Program letterhead explained optimistically that even though registration was just opening to the public, many beds for the restored ornithology workshops had already been spoken for. He also put out an all-call for available Friends of Hog Island volunteers to come help open and close the camp as well as providing kitchen and cleaning assistance during the sessions. And as always, smiling volunteers came forward, but it would be the last roundup for the Friends of Hog Island organization formed twelve years earlier by Bart and Ginny Cadbury and their friends. More change was on the horizon.

One of those volunteers who stepped up summer 2010 was Juanita Roushdy, a neighbor from down Keene Neck Road. Roushdy was new to the Midcoast region, a retiree birder from North Carolina with a United Kingdom pedigree, who came to Maine in search of Bicknell's thrush. She first attended camp in 2007, Maine Audubon's penultimate summer of sessions. She fell in love with Hog Island in the process, so she signed up for an ornithology workshop the next spring. After that spring week on her way out, on Keene Neck Road, she noticed a house of interest for sale. Having thought about relocating for a time, she knocked on the door at 7:30 a.m., and after mild protest from the owners in their pajamas, got a brief look at the interior and a quick tour of the picturesque property that abuts Greenland Cove. Roushdy recognized possibilities in what she saw, but when a female American redstart hauling nesting material flew by, she decided, "Okay! That's it!" Realtors negotiated the details and by fall, the Keene Neck Road property came under contract just about the time Roushdy got word that Maine Audubon was closing the camp on Hog Island.

Due to several complications, including a national economy that was in the process of tanking, it wasn't until fall 2009 that Roushdy moved her furniture to Bremen. Just a few months later she heard about Project Puffin reprising birding workshops at the camp, so, very interested, she drove down the road to sign up. There she met "Seabird" Sue Schubel who was willing to take registration information but stressed how important volunteers were to the success of that summer's sessions. Paid intern help, like the kitchen boys of old, was not included in the lean budget. Project Puffin was relying on volunteers to pick up the slack. Roushdy ended up volunteering for not only the opening and closing work sessions but all four weeks of birding workshops.

Over the course of the summer, Roushdy and the staff talked about the future of the camp and in time she offered Steve Kress a "five figure sum of money." Kress was pleased with the news and explained how her gift would help get the camp up and running for the next season. But in the discussion, something sounded odd to Roushdy. Upon further questioning, Kress divulged that it looked like the camp's management was going to be transferred from Audubon to Camp Kieve in an attempt to rectify the money problem. Audubon, under Project Puffin, would still run ornithology workshops on Hog Island, though the peninsula would come under Kieve-Wavus education management. In fact, she learned December 11, 2010, was the date set for the ownership transfer papers to be signed.

Juanita Roushdy didn't like the idea of Audubon giving up control of Hog Island and told Kress her generous gift was off the table if it took place. She didn't like the idea, either, that negotiations to jettison the camp had been so quiet that stakeholders, like the Midcoast Audubon chapter, were left in the dark. One afternoon soon after, Steve Kress invited Roushdy to join a handful of other significant decision-makers in a casual discussion on his summer residence deck to think through the Hog Island financial conundrum one more time. What hadn't they tried? What might work? It was lamentable that campers' passion for the island didn't extend into "deep pockets," but such was reality. Maine

Audubon's consulting firm had concluded the only viable way out for the camp's financial woes was for it to enter a long-term partnership, and Camp Kieve seemed the best and, frankly, only fit.

Roushdy queried how much money was needed to keep camp management under Audubon control. Kress responded that a $50,000 influx of funds would be a starting point for the next summer. If that was what it would take, Roushdy promised, she would be good for the whole gift. But then she asked if the camp had ever considered organizing as a non-profit 501(c)3 entity that could offer tax breaks to donors. Kress responded that he had not and wondered if such was possible for a stand-alone Audubon-related organization. Roushdy said, "Sure. Why not?" Others on the deck thought the paperwork would be too much of a challenge and fundraising even more so. But they listened, and before the meeting was over, the gentlemen present learned a valuable lesson about what happens when you tell a capable woman what she *can't* do. Roushdy agreed to take on the non-profit incorporation and fundraising initiatives in what she knew was a very limited period of time. She had eleven weeks to work a miracle.

The new organization would need officers, a board of advisors, and a name. Ideas for that name were cast about and "Friends" was thought best. After searching for leaders of the defunct Friends of Hog Island association to learn if the name had already been incorporated, Roushdy found Betsy Cadbury, who advised that, no, FOHI had only been adjunct to National and Maine Audubon. They were never a fund-raising, tax-return-filing organization, nor was their name copyrighted. All the work their volunteers had done was under the authorization of either National or Maine Audubon and money raised was deposited in those accounts. The decision was soon made to retain the Friends of Hog Island name in honor of the "legacy people," and in the hope they would step forward to come to the aid of their beloved Audubon Camp.

By late October 2010, the new Friends of Hog Island organization picked up support when the Island Institute posted news online under the headline, "Audubon turning Hog Island over to Camp Kieve."[31]

Midcoast Audubon members were quoted as being unhappy, complaining the decision was made without their consultation. Roushdy went on record in the article saying her concern was that Camp Kieve was about character building, not conservation or ecology education. Kieve camp director Henry Kennedy, who was encouraged by Kieve-Wavus's first extended use of Hog Island the previous summer, countered that when their kids learn responsibility, respect and awareness for the environment will follow. Maine Audubon's Bos Savage added that he was convinced both sides would benefit from the transfer, although no money would change hands for the estimated $5 million property. Camp Kieve would get a mostly undeveloped island for their student experiences while Audubon could continue to run birding workshops during the shoulder seasons. The article ended with the acknowledgment that negotiations were still ongoing, though a final decision was expected "in the next few months."

Juanita Roushdy never thought of herself as a fundraiser, but she did give herself credit for her skill in mobilizing people. She also recognized that if something needed to be done, contact the head of the organization. Going through secretaries and lower-tiered managers only "wastes time." After she got the non-profit paperwork started, she made personal calls on Camp Kieve's Henry Kennedy, Maine Audubon's Ted Koffman, and National Audubon's new president, David Yarnold. She learned in those meetings that money collected for Hog Island's capital campaign would stay with Maine Audubon and would not be available to any new iteration of the camp in Maine. Proceeds from the *Puffin V* sale, likewise, would be put to other use for Maine Audubon. Henry Kennedy had doubts the new FOHI could raise the money necessary since success had been limited in prior campaigns. Still, Kennedy was open to more discussion if requested.

The Project Puffin folks and the revitalized FOHI realized that if the camp was to be resurrected, it would have to be under the auspices of National Audubon, not Maine Audubon. Roushdy realized that her personal appeal to David Yarnold, who had just been installed as National's president weeks prior, was the most important of the three. She was able to schedule ninety minutes of Yarnold's time in Audubon's New York City office the week before Thanksgiving when she presented a copy of the non-profit paperwork that had already been filed; a FOHI business plan; stationery; talking points that included FOHI was compiling a list of five thousand potential lost legacy donors; and a draft of FOHI by-laws. She wanted to be sure "he knew we were serious and we were in motion." She further explained that Steve Kress and Project Puffin felt a $50,000 FOHI organizational gift annually would keep the Audubon Camp afloat, and if needed, she was prepared to write that check herself on the spot. National Audubon's president was impressed. On their way out of the office, Yarnold told his chief financial officer to give Roushdy any records she requested and to send him duplicates. Signs were positive that Friends of Hog Island just might be, as Ted Koffman wondered, "the financial champion who came charging over the hill."

A few days later, barely a week before the December 11 transfer deadline, David Yarnold called Juanita Roushdy and asked frankly if she could write a business plan for the Audubon Camp operation and raise $1,000,000 by the first of May. If so, he would present the new plan for the camp before his board of directors and he was sure they would approve upon his recommendation. Without hesitation Roushdy responded, "Yes. That will be fine. That is not a problem." Yarnold suggested staff in his financial office work with her to write the business plan, but she insisted on drafting it herself, though she agreed to try to follow Audubon bookkeeping protocol in the process.

With Roushdy's pledge taken into consideration, David Yarnold announced that he would contact Kieve-Wavus Education to say that "new people were on board" and Audubon would like more time to think about the partnership proposal. The following May, when Yarnold presented Roushdy's business plan for the camp's operation and a substantial promised endowment, including a $500,000 gift from an anonymous donor, National Audubon's board of directors voted to approve the agreement and the Audubon Camp in Maine on Hog Island was back in business.

With that good news, the real work of the new Friends of Hog Island shifted into high gear. A volunteer database was built around old rosters while adding hundreds of new names. A development letter was sent out over Kress's and Roushdy's signatures that stated, "In today's economic climate, it is key that we demonstrate to the National Audubon Society that we have the capacity to continue successful programs at the Hog Island camp ... and that the camp will not be a drain on Audubon's finances." That first season under Project Puffin was profitable, they continued, in part due to "renewed energy found in volunteers." Volunteers were asked yet again to become the heart and soul of Hog Island with generous contributions of time and treasure. While larger donations were appreciated, Roushdy and Kress asked for 750 members to pledge at least $75 for each of the next five years to build a dependable financial base that would provide not only the $50,000 annual subsidy but would also add revenue for camp upgrades. Before long FOHI funded significant island expenditures like a state-of-the-art media system, solar power cell installation, and Bingham cottages restoration while always staying on the outlook for the next essential system to be replaced.

Camp Kieve was not left out of the revived Hog Island picture entirely, however. Seth Benz remembers how Kieve-Wavus had wanted the island for the month of July "for years," and that perhaps part of Audubon's solution had been staring them in the face all that time. In any case, as of 2011, Kieve-Wavus scheduled the island for July with Audubon Camp workshops on the calendar before and after. Also, from Benz's point of view, the loss of the *Puffin V*, thought by many to be catastrophic, was really a blessing in disguise. Program boats are very expensive to run when gas, maintenance, radio and weather radar systems, winter storage, and insurance are all added together. Without a passenger boat expense of their own, the Audubon Camp had shed a major factor in cost overruns. Instead, the camp budgeted to contract with Camp Kieve for the use of their captain, a mate, and the *Snow Goose III* when needed. Under this new arrangement, Audubon shed its boat worries while Camp Kieve found a partner to help underwrite their own vessel expenses. It was a win-win situation on multiple levels.

Under Juanita Roushdy's leadership, Friends of Hog Island not only kept their promise to provide annual underwriting for the camp's operation but energized a renewed cadre of volunteers. Roushdy makes it clear whenever she can, to whomever will listen, that FOHI volunteers have "kept all the threads in the seams. Without that, I really don't think the Camp would be here right now." She is fond of reminding everyone how much an hour of volunteer work is worth, then highlighting the over 7,200 hours FOHI volunteers provide every year. Most volunteers are retired, but many educators return, and in 2017, the youngest volunteer was a fourteen-year-old who had aged out of family camp but just had to return, even if it meant working in the kitchen and emptying trash cans.

In the ensuing years since 2010, summer camp programs have found a renewed lease on life along with new elements added to what could be considered a year-round curriculum. After a nesting platform was erected beside a maintenance shed on the camp peninsula in fall 2006, osprey pairs have taken up residence there just about every summer since. With cameras and internet streaming provided by explore.org, osprey couple Steve and Rachel became a bit of a national sensation, drawing thousands of viewers, many of whom have never, nor will ever, set foot on Hog Island. An active online community that shares posted comments has grown at the website, reaching peak audience annually when osprey return in the spring and when chicks hatch two months later. Ten years of record keeping indicate that during seasons when the nest is harassed and chicks preyed on by owls and/or bald eagles, the online community contracts.[32]

Also of note is the Audubon Artist Residency at Hog Island program begun in 2014, which selects artists and writers to work with the island muses in solitude while living in the FOHI-restored Bingham cottages. Accommodations are still rustic, complete with a pit toilet, but participants don't seem to mind. Along with whatever else comes of their work, participants are commissioned to create some product for the camp in their process. First artist-in-residence, writer Rebecca Gilman, worked on her one-woman play about Hog Island matriarch Mabel Loomis Todd while living in the actual summer cottage Mrs. Todd so loved. Gilman's *Woman of the World* made its New York off-Broadway debut in October 2019.[33]

When David Yarnold came to Hog Island for the first time in 2011 for the camp's seventy-fifth anniversary celebration, he observed that through the camp's rich and innovative history, it had been tempered into Audubon's "true north." Though Audubon has seen myriad changes over its century of awareness-raising, education, and advocacy, David Yarnold came to understand that the convocation of souls who gather on Hog Island to celebrate birds, wilderness, and so much more embodies the essence of what the National Audubon Society has become. Thanks to the contributions of so many of Nature's People, the future of the Hog Island Audubon Camp is assured for future generations.[34] From Camp Mavooshen through Mother Church to Audubon's "True North," Hog Island represents some of the best of what authentic love for nature can accomplish, and planet Earth is a better place for it.

Chapter 7 Notes

[1] In various interviews made for this book, Elvis Stahr was remembered at camp in a humorous way when he came for the dedication of the Allan Cruickshank Sanctuary on Eastern Egg Rock in 1976 inappropriately wearing "street shoes." Still, Stahr accomplished much as Audubon chief executive, including lobbying for the passage of national legislation that permitted environmental groups wider latitude in promoting their positions in public without losing tax-exempt status. Frank Graham, Jr., *The Audubon Ark: A History of the National Audubon Society* (University of Texas Press, 1990), 241.

[2] I am disappointed I didn't have more to write in my journal about the Carl Buchheister visit that summer. I am not sure Harriet accompanied him on that trek to the island. Both were already fighting various maladies and when I visited them at their home in North Carolina the following spring, Harriet was bedridden. Still, in the feisty characteristic I've learned was natural for her, an hour or so into the interview she called from the other room to inform Carl and me that enough time had been spent and the interview was over. She didn't want Carl to get too tired. In any case, I was impressed enough to write in my journal on that August Friday on Hog Island, "Carl Buchheister visited and hiked to Bingham cottages—I felt like a disciple sitting on … his words."

[3] The idea of restoring nesting birds to a previously inhabited breeding area was revolutionary in 1981. During my session that summer a *Newsweek* photographer came along on our all-day trip into the bay. His photographs accented an article run later that year about the Audubon Camp and the Seabird Restoration Project. I framed my copy of the article and hung it in the Fish House. It was still there the last time I checked.

[4] Some of these Audubon budget cuts came under Russell Peterson, others under Peter A. A. Berle. Graham, *Ark,* 281 and 303.

[5] See Roger Tory Peterson's "The Maine Story" in *Bird Watcher's Digest,* November/December 1986.

[6] In the post–Baker-Buchheister era, National Audubon's action agenda shifted from student-based education to habitat management and

providing a voice to various national environmental concerns. The unprofitable Junior Audubon clubs program, with its bird data cards and other nature paraphernalia, made way for *Audubon Adventures*, a seasonal classroom periodical aimed at upper elementary students that was funded largely by chapters, not by National Audubon. Peterson instead focused more of the society's attention and budget on the new media wave in television, which came to include the highly acclaimed TBS series, *The World of Audubon*. Society naturalists are no longer head-quartered at Audubon's New York office as in days of yore, but in the handful of nature centers operating around the country, where they developed their own curriculum with a local flavor. Frank Graham concluded in his sterling Audubon history, *The Audubon Ark*, that education reached its nadir at Audubon in the early to mid-1980s.

[7] Golf course managers who use the Audubon name to indicate a more environment-friendly use of chemicals on their links are not connected to the National Audubon Society. See Audubon International (auduboninternational.org). Likewise, The Audubon Nature Institute in New Orleans, which is better known as the Audubon Zoo, is not connected to the National Audubon Society. See https://audubonnatureinstitute.org.

[8] Un-cited quotations from Friends of Hog Island founding materials are from various unpublished printouts, emails, and meeting minutes.

[9] Suggested levels of giving for the Audubon Camp in Maine Friends fundraiser: Heron, $250; Egret, $750; Eider, $1,500; and Osprey, $5,000.

[10] Harbor Island in Muscongus Bay is a popular stopping point on all-day Camp trips and home to the Duryea Morton Audubon Sanctuary.

[11] As posted in the first Friends of Hog Island newsletter mailed December 1998, the first executive committee was comprised of president Tally Avener (Midcoast Audubon Society chapter) and directors Bart Cadbury, Betsy Cadbury, Joe Gray (former camper), Brian Harrington (former student assistant), Barbara Levine (former camper), Robbie Rubly-Burggraff (former staff), Rick Ylagen (current staff), and camp director Sam Hands (ex-officio).

[12] Though Bart Cadbury singled out himself, wife Ginny, Sam Hands, and Robbie Rubly-Burggraff as those who first discussed a Friends of

Hog Island organization, the roster of those in attendance for that first annual meeting compose a broader charter member or "founders list." Those in attendance: Tally Avener, Andre Breton, Bart Cadbury, Betsy Cadbury, David Cadbury, Ginny Cadbury, Karen Cadbury, Peggy Cadbury, John Flicker, Joe Gray, Sam Hands, Brian Harrington, Barbara Levine, Steve Kress, Alesia Maltz, Marci Mowery, Joei Randazzo, Pete Salmansohn, Lynn Saunders, Scott Saunders, Joe Spaulding, Hank Tyler, Ching Wong, Rick Ylagen, and Wendy Ylagen.

[13] This excerpt from the March 1998 *Across the Narrows* addressed camp upgrades: "Renovations of the Queen Mary, which began last year, are expected to be completed this summer. The Saunders family, Jason Chapman, and Dan May have worked very hard to restore the safety and longevity of the Queen Mary while preserving her historic and charming character. The sewage treatment system on the island will be modernized and upgraded by fall. The effort will be equally funded by National Audubon and bond monies approved for such projects by Maine voters."

[14] Talbert Spence, who had been an advocate for FOHI and the camp, left Audubon employ in early 1999.

[15] Establishing an educational seabird center along the Maine coast was an Audubon concept developed by Steve Kress. With the donation of the Zahn property, thoughts of a seabird establishment down Keene Neck Road was a natural. Turned out mainland neighbors were opposed to the additional traffic a Seabird Center would draw. After some deliberation, it was determined a storefront in Rockland would be better suited for what became known as the Project Puffin Visitor Center. See https://projectpuffin.audubon.org/visit-us/project-puffin-visitor-center.

[16] Audubon Camp in Maine directors: Carl W. Buchheister (1936–57), B. Bartram Cadbury (1958–68), Robert "Doc" Houston (1969–70), Duryea Morton (1971–77), Mike Shannon (1978–80), Manlius and Mary Sargeant (1981), Steve Kress (1982–86), Eugene Beckham (1987–88), Robert Dorrance (1989–91), Mike Shannon (1992), Donald Burgess (1993–95), Sam Hands (1996–98), Seth Benz (1999–2008), and Steve Kress (2010–19). Upon Steve Kress's retirement from Audubon in 2019, new Seabird Institute directors were Donald Lyons (Director of

Conservation Science) and Tiffany Huenenfeldt (Managing Director). The Seabird Institute includes three Audubon operations: the Seabird Restoration Program (Project Puffin), the Hog Island Audubon Camp, and the Puffin Visitor's Center in Rockland.

[17] Project Puffin summer staff on Eastern Egg Rock became known as "puffineers." Since only terns were tended on Stratton Island, Seth Benz chuckled about being a "terneer."

[18] Varied details here culled from an interview with Seth Benz.

[19] The official name of the Hog Island camp changed over time, though no record of just when those changes took place is recorded. At its opening in 1936, it was called the Audubon Nature Camp for Adult Leaders. By the early 1980s, that name had evolved into the Audubon Ecology Workshop in Maine. Maine Audubon would rename it the Hog Island Audubon Center. When National Audubon returned to the scene it was changed to its current iteration, The Hog Island Audubon Camp.

[20] The camp's mailing address was on Keene Neck Road until its end of the street was renamed Audubon Road.

[21] *Across the Narrows* editors appointed at the 1999 annual meeting were none other than your humble author, Tom Schaefer, and his wife, Cindy Cooke. Volume 2, number 1, which was the first FOHI newsletter under the *Across the Narrows* banner, was mailed fall 1999. Cindy and I published seven editions through fall 2002, just months before the fateful meeting at the Sharon Audubon Center in January 2003.

[22] Seth Benz revealed in his interview that Maine Audubon was not in favor of Friends of Hog Island "from the get-go" in 2000.

[23] The FOHI executive team present at the January 2003 meeting with Maine Audubon representatives came to call that day's meeting in Connecticut the "Sharon Massacre."

[24] More detail from the Hog Island Audubon Center Capital Campaign May 7, 2007 printout: "Phase I: $400,000 - Completed! 1. Purchased *Puffin V*, a used 49 passenger program boat, and certified *Osprey III* for passenger use. ($200,000) 2. Upgraded island electrical systems and circuit breaker capacity; improved exit safety from top floor of Queen Mary dorm; funded marketing consultation;

and, hired development personnel. ($200,000) <u>Phase II: $1 million:</u> 1. Renovate program space by reconfiguring Crow's Nest to 'high end' guest accommodations and renovate Foc's'cle for guest/staff use. ($300,000) 2. Complete deferred maintenance items such as repairs to Porthole dorm foundation and bathrooms. ($100,000) 3. Renovate the Bridge—the signature farmhouse and island hub of the center. Upgrade kitchen, dining room, and add public restroom. ($600,000) <u>Phase III: $1 million:</u> 1. Improved staff, instructor, and guest housing to provide updated and appealing accommodations. ($425,000) 2. Complete deferred maintenance items and improvements to mainland grounds and facilities. ($500,000) 3. Make waterfront improvement to boathouse, piers, floats, docks, smaller boats, and equipment. ($75,000) <u>Ongoing: $500,000 to $1 million:</u> Leverage planned giving to create an endowment to help support scholarships and innovations in programming."

[25] In April 2009, ConsultEcon from Cambridge, Massachusetts, was selected to develop the business plan for Hog Island's future.

[26] Maine Audubon absorbed the more than $600,000 raised in the Hog Island Center Capital Campaign into other accounts to offset losses incurred while managing the camp. Friends of Hog Island's donors weren't happy about the sale of the *Puffin V* or the lost endowment funds. National Audubon, once again island managers via Project Puffin, placated the criticism with the knowledge that new efforts were already afoot that had the potential to save the island's prized summer programs.

[27] By fall 2013, the Seabird Restoration Program reported "more than 47 seabird species have been protected in 100 locales in 14 countries across the world" through their innovative techniques. "Follow the Leader" (*Audubon*, September–October 2013), 34.

[28] While this subsection of the Hog Island story focuses on Steve Kress's influence on the camp in Maine, note that one of Hog Island's influences on Kress is a product of legacy staff member Allan Cruickshank. In cool weather, Allan always wore a tam o'shanter which became a kind of personal trademark. Steve honors Mr. Cruickshank's memory by wearing a tam, too.

[29] The restoration contractor on the Camp Mavooshen building was Allen Davis. Kress advised the two Bingham buildings near the shore were moved for security and longevity issues. Unattended buildings on islands proved problematic. Also, time was taking a toll on both buildings. If not tended, they would surely fall as the Osprey cottage had done not many years prior. Foundations of other defunct Bingham buildings were already lost in the ferns.

[30] Colin Woodard, "Talk of Maine: Saving Hog Island" (*Down East,* April 2010).

[31] Steve Cartwright, "Audubon turning Hog Island over to Camp Kieve" (*Working Waterfront,* October 27, 2010).

[32] For year-round osprey platform observation, go to explore.org and search for "Audubon Osprey Nest, Hog Island, Bremen, Maine, USA." Birds are on the nest from mid-April through August. Osprey pair Rachel and Steve were named in honor of Rachel Carson and Steve Kress. The online community grieved in April 2020 when Rachel failed to return. Steve took on a new partner, Phoebe, named in honor of Phoebe Snetsinger, an American birder notorious for having been the first to observe over eight thousand species.

[33] Application details for the Audubon Artist Residency at Hog Island can be found at https://hogisland.audubon.org/programs/artist-residency-information.

[34] In 2019, Friends of Hog Island found new leadership with Scott Weidensaul's election as president. Weidensaul's regular "Migrations" columns in *Bird Watcher's Digest* give focus to Hog Island programs on occasion. For example, see his take on International Guillemot Appreciation Day, a tongue-in-cheek celebration conjured by Project Puffin staff, or as Weidensaul explains, "seabird biologists marooned for months on a lonely island off the coast of Maine." See "IGAD! Attention Must Be Paid" (*Bird Watcher's Digest,* May/June 2020).

Afterword

As Tom Schaefer has so lovingly detailed in this book, the history of Hog Island over the past 150 or so years has been one of many unexpected twists, from farm and maritime store to Camp Mavooshen to rusticator resort to Audubon. Few changes, however, have been as dramatic as the turn-around since the camp's closure in 2009, when Steve Kress and a reconstituted, re-energized Friends of Hog Island, led by Juanita Roushdy, rode to the rescue.

As a longtime Hog Island instructor, and the current president of FOHI, it's my pleasure to bring the story full circle. Tom's narrative ends with the slow rebuilding of the camp program after Hog Island reopened in 2010, and I'm pleased to say that the partnership of National Audubon and the nonprofit FOHI has brought us back to full operations, and with even the COVID-19 pandemic proving only a temporary hurdle with the loss of the 2020 camp season. (Yet, as we'll see, even that very dark cloud had a silver lining.)

FOHI, through its legion of members, continues to serve as a bulwark for the camp in terms of direct financial support, in-kind contributions, and the efforts of almost two hundred volunteers who every year provide housekeeping, food service, and maintenance help—all while having a great time doing it. In the decade since camp reopened, FOHI volunteers from around the country have come to Hog Island on their own nickel, year after year, and have contributed more than 75,000 person-hours of hard, important work.

Between 2010 and 2022, FOHI has also provided National Audubon with a little over $1 million in direct cash support, and in-kind and material donations that touch literally every facet of the island's infrastructure and camp programming. Some have been very big-ticket items, like the restoration of the Bingham Cottages at old Camp Mavooshen for the artist-in-residence program, refitting the Fish House with state-of-the-art AV systems, new lighting, and the solar array that now provides 100 percent of the camp's electricity; resupplying the entire kitchen including three new stoves, a chest freezer and the walk-in refrigerator, right down to aprons, salad spinners, flatware, and place settings, as well as granite-topped stone tables for outdoor food service; specimen cabinets for the island's extensive bird skin collection, taxidermy mounts and microscopes for the Queen Mary Lab; geolocator tags for tracking migrating thrushes; a pontoon boat and sixteen-foot Carolina skiff with motor; support for the purchase of two sixteen-passenger vans and backhoe and tractor; and the digitizing the Hog Island historical documents and photographs that are now publicly available on FOHI's website (www.fohi.org).

The future holds fresh challenges, of course. One of pressing importance to an island facility like Hog is sea level rise, which has become starkly evident in recent years.

At the isthmus between the peninsula and main island, where Long Cove and Midden Cove (as Indian Cove is now known) almost meet, lunar high tides now all but create two separate islands—and as the sea continues to rise, that split will become more and more constant. Island facilities manager Eric Snyder has been employing creative, environmentally sensitive ways to slow the accelerating shoreline erosion that has significantly chewed back the edges of the peninsula, especially on the northeast side.

More immediately, it became clear in the past decade that the Queen Mary, the old ship's chandlery perched right out over the water, was at rapidly increasing risk of flooding, especially during winter nor'easter storms whose winds push extra water into Muscongus Bay on top of already high tides. On more than one occasion, flood waters came *right* up to the floorboards, though catastrophe was narrowly averted.

Something had to be done, and that something was to raise the Queen Mary a full three feet above its original level. Such a job, on a very large and historic structure, proved to be both an engineering and financial challenge. Over time, and in part because at some point in the past internal bracing beams on the first floor had been removed to create a more open feel to the lab area, the Queen Mary had begun to list off the perpendicular. Eric oversaw a multi-step process to bring the old girl back into square, using braces and cables to slowly and gingerly, and over the course of several years, pull the Queen Mary back into true.

Even the COVID-19 pandemic shutdown in 2020 proved a bit of a blessing. With no campers on the island for that summer, Eric and his assistant, Adrian Bregy, had the freedom to gut the lab floor, reinstall brace beams, and move the entrance door to the east wall, the better to handle the eventual change in elevation and ramps that a lift would entail. Meanwhile, Eric was navigating a maze of town, state, and federal permit requirements—in essence blazing a trail for others to follow, since in many cases this was the first such lift project driven by the sea-level rise that the permitting authorities had dealt with. It will hardly be the last along the Maine coast.

Nor is such an enterprise cheap. The actual lift work, along with all the advance engineering and the permitting, came to $278,000, the cost of which was covered by donations to FOHI, including a significant portion from a single gift from longtime FOHI board member and Hog Island supporter Walt Pomeroy and his wife, Lin. Walt, a nationally respected conservationist, recognized early the challenges that climate change and rising seas posed to Hog Island. Sadly, Walt did not live to see the Queen Mary successfully raised in the autumn of 2022, but the landmark building, safe now from the tides, stands as a memorial to his dedication to the camp.

Somewhere, I'd like to think Mabel Loomis Todd, David Todd, and Millicent Todd Bingham—and the legions of former campers, instructors, and all who have been touched by Hog Island—are smiling.

— Scott Weidensaul
Naturalist and Pulitzer Prize finalist
Author of *A World on the Wing: The Global Odyssey of Migratory Birds.*
Milton, New Hampshire
November 2022

Works Engaged

Mabel Loomis Todd

Todd, Mabel Loomis and David Peck Todd. "An Ascent of Mount Fuji the Peerless." *The Century Magazine*, January 12, 1906.

Todd, Mabel Loomis. *Corona and Coronet: Being a Narrative of the Amherst Eclipse Expedition to Japan, in Mr. James Schooner-yacht Coronet, to Observe the Sun's Total Obscuration*, August 9, 1896. Houghton Mifflin, 1898. General Books reprint, 2009.

_____, ed. *A Cycle of Sonnets*. Roberts Brothers, 1896.

_____. *A Cycle of Sunsets*. Small, Maynard and Co., 1910.

_____. "A Great Modern Observatory: Harvard's Astronomical Work." *The Century Magazine*, June 1897.

_____. "The Epic of Hog." Millicent Todd Bingham Papers (MS 496D), Manuscripts and Archives, Yale University Library, unpublished.

_____. "In Aino-Land." *The Century Magazine*, July 1898.

_____. "In Quest of a Shadow: An Astronomical Experience in Japan." *The Atlantic Monthly*, September 1897.

_____, ed. *Letters of Emily Dickinson*. Vol. 1. Roberts Brothers, 1894.

_____. "Muscongus Island, Maine." Mabel Loomis Todd Papers (MS 496C), Manuscripts and Archives, Yale University Library, unpublished.

_____. Personal journals and diaries. Mabel Loomis Todd Papers (MS 496C), Manuscripts and Archives, Yale University Library, unpublished.

_____, ed. and Joel Dorman Steele. *Popular Astronomy: Being the New Descriptive Astronomy*. "Revised and brought down to date by Mabel Loomis Todd." American Book Company, 1884.

_____. *Total Eclipses of the Sun. The Columbian Knowledge Series.* David P. Todd, ed. Roberts Brothers, 1894.

_____. "The Great Red Planet in the West (Mars)." *Saint Nicholas: A monthly magazine for boys and girls,* June 1899.

_____. *The Thoreau Family Two Generations Ago.* Foreword by Millicent Todd Bingham. Thoreau Society Booklet #13, 1958.

_____. "The Village Beautiful." Annual Report of the Secretary of the Connecticut Board of Agriculture, 1902.

_____. "The Village Problem." *The Federation Bulletin: Official organ of the Massachusetts State Federation of Women's Clubs,* April 1904.

_____. *Tripoli the Mysterious.* Grant Richards (publisher), 1912. Elibron Classics series (facsimile), 2005.

_____. "The Witch of Winnacunnett." *New England Magazine,* January 1891.

_____. *Witchcraft in New England:* Read before the Connecticut Valley Historical Society, January 12, 1906. University of California Libraries reprint, 2011.

Millicent Todd Bingham

Bingham, Millicent Todd. *Ancestor's Brocades: The Literary Debut of Emily Dickinson.* Harper & Brothers, 1945.

_____. "Beyond Psychology." *Homo sapiens Auduboniensis: A Tribute to Walter Van Dyke Bingham.* National Audubon Society, 1953.

_____. "Chasing Eclipses in Four Continents." Speaking notes. The Patriot's Club, Bremen, Maine, July 13, 1950.

_____. *Eben Jenks Loomis: A Paper Read by His Granddaughter, Millicent Todd, to a Group of Friends, February 8, 1913.* Riverside Press, 1913. BiblioLife Reproduction.

_____. *Emily Dickinson: A Revelation.* Harper & Brothers, 1954.

_____. *Emily Dickinson's Home: Letters of Edward Dickinson and His Family.* Harper & Brothers, 1955.

_____. "Gift of an Island Wilderness." Excerpts from addresses made upon the gift of Hog Island to the National Audubon Society. Essays by Irston R. Barnes, Millicent Todd Bingham, and Paul B. Sears. Photographs by Shirley A. Briggs. *Atlantic Naturalist*, October–December 1960.

_____. "History of Audubon Camp in Maine given to campers in the Fish House at Hog Island." National Audubon Society audio tape, July 10, 1950.

_____. "History and Possible Future Use of the Todd Wildlife Sanctuary." Millicent Todd Bingham Papers (MS 496D), Manuscripts and Archives, Yale University Library, unpublished.

_____, ed. "Letters from Mrs. J. A. Ambrose." Millicent Todd Bingham Papers (MS 496D), Manuscripts and Archives, Yale University Library, unpublished.

_____. *Mabel Loomis Todd: Her contributions to the Town of Amherst*. Private printing. 1935.

_____. National Audubon Society. Letter to the Directors and President, August 9, 1960.

_____. "Rescuing an Island." *Natural History*, May 1937.

_____. "The Story of Hog Island. June 26, 1936." Millicent Todd Bingham Papers (MS 496D), Manuscripts and Archives, Yale University Library, unpublished.

_____. "The Story of the Spiral." Millicent Todd Bingham Papers (MS 496D), Manuscripts and Archives, Yale University Library, unpublished.

_____. "The Todd Wildlife Sanctuary." *Bird-Lore*, September–October 1935.

_____. "July 25, 1955/History." Millicent Todd Bingham Papers (MS 496D), Manuscripts and Archives, Yale University Library, unpublished.

Bingham, Millicent Todd and Mabel Loomis Todd. *Bolts of Melody: New Poems of Emily Dickinson*. Harper. 1945.

David Peck Todd

Todd, David Peck and Mabel Loomis Todd. "An Ascent of Mount Fuji the Peerless." *The Century Magazine,* August 1892.

Todd, David Peck. *Astronomy: The Science of the Heavenly Bodies.* Harper, 1922.

_____. *American Eclipse Expedition to Japan, 1887: Preliminary Report of the Total Solar Eclipse of 1887.* Amherst College Observatory, 1888. Kessinger Publishing's Legacy Reprint series.

_____. *A New Astronomy.* American Book Company, 1897.

_____. *Stars and Telescopes: A Hand-Book of Popular Astronomy, Founded on the 9th Edition of Lynn's Celestial Motions.* Little Brown, 1899. Nada Public Domain Reprint, 2011.

_____. *The Story of the Starry Universe: The Science of Astronomy—The Size, Motions, Relative Positions and Other Heavenly Phenomena of the Heavenly Bodies.* Revised by John E. Merrill. Popular Science Library series. Six volumes. Garrett P. Serviss, ed. P. F. Collier & Son, 1922 and 1939.

Walter Van Dyke Bingham

Bingham, Walter Van Dyke. *Aptitudes and Aptitude Testing.* Harper, 1937.

_____. "Preliminary Notes on Behavior and Ethology of *Homo Sapiens Auduboniensis* in the Muscongus Bay Region." National Association of Audubon Society reprint, 1937.

_____. *Homo Sapiens Auduboniensis: A Tribute to Walter Van Dyke Bingham.* Millicent Todd Bingham, ed. National Audubon Society, 1953.

Bingham, Walter Van Dyke and Bruce Victor Moore. *How to Interview.* Harper & Row, 1941.

"Walter Van Dyke Bingham." Beloit College Library Archive. Obituary excerpt from *New York Times,* July 9, 1952, http://www.beloit.edu/-libhome/Archives/acoll/bingham.html. Downloaded September 20, 2006.

"Walter Van Dyke Bingham Collection." Carnegie Mellon University Libraries. Staff and Faculty Papers, Carnegie Mellon University Archives, http://www.library.cmu.edu/Research/Archives/UnivArchives/BinghamAid.html. Downloaded September 20, 2006.

Eben Jenks Loomis

Loomis, Eben Jenks. *An Eclipse Party in Africa: Chasing Summer Across the Equator in the* U.S.S. Pensacola *(1896)*. Roberts Brothers, 1896. Kessinger Publishing's Legacy reprints.

Sereno Edwards Todd

Todd, S. Edwards and Thomas Bridgeman. *The American Gardener's Assistant in Three Parts. Containing Complete Practical Directions for the Cultivation of Vegetables, Flowers, Fruit Trees, and Grapevines.* William Wood (publisher), 1869. Nabu Public Domain reprint.

Todd, Sereno Edwards and James P. Boyd. *Todd's Country Homes and How to Save Money: A Practical Book by a Practical Man* (1885). Kessinger Publishing Legacy reprint.

Todd, Sereno Edwards. *The Young Farmer's Manual: Detailing the Manipulations of the Farm in a Plain and Intelligible Manner; With Practical Directions for Laying Out a Farm and Erecting Buildings, Fences, and Farm Gates.* Saxton, Barker & Co., 1860. Forgotten Books reprint.

Various unpublished works from Todd Bingham Family Papers, Manuscripts and Archives, Yale University Library.

"1912 List of Plants on Hog Island Made by M. L. Todd."

Advertisement from *American Forests* magazine for "Vacation Opportunity" re: help on "just inherited island of wild and untouched beauty off Maine coast." May 1933.

Letter from **Andrew Carnegie** in response to David Peck Todd's sending an "interesting book your daughter has written." December 21, 1909.

Christmas card featuring line drawing of Camp Mavooshen, Muscongus, Maine.

"**Dawn Redwood**: Copy of card from David Challinor." Undated (c. 1964) With explanation from Millicent Todd Bingham attached.

Various **invoices** from local merchants for materials used at family camp.

Two deed documents via **Etta Glidden** c. 1909.

Written agreement with **Charles K. Nash** for access at Keene Neck and boat storage. October 10, 1928.

Untitled remarks by **Myra Nash.** September 3, 1936. re: Keene and Nash families and Hog Island history. Another document dated September 17, 1937. re: Keene family. Millicent Todd Bingham, ed.

Various documents from Yale re: Todd Wildlife Sanctuary/Hog Island as a research station. c. 1962–1965.

Other Significant Titles

Allegany School of Natural History application packet. Program conducted by Buffalo Society of Natural Sciences, the University of Buffalo, and the Allegany State Park Commission, 1940.

The American Environment: Readings in the History of Conservation. Second edition. Roderick Nash, ed. Addison-Wesley, 1976.

"The Audubon Nature Camp." *Bird-Lore,* January–February 1936.

"The Audubon Nature Camp." *Bird-Lore,* September–October 1936.

Baker, John H., ed. *The Audubon Guide to Attracting Birds.* Doubleday, Doran and Company, 1941.

Baker, John H. "Saving Man's Wildlife Heritage." *National Geographic,* November 1954. National Audubon Society reprint.

Barcott, Bruce. "Follow the Leader." *Audubon,* September/October 2013.

Barnes, Irston R. with Millicent Todd Bingham and Paul B. Sears. "Gift of an Island Wilderness." Shirley A. Briggs, ed. *Atlantic Naturalist,* October–December 1960.

Benfey, Christopher. *The Great Wave: Gilded Age Misfits, Japanese Eccentrics, and the Opening of Old Japan.* Random House, 2003.

_____. *A Summer of Hummingbirds: Love, Art, and Scandal in the Intersecting Worlds of Emily Dickinson, Mark Twain, Harriet Beecher Stowe, and Martin Johnson Heade.* Penguin, 2008.

Beston, Henry. *Northern Farm: A Chronicle of Maine.* Illustrated by Thoreau McDonald. 1949. Chimney Farm and Blackberry Books reprint.

_____. *The Outermost House: A Year of Life on the Great Beach of Cape Cod.* Holt, 1928 and 1992.

Bianchi, Martha Dickinson. *The Single Hound: Poems of a Lifetime: Emily Dickinson.* Hesperus Press, 2005. Originally published 1914.

Bollier, Peter and Randall Jimerson. "Guide to the Mabel Loomis Todd Papers, Manuscript Group 496C." Manuscripts and Archives, Yale University Library, 2003.

Buchheister, Carl. Various documents from the family archive, offered by his daughter, Mary Carol Massinneau.

Cadbury, Bart. "Audubon Camp: A Brief Historical Sketch." January 31, 1979. Unpublished.

Cadbury, B. Bartram. "Audubon Sanctuary Dedicated in Memory of Wildlife Writer, Photographer." *Courier-Gazette* (Rockland, Maine), July 16, 1976.

_____. *The Community of Living Things in Fresh and Salt Water.* In cooperation with the National Audubon Society. Creative Educational Society, 1956–1967.

_____. "The Maine Idea." Haverford College Alumni Newsletter, undated.

_____. *Life in Shallow Sea Water.* In cooperation with the National Audubon Society. Nelson Doubleday, 1954.

Carpenter, Murray. "Native American secrets are buried under shells." *New York Times* via *Dayton Daily News,* October 10, 2017.

Carson, Rachel. *Silent Spring.* Fawcett, 1962.

Cartwright, Steve. "Audubon turning Hog Island over to Camp Kieve," *Working Waterfront,* October 27, 2010. Reprinted with permission at fohi.org. See https://fohi.org/2010/11/01/working-waterfront/.

Cary, Austin. "Forty Years of Forest Use in Maine." *Journal of Forestry,* April 1935.

Charyn, Jerome. *A Loaded Gun: Emily Dickinson for the 21st Century.* Bellevue Literary Press, 2016.

____. *The Secret Life of Emily Dickinson: A Novel.* W. W. Norton, 2010.

Clerke, Agnes M. *A Popular History of Astronomy During the Nineteenth Century.* First edition 1885. Fourth edition 1908. Kindle edition/ download February 21, 2014.

Conkling, Philip W. *Islands in Time: A Natural and Cultural History of the Islands of the Gulf of Maine.* Revised edition. Island Institute, 1999.

Conservation and the Gospel of Efficiency: The Progressive Conservation Movement, 1890–1920. Samuel P. Hays, ed. Atheneum, 1980.

Cotter, Holland. "My Hero, the Outlaw of Amherst." *New York Times,* May 11, 2010.

Cronon, William. *Changes in the Land: Indians, Colonists, and the Ecology of New England.* Hill & Wang, 1983.

Cruickshank, Allan D. *Birds Around New York City: Where and When to Find Them.* American Museum of Natural History Handbook Series, No. 13. American Museum of Natural History, 1942.

____. *Cruickshank's Photographs of Birds of America.* Preface by Helen G. Cruickshank. Dover Publications, 1977.

____. *The Pocket Guide to Birds: Eastern and Central North America.* Pocket Books, 1954.

____. *Summer Birds (June through September) of Lincoln County, Maine (including all of Muscongus Bay).* National Audubon Society. Undated (early 1950s).

____. *Wings in the Wilderness.* Oxford University Press, 1947.

Cruickshank, Allan D. and Helen Cruickshank. *1001 Questions Answered About Birds*. Dodd, Mead & Co., 1958.

Cruickshank, Allan D., et al. *Hunting with the Camera: A Guide to Techniques and Adventure in the Field*. Harper & Brothers, 1957.

Cruickshank, Helen Gere. *Bird Islands Down East*. Macmillan, 1941.

_____. *Flight into Sunshine: Bird Experiences in Florida*. Photographs by Allan D. Cruickshank. Macmillan, 1948.

_____. *A Paradise of Birds: When Spring Comes to Texas*. Photography by Allan D. Cruickshank. Dodd, Mead & Co., 1968.

_____. *Wonders of the Bird World*. Photography by Allan D. Cruickshank. Dodd, Mead & Co., 1956.

Dickinson, Emily. *Favorite Poems of Emily Dickinson*. Mabel Loomis Todd and T. W. Higginson, ed. Originally published as *Poems* (1890). Avenel, 1978.

_____. *The Complete Poems of Emily Dickinson*. Thomas H. Johnson, ed. Little, Brown & Co., 1960.

_____. *Final Harvest: Emily Dickinson's Poems*. Thomas H. Johnson, ed. Little, Brown & Co., 1962.

_____. *Letters of Emily Dickinson*. Volume 1. Mabel Loomis Todd, ed. Roberts Brothers, 1894. Kessinger Publishing reprint, 2016.

_____. *Poems by Emily Dickinson*. *Second series*. Mabel Loomis Todd and T. W. Higginson, ed. 1893. Kessinger Publishing reprint, 2011.

_____. *Poems by Emily Dickinson*. *Third series*. Mabel Loomis Todd, ed. 1896. Kessinger Publishing reprint, 2011.

_____. *Poems by Emily Dickinson*. Martha Dickinson Bianchi and Alfred Leete Hampson, ed. Little, Brown & Co., 1914.

_____. *The Poems of Emily Dickinson: Reading Edition*. R. W. Franklin, ed. Belknap Press, 2000.

Emily Dickinson's Garden: The Poetry of Flowers. The New York Botanical Garden, 2010.

Emily Dickinson: Selected Letters. Thomas H. Johnson, ed. Belknap Press, 1971.

Emily Dickinson: The Gorgeous Nothings. Marta Werner and Jen Bervin, ed. Christine Burgin/New Directions Books, 2013.

Dobrow, Julie. "Amour in Amherst." *Tufts Magazine*, winter 2013.

_____. "Early 20th Century 'Tree Huggers': Mabel Loomis Todd, Millicent Todd Bingham and the Development of their Conservation Impulses. Keynote address at the 80th anniversary celebration of Hog Island Audubon Camp." Friends of Hog Island publication, August 5, 2016.

_____. *After Emily: Two Remarkable Women and the Legacy of America's Greatest Poet.* W. W. Norton & Co., 2018.

_____. "Saving the Land: Thoreau's Environmental Ethic and Its Influence on Mabel Loomis Todd and Millicent Todd Bingham." Written for Thoreau Society, unpublished.

"Dr. James M. Todd: One of Boothbay Harbor's Great Benefactors." Boothbay Region Historical Society (Maine), undated.

Duncan, Robert F. *Coastal Maine: A Maritime History.* W. W. Norton & Co., 1992.

Emerson, Ralph Waldo. "Nature." 1836.

Farr, Judith with Louise Carter. *The Gardens of Emily Dickinson.* Harvard University Press, 2004.

Farr, Judith. *I Never Came to You in White.* Houghton Mifflin, 1996.

Flicker, John. *Audubon: The Second Century Connecting with Nature.* National Audubon Society, 2002.

Gay, Peter. *Education of the Senses. Vol. 1 of The Bourgeois Experience, Victoria to Freud.* W. W. Norton, 1984.

Gay, Ruth. "Guide to the David Peck Todd Papers, MS 496B." Manuscripts and Archives, Yale University Library, 1976.

Gelarden, Joe. "A Historic First on Louds Island." *Lincoln County News,* July 8, 2009.

Gibbs, Iris and Alonzo. *Bremen Bygones.* Town of Bremen (Maine), 1976.

Glidden, Etta. Personal correspondence to Mabel Loomis Todd. August 4, 1908. Manuscripts and Archives, Yale University Library.

Goad, Meredith. "By the end you feel so good." Blethen (Maine) Newspapers, August 27, 2006.

Gordon, Lyndall. *Lives Like Loaded Guns: Emily Dickinson and Her Family Feuds.* Viking, 2010.

Graham, Frank, Jr. *The Audubon Ark: A History of the National Audubon Society.* University of Texas Press, 1990.

_____. *Man's Dominion: The Story of Conservation in America.* Evans, 1971.

Gross, Alfred. O. "Along Maine's Coast: Where and how to see some of our most striking bird colonies." With "An Ornithological Map of Maine." *Bird-Lore,* May–June 1935.

Hanna, Thomas. *Shoutin' into the Fog: Growing up on Maine's Ragged Edge.* Islandport Press, 2006.

"Her gift, an island: Mrs. Bingham donates Maine haven." *Sunday Star* (Washington, DC), August 14, 1960.

Hillcourt, William. "An Isle A-Calling You!" *Bird-Lore,* March–April 1940.

Holmes, Wyman. "Mrs. Bingham's Island." *Down East,* April 1992.

Hudson, Charles J. "David Todd (1855–1939): An Appreciation." Reprint from *Popular Astronomy,* November 1939.

Huth, Hans. *Nature and the American: Three Centuries of Changing Attitudes.* University of Nebraska, 1952.

Jabr, Ferris. "The Lost Gardens of Emily Dickinson." *New York Times,* May 13, 2016.

Jakubchak, Chuck. "Hog Island Audubon Camp." *Bird Watcher's Digest,* January–February 2016.

Jimerson, Randall C. "Guide to the Millicent Todd Bingham Papers." Manuscripts and Archives, Yale University Library, 1979.

Johnson, John. *A History of Bristol and Bremen in the State of Maine.* Joel Munsell, 1873.

Johnson, Thomas H. *Emily Dickinson: An Interpretive Biography.* Belknap Press, 1955.

_____, ed. *Emily Dickinson Selected Letters.* Belknap Press, 1958.

Jones Library. Amherst, Massachusetts. Emily Dickinson display. September 2006.

Klinger, David. Personal letter recounting term as FOHI president. April 4, 2018.

Kress, Stephen W. and Derrick Z. Jackson. *Project Puffin: The Improbable Quest to Bring a Beloved Seabird Back to Egg Rock.* Yale University Press, 2015.

"The Legacy of Hog Island." hogisland.audubon.org., February 2016.

Liebling, Jerome. *The Dickinsons of Amherst.* University Press of New England, 2001.

Longsworth, Polly. *Austin and Mabel: The Amherst Affair & Love Letters of Austin Dickinson and Mabel Loomis Todd.* Farrar, Straus, & Giroux, 1984.

_____. *The World of Emily Dickinson: A Visual Biography.* Norton, 1990.

Lyons, James W. "Appraisal Report and Valuation Analysis: Property of Mrs. Millicent Todd Bingham Situated at Hog Island, Bremen, Maine." August 17, 1953.

Marx, Leo. *The Machine in the Garden: Technology and the Pastoral Ideal in America.* Oxford University Press, 1964.

Mathews, F. Schuyler. *Field book of American Wild Flowers.* Knickerbocker Press, 1902. Sterling Publishing reprint, 2001.

McBride, Bunny and Harald E. L. Prins. *Indians in Eden: Wabanakis and Rusticators on Maine's Mount Desert Island, 1840s–1920s.* Down East, 2009.

McDowell, Marta. *Emily Dickinson's Gardens: A Celebration of a Poet and Gardener.* McGraw Hill, 2005.

McLane, Charles B. *Islands of the Mid-Maine Coast: Muscongus Bay and Monhegan Island.* Vol. 3. The Island Institute. Tilbury House, 1992.

Merchant, Carolyn, ed. *Major Problems in American Environmental History: Documents and Essays.* Heath, 1993.

Miller, Samuel L. *History of the Town of Waldoboro, Maine.* Emerson, 1910.

Minton, Tyree G. *The History of the Nature-Study Movement and Its Role in the Development of Environmental Education.* Excerpt from doctoral dissertation. University of Massachusetts, 1980.

Misch, Anthony. "Reanimating the 1882 Transit of Venus." *Sky & Telescope,* July 2012.

Morton, Duryea. *Audubon Camp in Maine Opening Program, 1971–1977.* Video/DVD, unpublished.

_____. *Who Lives in a Field.* Douglas Howland, illustrator. Coward-McCann, 1959.

_____. *Young Naturalist's Handbook.* Audubon Naturalist Society of the Central Atlantic States, 1960.

Murphy, Robert Cushman. *Land Birds of America.* Photography by Allan D. Cruickshank and Helen G. Cruickshank. McGraw-Hill, 1973.

Murray, William H. H. *Adventures in the Wilderness.* The Adirondack Museum and Syracuse University Press, 1989.

Nash, Roderick. *Wilderness and the American Mind.* Yale University Press, 1967.

National Audubon Society. *Audubon: 100 Years of Conservation: The Story of Audubon.* Video. 2005.

Nicholson, William. *Amherst.* Simon and Schuster, 2015.

Nijhuis, Michelle. "Comeback! A puffin success story." *Smithsonian,* June 2010.

Orr, Oliver H., Jr. *Saving American Birds: T. Gilbert Pearson and the Founding of the Audubon Movement.* University Press of Florida, 1992.

Parke, Rob. Personal email. July 14, 2008.

Peavey, Elizabeth. "Going Whole Hog on Hog Island." *Down East,* July 1999.

The Poetry of Emily Dickinson. Readers Guide. National Endowment for the Arts. The Big Read series, 2010.

Popova, Maria. "What to look for during a total solar eclipse: Mabel Loomis Todd's poetic 19th-century guide to totality, with help from Emily Dickinson." brainpickings.org., August 9, 2017.

Perspectives on Conservation: Essays on America's Natural Resources. Johns Hopkins Press, 1958.

Peterson, Roger Tory. *All Things Reconsidered: My Birding Adventures.* Houghton Mifflin, 2006.

_____. "The Maine Story." *Bird Watcher's Digest,* November–December 1986.

Rasenberger, Jim. *America, 1908.* Scribner, 2007.

_____. "1908." *Smithsonian,* January 2008.

Ridington, Candace. *Rubicon: The Love Story of Emily Dickinson's Brother, Austin, and Mabel Todd, the Woman Who Saved Emily's Poetry.* Arlington Press, 1998.

Roosevelt, Eleanor. "My Day" newspaper columns. United Features Syndicate, August 14, 1936, and August 28, 1951.

Roosevelt, Theodore. "Conservation as a National Duty" (speech text). Governor's Conference on the Conservation of Natural Resources, May 13, 1908, http://voicesofdemocracy.umd.edu/theodore-roosevelt-conservation-as-a-national-duty-speech-text/

Rosenthal, Elizabeth J. *Birdwatcher: The Life of Roger Tory Peterson.* Lyons Press, 2008.

Ryden, Kent. *Landscape with Figures: Nature and Culture in New England.* American Life and Land Series. University of Iowa Press, 2001.

Sanger, David. "Ancient Times in the Hockomock Point Area: Archaeology at the Todd Site." University of Maine, undated/unpublished, http://hogisland.audubon.org/documents/ancient-times-hockomock-point-david-sanger.

Schaefer, Thomas J. *"The Epic of Hog": The Todd-Bingham Family and the Establishment of the Audubon Camp in Maine.* Master of Humanities program, Wright State University, 1985.

_____. "The Reach of the Humanities." fohi.org. *Voices Through Time* segment.

Schuman, Jo Miles and Joanna Bailey Hodgman, ed. *A Spicing of Birds: Poems by Emily Dickinson.* Wesleyan University Press, 2010.

Sears, Paul B. "The Audubon Camp Philosophy." *Audubon,* March–April 1954.

Sewall, Richard B. *The Life of Emily Dickinson.* Farrar, Straus & Giroux, 1974.

Shain, Charles and Samuella Shain, ed. *The Maine Reader: The Down East Experience from 1614 to the Present.* David R. Godine, 1991.

Smith, David C. *A History of Lumbering in Maine: 1861–1960.* University of Maine Studies #93. University of Maine Press, 1972.

Sottili, Carol. "The Maine Course." *Washington Post,* August 8, 2004.

Speh, Chris. "The Hog Island Experience." Personal reflection, unpublished. July 2005. Follow-up email, June 2006.

_____. "Willow's remembrance." Personal reflection, undated/unpublished.

Stahl, Jasper J. *History of Old Broad Bay and Waldoboro. Vol. Two: The Nineteenth and Twentieth Centuries.* Bond Wheelwright Company, 1956.

Stout, Prentice K. "Helen Cruickshank." *Bird Watcher's Digest,* January–February 1994.

Thaxter, Celia. *Drift-Weed.* Houghton, Osgood, and Co., 1879.

_____. Selections from *An Island Garden.* From *At Home on This Earth: Two Centuries of U.S. Women's Nature Writing.* Lorraine Anderson and Thomas S. Edwards, ed. University Press of New England, 1941.

"The Puffins Await You!" *Bird-Lore,* May–June 1936.

Treat, Dorothy. "June comes to Hog Island." *Audubon,* July–August 1941.

_____. Unpublished correspondence with John H. Baker. December 1963.

Tupper, Asa D. "Dr. James M. Todd: One of Boothbay Harbor's great benefactors." *Boothbay Register,* undated.

Vogt, William. "We're Coming Back!" *Bird-Lore,* July–August 1936.

Vosburgh, John. "Our Maine Camp." *Audubon,* March–April 1963.

Walker, Barbara. "Hog Island 1936." *Wing Beat.* Clearwater (Florida) Audubon Society, October–November 2008.

Ware, Leslie B. "Grassroots Television." *Audubon,* January 1986.

Weidensaul, Scott. *Of a Feather: A Brief History of American Birding.* Harcourt, 2007.

_____. "IGAD! Attention Must Be Paid." *Bird Watcher's Digest,* May–June 2020.

"Wilbur Wright: A Life of Consequences." Wright State University Libraries Special Collections and Archives, January 2012.

Wiley, Farida A. *Ferns of Northeastern United States: Illustrations and Descriptions of All Known Species in the New England and Middle Atlantic States.* Dover, 1936 and 1964.

Winslow, Helen M. "The Story of the Woman's Club Movement." *New England Magazine,* July 1908.

Wolff, Cynthia Griffin. *Emily Dickinson.* Alfred A. Knopf, 1987.

Woodard, Colin. "Talk of Maine: Saving Hog Island." *Down East,* April 2010.

_____. *The Lobster Coast: Rebels, Rusticators, and the Struggle for a Forgotten Coast*. Penguin, 2004.

Young, Terence. "The Minister Who Invented Camping in America: How William H. H. Murray's accidental bestseller launched the country's first outdoor craze." Smithsonian.com, October 17, 2017.

Recordings of Hog Island Proceedings via National Audubon Society (Audio Tapes)

July 10, 1950. **Millicent Todd Bingham.** "History of Audubon Camp in Maine Given to Campers in the Fish House at Hog Island."

July 26, 1972. **Carl W. Buchheister**. "Audubon Camp in Maine."

Summer 1975. **Carl and Harriet Buchheister.** "History of the Audubon Camp in Maine."

Summer 1976, Final Field Trip Session IV. "**Dedication Allan D. Cruickshank Sanctuary**, Eastern Egg Rock, Muscongus Bay, Maine."

July 28, 1977. **Carl W. Buchheister**. "History of the Audubon Camp in Maine given to campers in the Fish House at Hog Island. **Duryea Morton** (camp director) gives the introduction."

July 18, 1978. **Carl W. Buchheister**. "Early History."

June 25, 1982. **Carl W. Buchheister** and **Stephen Kress**. "National Audubon Society's President's Council Meeting, Hog Island."

August 14, 1984. **Carl W. Buchheister**. "History of the Audubon Camp in Maine given to 3rd Session campers in the Fish House at Hog Island. **Dr. Stephen Kress** (camp director) gives the introduction."

Interviews Recorded by the author

Benz, Seth. Camden, Maine. September 9, 2017.

Buchheister, Carl W. Carol Woods, North Carolina. March 28, 1983.

Cadbury, Bart. Cushing, Maine. August 6, 1982.

Cadbury, Bart and Ginny. Hanover, New Hampshire. July 7–8, 2004.

Cadbury, Bart Memorial. Hog Island, Maine. June 15, 2005.

Cadbury, Ginny and Betsy Cadbury and Art Borror. Pittsfield, New Hampshire. April 3, 2007.

Johansen, Joe. Brooksville, Florida. March 28, 2005.

Kress, Steve. Ithaca, New York. May 7, 2015.

Massonneau, Mary Carol. Burlington, Vermont. September 26, 2006.

Morse, Doug and Elsie. Providence, Rhode Island. April 5, 2007.

Morton, Duryea and Peggy. Interviewed by Tom Schaefer and David Klinger. Williamsburg, Virginia. October 17, 2005.

Roushdy, Juanita. Bremen, Maine. September 9, 2017.

Salmansohn, Pete. Hog Island Audubon Camp, Bremen, Maine. September 10, 2017.

Appendix A

The Epic of Hog: Sketches of the Natural World

A series of unpublished, undated essays
by Mabel Loomis Todd

Osprey

When we got back to the island in early June, we heard from the permanent inhabitants many stories of the ospreys which had built a nest on the point nearest to us. And the next time we went for some of the delicious ice cold water from the hidden spring near the point, we had ocular and aural proof of the ospreys' nearness. They strenuously objected to our coming to their neighborhood, and when we tried to see their nest a little nearer, we were distinctly told in fierce bird language to retreat. Indeed, if I had been much smaller and not strong, as a little child, I should have been genuinely alarmed at venturing in their vicinity. As it was, we did retreat, for that time, but we continued to feel a great interest in our vigilant neighbors.

Always there was one of the pair in evidence, on watchful guard, and when we continued to advance, he or she would be reinforced by the mate, both of whom combined to try to drive us away. Sometimes, though, we came just as one or the other parent was arriving at the nest with spoil from the sea, and then we watched the great bird fly to the huge nest in the very top of the Japanese-looking pine, there to feed the row of little heads, apparently all mouth, with the hapless fish tweaked from his peaceful haunts in the quiet sea. As the sweet, still sunset came on over the reflecting sea and above the dreaming hills, the pair abandoned their warlike attitude, and permitting us to float undisturbed near the point, curved with great sweeps silently around us, and became one with the calm evening.

Gradually they became aware that we should not injure them. And then we were able to see the cruel curve of their efficient beaks, and learned the white and beautiful spots under their strong wings. The little ones in the great nest grew apace. Finally there was a row of wondering sons and daughters standing up bravely on the edge of the nest, and resting rather uncertainly upon newly discovered legs. And just about this epoch we had a genuine fright. A young neighbor on the main land, unduly efficient with a gun, showed us proudly one evening the helpless remains of a large hawk of his killing.

"Our osprey!" we exclaimed with terror. But the neighbor was quite certain it was not our odd friend, showing us his beautiful tawny color, the unbroken tint on the under side of the wings, and adding that it was a famous hen-hawk, the enemy which had haunted the chicken yard for many a long evening, the successful poacher on friendly preserves. So we returned to our happy observations of "Osprey Point" as we termed the home of the pervasive family, and found that the whole family had flown. While we were sitting in the boat, disconsolate, an episode in the sky was approaching. Gracefully, slowly, in long, beautiful curves, came five splendid birds, even majestic in their sweep, aiming for the deserted nest in the top of the great pine, and as we watched, one by one they alighted on its edge, settled with a huge folding of wings into its depths, and as the large round moon began to show through the trees, there was only the shape of the nest left to our eager eyes. The babies had grown, almost in a night, to the parental size and fierceness.

Our friend the artist had watched them with undisguised admiration, and one happy morning we came into our living room for a whiff of the wood fire we so enjoy, and there on the gable wall stood the king-like osprey in all his magnificence, the rough pine tree under him, and his attitude of parental watchfulness as he alighted on the nest, reproduced in all its glory. The artist's art had preserved for us for all time this magnificent incident.

Cobwebs

The Spider as an Artist
Has never been employed -
Though his surpassing Merit
is freely certified

By every Broom and Bridget
Throughout a Christian Land -
Neglected Son of Genius
I take thee by the Hand
—Emily Dickinson

Though we have little use for brooms, and quite none for Bridgets, we do have the most remarkable artists among spiders that any camp ever boasted. And glad indeed am I that no ignorant brooms lie in wait for the exquisite workmanship that decks bush and tree and every unlikely vantage point on those wet mornings when we are proceeding from one house to another.

I suppose the charming cobwebs are there on ordinary mornings as well, but they do not show their beauties except in fogs, or some other kind of dampness which brings out the almost infinitesimal lines and angles and mechanical perfectness which make of them such surpassing works of art.

Another subject which I ought to have pursued years ago! Only—how was a young girl to pursue to specialist attainment all or even half the subjects which enthrall her! Botany, ornithology, biology, geology, the lighter aspects of geography, ethnology, anthropology, archeology, fishes, sea mosses, lichens, mushrooms, spiders, butterflies—all the myriad subjects which make of this wonderful island a compendium of no less than half the exciting subjects in the world! But even to notice each exquisite object as one passes gives delight and satisfying happiness even without the perfect knowledge which would make of them tale-bearers of a long past to ears attuned to their story.

For many days we watched the "boojum," a peculiar spider which issued forth from his hole in the ground with great regularity when the sun was shining, holding aloft in his "paws" a large round mass which we at once decided was a package of eggs, held with tenacious care, and turned slowly once in a few minutes toward the friendly sun. And "boojum" we continued to call him for weeks. He appeared extremely timid, for when some one approached and had come even within fifteen or twenty feet, he seemed to have an uncanny premonition of their nearness, and proceeded to disappear with extreme celerity into his hole, eggs and all. Then if we wished to see him again it behooved us to sit in complete quietude sometimes for no less than half an hour, or even longer, when he would be seen emerging with much watchfulness, putting his precious burden again directly in the sun's rays, and ever on the watch for some other supposedly enemy approach.

Some weeks later I chanced upon a scientific description of our own "boojum" which remained no longer distinguished by that somewhat disrespectful cognomen, when we had learned that his proper name was *Lycosa pictu*, a variety of the wolf spiders which are fairly abundant in our northern latitudes. The bag of eggs was supported by the spinnerets, or the two very short forward protuberances which might be supposed extra legs if one did not know that spiders have eight legs—something my desultory reading had informed me long ago. When soft rain has filled the woods with dampness, and all the wonderful cobwebs have caught the moisture, one can realize the beauty of those airy structures, but they are hardly apprehended at other times. This morning I lay upon my back, in rest from some arduous labor, looking up into the sweet greenness of the spruce trees above me, when my eye caught an ordinary, rough cobweb, with a heavy gray watcher in the center, his circle imperfect, broken in spots, but apparently effective for victims. And then, far above, a wonderful circle, with no less than twenty or thirty spokes, their connecting lines as even as machinery could have made them, with a tiny, almost invisible little master of the dainty thing staying in the center, and watching, I suppose, as vigilantly as his coarser neighbor for the unwary passer in the sunshine. At first all I could see of the delicate connecting lines between the spokes of the wheel was a faint grayness, indicative of some manufactured substance, but speedily it resolved itself into the separate little lines, carefully placed in a circular pattern. The marvelous little wheel swayed in the sunshine, and a myriad exquisite tints strayed across the whole. Violet, purple, bronze, and occasionally copper in a glowing hint, made the lovely thing fairy-like. Two stout cables on each side connected it and made it stable and firm, and on the top one other anchored it to the spruce tree which was that spider's whole world. Dainty, elusive thing! Looking with eyes now attuned to the delicacy, I soon spied six others as perfect, as beautiful and as colorful as this first one, only high up in the tree, away from casual injury. Sometimes in crossing one of our well-worn paths in the woods, a cobweb of surprising toughness obstructs our passage, and stopping to remove it from our persons, we are forcibly reminded of the immensely tougher threads of the huge spiders in and near Sumatra, where we once spent several months trying to catch the elusive eclipse of the sun. I often took rather daring walks into the jungle of the little island of Singkep, where my husband's telescopes and other astronomical instruments were carefully set up for what was to be the longest eclipse ever observed—six minutes and thirty seconds. Before the celestial happening, however, the curious aspects of the lovely tropical island and its inhabitants were never-endingly wonderful and beautiful to me.

One night at our dinner, commonly served about nine o'clock in the evening, I noticed a little bird, one in constant flight during the day about the house of the Manager of the tin company, who was our host on that delightful trip. This bird had retired for the night, swinging himself happily in a corner of the dining room, open on all sides to jungle murmurs and the soft darkness of the tropics. What was that little bird sitting on? What supported him apparently without foothold in the dusky corner of the room?

After dinner, and looking at him curiously during the remainder of the elaborate meal, as he swung happily back and forth, I went over to him and investigated. He was sitting in a cobweb! Dear little visitor, who wisely improved such opportunities as presented themselves, for a completely home-like environment!

The Little Lids of the Winkle
(No Relative of Nathaniel)*

Walking along the highest ridge of the island one day, I found what was apparently a most dainty shell, about an inch long, of a beautiful soft brown in color, highly polished, and lying on a delicate moss background. The first one of the kind that I had seen I was naturally greatly interested and took it back to the camp after the walk was finished.

A few days later another of the same fairy variety was found, but this time not on a ridge of the island; instead, down on the shore, close to the incoming tide, shining delightfully, and almost transparent, like the first one. I thought I had made a great discovery, and for many days thereafter I kept a wary eye out for a beautiful, shining thing, but found no more for a long time.

The third one was found in a most unlikely place for shells, and I could hardly think it one, but still it possessed the absolute character of a sea shell so unmistakably that I still believed it one. It was in the deep woods, a delicious dark spot among the spruces, lying amid a clump of mosses almost buried from sight.

A year or two passed, during which I found possibly eight or ten more, each guarded like a precious possession, and held as specimens of the riches of Hog. They were, each of them, found in places differing greatly—on ledges high up above the water, on mossy banks, on sharp rocks, sometimes in the waves just breaking on the shore, or amid the riches of the sea, just above the up-reaching tide, and some like the first, in the depths of the island forests. At last I began to be curious about my exquisite shells, and I sought the fisherman lore of the region.

"Oh, them's winkles!" said the old salt of whom I asked about them.

"Winkles?" I said in some wonder.

"Yes, winkles the crows has et," he said. "I'll bring you some next time I'm goin' by."

And he brought me a bucket of the pretty crustacean on his next advent. They had wound themselves out of their little houses, until all the soft, most exquisitely smooth flesh lay in the water, and on the outer end were the same brown "shells" I had ignorantly found.

A few days' study of the odd guests made me comparatively familiar with their uncomplicated existence. They wove themselves in and out of their curled houses most deliberately, the little lids occasionally shutting them in apparently solidly, when they presented the appearance of the periwinkles I had known slightly for many years, but never especially cared to become intimate with, having completely missed the one charming beauty of their life. Now the excitement of studying them was a reproach to all the careless years.

The crows, which live happily in the fastnesses of Hog, are largely responsible for these beautiful "shells" being scattered all over the island. Taking the outer shell of the winkle, his whole house in fact, in their beak, the crow flies with his victim into the interior of the island until he finds a good, hard rock below, when he drops the poor victim down hard on the unresponsive ledge, which cracks the outer shell completely, and the crow proceeds to enjoy a comfortable meal, of course not swallowing the little brown lid, which the poor winkle had always relied upon for his protection from enemies, but which can not fight crows in their uncanny knowledge of the ways of their victims. Sometimes the sea-gulls take winkles up on undesired trips in the sky, and they invariably drop them on ledges at sea, near the shore, but the ones in the island are chiefly the subjects of the crows.

No matter how weather-stained and cracked, how thoroughly discouraged the outer white shell of the winkle may get through years of lying about on the island, the little brown lid remains as dainty as a lady's jewel, always brilliantly polished, always delicately marked and curved, and always curved in the same direction, an opposite turn being as rare as a four-leaved clover—even rarer than my finding of those irresistible tokens of good luck, in a so-called luckless world. They are as beautiful as the finest tortoise shell, and they really look as if they had been carved very wonderfully from the brown semi-precious shell.

Dear little lids of the unhappy winkle! You have delighted me for many a year, and even yet I cannot resist an upward leap of the heart whenever I see the beautiful gleam of your shining shell in the midst of—who can say what foreign surroundings!

There were the broken shells of mussels which had changed to the most exquisite shades of pale blue in their unexpected island retirement, occasionally one of a beautiful lavender, which gleamed among the foreign greens like some rare jewel; and there were the helpless claws of discouraged crabs, as well as their backs, entire, and the sun-dried white of clam shells, which fail to bring any suggestion of pathos in their untimely end. And among all the welter of the dining remains of these careless crows were the broken coils of the periwinkles. Think of the poor little twists of feeling! When they felt themselves jerked up into the unfamiliar ether, they would have closed their little houses up tightly, shutting their lids down in the vain attempt to offset the accident, so terribly attacking them; and then the tragedy came upon them and they were dropped from a great height upon the cruel rocks below, all the lids of all the winkles helpless to avert the woe. There they lay, bleaching in the sun, all over the island, but the little lids, the only clear, beautiful untouched relic of all the pain and disappointment.

After this I found myself looking about for the broken tokens of the winkle, and then, in the same general region, somewhere I always came upon the lovely brown lid. I have over a hundred of them now, of different sizes, and I feel richer for my collection.

[***Editor's note:** Nathaniel Winkle, character in *The Pickwick Papers*, the first novel of Charles Dickens.]

Jellyfish

We always knew that the island is like Paradise in many of its delightful characteristics, but this morning when I came to the little lobster house, I found the beach literally paved with shining crystal. It was like a pavement of cobble stones, only instead of the unknowing stone "whose coat of elemental brown, A passing universe put on," the individual stones were of the purest, most transparent clear glass. As the rising sun shown more and more clearly on this fairy floor, iridescent colors shot here and there making the whole beautiful substance more exquisite than imagination could have pictured.

I stood, looking at it in silence for a long time; finally it occurred to me to examine into the texture and substance of this wonderful gift to the beauty, already so compelling that I can hardly do the few necessary things to the houses day by day. And it proved to be merely jelly fishes, in the regiment of individuals, massed in such numbers as to defy computation, but I did take a general survey with the idea of estimating their number. Seven hundred was the smallest number I could assign, and that was on only a part of the little beach.

Poor bits of unknowing, unfeeling protoplasm! Before this we had watched them floating about in the sea when we were sailing, had pitied the stranded ones, uselessly, I suppose, and had admired the giant members of their family, floating in majesty in royal crimson, their powers of propulsion very active, and countless little feathers and threads of crimson in constant motion, with what use we knew not, but here was the jelly-fish story, spread for our delectation upon our very beach!

They lasted all day, and with diminished glory into the next day. Then gradually they melted from sight, and so largely is their substance composed of water that as they melted there was almost no residue from their curious, useless little lives to pollute the beach, or leave any indication to eye or other sense of their wholesale stranding.

We have had no heavenly pavement since, but the memory of the past glory does irradiate the beach.

Island Tragedies

We have very few snakes on the island. The great fire of eighty or ninety years ago seems to have disposed of the numerous community which is apt to haunt country places, and which gives such perennial fear to old ladies who take their summers in really rural resorts. But on the island, we now have only a few dainty little green ones, my delight. I always remember as a little girl, my exultation of spirit when dear Celia Thaxter told me she loved them, and when some of our men friends related with much perturbation of spirit how she often used to twine them into necklaces and bracelets to wear at the hotel dances, when their little heads would be raised in somewhat alarmed curiosity at the music and the pressure of a crowd. Her partners had need to be men of courage, indeed, said those men!

I have loved them for years, and always watched them on the island with genuine interest. But a few days ago I came upon one of them most cruelly murdered, in the pathway, his little head crushed out of all likeness to his pretty self as I knew him. Some guest of ours, of our own friends, had committed the crime, and gloried in it, when I tried to find the villain. Poor little green beauty—I grieve for you!

The next island tragedy was really an accident. The June days had been very perfect, each one like an ocean cameo, but one night we heard the rain descending, and in the morning we were really glad to find our barrels partly filled with water. For two days we enjoyed the feeling that we were not really dependent upon the spring, a short distance down the coast, but had the rare water at our very doors. And then one morning as I went happily down to the beach house for my morning cereal, there lay a quiet little body, completely drowned in the rain barrel! One of our men speedily rescued what was left, which was very wet and bedraggled, but showed a new kind of inhabitant of the island. It was a flying squirrel, with the tiny wing-like forepaws, the curious back ones, and the bushy tail, alas, not bushy that morning, but the whole little animal so discouraged that I could not bear his sad effect, and turned away with a genuine sigh for a life which I did not know at all, and would have been so glad to study and appropriate for my own knowledge. I remembered the huge flying-foxes which used to haunt our bungalow in the island of Singkep, almost exactly upon the other side of the world from this domestic island, and of his really terrifying descents as twilight settled into the swift tropical night. We shot one before leaving there, and found him over four feet from tip to tip. His thick hair was of a reddish brown, and his head curiously like that of a fox. Poor little flying squirrel, the first of his kind on the island, and to die so unheralded and unknown!

But the third tragedy which I must tell is a strange one. This morning I went out in a rowboat with the Master of Ceremonies, and saw after a while ahead of us a good, thick plank of pine. As pine is a rare fire-wood for us on an island of spruce, I tried to rescue my treasure trove, and finally brought it into the boat in triumph. But suddenly I saw on the boat's floor just at my feet, a tiny elongated sphere of green which looked exactly like one of the little floating bladders of the seaweed, only greener. It had detached itself from the stick, and suddenly giving a gasp like something alive, it gave me a galvanic shock. It was alive! Less than a quarter of an inch in length, this was apparently a perfect fish, with the agonized mouth of his kind when caught, and the convulsive tail. His eyes too were curiously bright and terrified, and a brilliant yellow. Fearing to pick him up, lest I should crush this minute stranger, I quickly took two small sticks from the pine I had just rescued with so much pride, and improvising a stretcher with them, I got him up on them and carefully conveyed him to the boat's side, just as he gave what I tremendously fear was his death quiver, and into the friendly water I laid him. But he went upside down, and his tiny white stomach and gleaming yellow eyes formed my view for two or three minutes, while I watched for his possible resuscitation. I fear that never came, and he sank from my view.

The unknown little green fish was the tiniest tragedy I have had on the island. Another being of our largest game. I was up very early one exquisite morning, simply "studying the weather" as the Master of Ceremonies amiably calls it when I am engaged in no visible occupation, but this time

I had just been visited by a hermit thrush, an arrival so unexpected and wonderful that I had remained in utter quietness for no less than fifteen minutes. This rare bird, like the other inhabitants of our island, stands in no fear of his human neighbors, and is friendly and dear under all our goings and comings. I had just started out again when there hopped into my ken one of our numerous rabbits. Not really intimate with that family, I went toward him to gently frighten him from the vicinity of my freshly starting ferns and other tempting objects to rabbits' teeth, when I saw that he was in a different state of mind and health from his ordinary condition. As I approached he retreated by one feeble bound, and then curled up in the sweet fern, with visibly beating heart and tremulous ears. Going once more toward him, he made one other faint retreat, and settled down that time for all his remaining minutes. His large, slightly protruding black eyes gradually closed, and as I looked, his brown fur settled down in a relaxed sort of way, and the rabbit had gone on—somewhere?

And a really sad little tragedy happened close to our living room. Coming in from a lovely sail one bright afternoon, I heard a mighty confusion of bird voices, as at least four white-throated sparrows were flying about madly, and attacking, or attempting to, one wicked little baby squirrel or chipmunk, who had actually taken from the nest one tiny birdlet, evidently just hatched, and was trying to make away with it. I rushed in and startled the small thief so much that he dropped his helpless prey and scampered off, while the little mass of frightened soft feathers with its poor little heart almost shaking its life out lay at our mercy on the soft moss. Picking it up tenderly we tried to smooth its tiny garments, and warm the little frightened body. After a good while, we laid it on another part of the moss and tried to ask its parents and friends to come to its rescue. They had stopped their vociferous cries already, as if they recognized us as attempting to help, and were flying about us and the baby bird. What finally became of the victim of that wretched little chipmunk never transpired. A few minutes later we went back, but no birds were to be seen or heard. The little one was gone, and peace and quiet were restored. I hope the parent birds had carried their baby off safely and that he will always remember his early adventure.

Hermit Crab

We came upon a tiny little cove the other day, which seemed the home of a forest of small hermit crabs, living happily but not quiescently in the shells of the snails. Just as we were taking our dory to go out, I noticed this community, and thereafter any trip was unthinkable. The snail shells were of different sizes, and their inhabitants correspondingly fierce. They were fascinating! After a whole afternoon spent with them, I tried taking one little crab out from his appropriated dwelling. He fought tremendously to retain his home, summarily taken from some innocent dweller, but I held him and threw the abandoned shell into the water. After a time I put the defenseless animal himself down into the clear and shallow water. He seemed bewildered, and went about sideways, without apparent purpose. After a moment, however, he seemed to understand his position, and began to hunt for another house. But he was apparently not a desired neighbor by his kind. Every shell he approached scuttled away with immense speed and he became somewhat ostracized. One or two, larger than he, thought to attack him, and drive him away, but he fought them. There were apparently no empty shells to be had. I left him still house hunting, with a fellow feeling for his perplexity.

Star Fish

Why have I not devoted my life to star fishes! They are exquisite, color as well as shape. The other day we went to Harbor Island for the day, and after luncheon we went out on the splendid rocks which protect the island from the ever-encroaching sea. First, I noticed hundreds of perfectly contented little snails, all in their gorgeous houses of yellow, shades of brown, white and other dainty tints, all clustered on rocks where the retreating waves washed completely over them every few seconds and poured off in iridescent tints of rainbow beauty. Then projected itself into my conscious vision rocks a bit lower, nearer the waves, covered with the beautiful star fishes. Their colors were truly amazing. Several of brilliant vermillion, two or three delicate green, a dozen of lavender in varied shades, and finally one which was a real purple of most dainty shade, which, while I looked, resolved itself into pink, turning, while I gazed at him enthralled, to the most airy lilac, finally showing all the tints at once in rainbow colors the most wonderful.

Waldoboro

At low tide in Waldoboro the river is but a small stream running out from under the bridge. Huge rocks fill its channel and scraps of thrown away material—the American method of disposing of discarded substances— may be descried all about. Down to the slippery and wet bed of the stream, came five little boys and a dog. Sticks were in their hands, and evidently an adventure of supreme interest was imminent. Three of the boys were little ragged town products, and the dog evidently belonged to them, but the other two were very nicely and neatly dressed, one in a pretty scarlet sweater, the other in a wide, handsome collar but they proceeded with their companions to attempt a crossing of the channel, albeit the bridge but was a few feet distant. Evidently the "going" was extremely slippery, as even the rough little shavers in front found great difficulty in keeping on their feet, but the little city children were manifestly appalled, and when the taller one, in the wide collar, fell flat into a deep pool, and emerging, shook his hands helplessly, and tried to get the water out of his clothing, his smaller companion just having tripped and gone down on his knees, both stopped, and with a long look at each other, unanimously started on a backward path. Gibes and definite remarks from their companions and the dog, served only to accentuate their retreat, and when these suc- cessful adventurers reached the other shore and cried out triumphantly, their voices but served to hasten the little city boys on their homeward march, which was never rapid and punctuated with many falls. Finally, I looked at the river, and its channel was full with the incoming tide. I hope the little city boys reached home and clean clothes in time for luncheon!

At Waldoboro I always let my good friends do all the shopping, while I sit in the boat or look about to see the many queer things that happen, even in that sleepy little town. This morning the tide was most horridly low—our boat scraped in the mud, and when we tied up to the float we were not less than twelve to fourteen feel below the land level. So I came up, and sat on the high granite at the foot of the steep hill. Very soon a little row boat arrived, with a gentleman in dark glasses, a shirt turned away at the collar, and short sleeves, puttees on his legs, and a very efficient manner. He picked up four fine wide boards lying at the top of the steps descending to the float, shouldered them, and entered his row boat with his property. Crossing the stream, he made a tough job of climbing up the wharf across, but finally accomplishing it, I saw him toiling through waist-high grass, going I could not imagine where. Presently, however, he came down nearly opposite me and stopped at a miserable, tumble-down boat house, at which he looked for a few minutes with much pride. One side had fallen from the perpendicular, the front toward me was largely open to the weather, it was black from years of disuse, the most hopelessly gone-to-decay edifice I have ever looked at. Laying his handsome boards down, he proceeded to look over the front openings. Taking a hatchet in his hand, he sounded the rickety front of the building and picking up the widest board of his new supply, he measured its length across the widest hole, driving in several nails with commendable energy. Then he walked away, almost into the muddy water before it, looking at it lovingly. Going quickly back, he nailed on a second board, then picked up several black and dirty (of course) boards lying beside the house, and with his hatchet nailed one of them on the side, letting its superior length project outward two feet or more. Suddenly he dived into his property by a tiny little hole on one side, the sound of vigorous pounding emerging thence stridently. Once more he emerged, his manly figure enlivened the landscape, and he put a third board across the front. My laughter apparently reached him over the narrow and muddy stream, for he stopped his exertions and looked across severely at me. Then shouldering his fourth board he strode away, up the hill, designing I thought to save it at his home, wherever that might be. But he thought better of that ere long, for turning abruptly, he began to come down the hill again, and diving into the small hole on the side of this gorgeous house, the long board apparently determined not to go also, but finally prevailed upon to go in with the master, he speedily came out, both hands free except for the hatchet. Going up the hill once more, with pride in his heart at the made-over boat house, which now had a corner, and three boards on the supposable front in addition to the half dozen black and worn-out ones which had been there before, he turned and surveyed me loftily. And then went home.

Two years later I had occasion again to wait on the high granite ledge, opposite the made-over boat house. But the landscape was empty of that architectural triumph. Even the weedy site retained no memory of the crazy structure, and as for my triumphant gentleman builder, he too seemed non-existent. Alas for the temporary character of artificial adjuncts of the scenery!

Barnacles

Barnacles are truly winning friends! And not for their society conversation, either. Nor their haste of motion; in fact, one hardly realizes any motion in the charming creatures, until he happens, as I did, to be looking into the water quietly when the tide is barely over the rocks where they live in great numbers, and there, when the sun strikes, you may see the tiny mouths open like a soft white flower to catch any food which may pass that way. Softly feeling the water, less than half an inch long, you may see their tentacles in the sweet morning air waving their share in the glory of living. Stirless from their rock home, they nevertheless have the power of motion and of joy in it. I can almost feel their delight in the lovely soft sunshine which strikes down to their dwelling place in these perfect September mornings and wish there were some sound they might make to speak of it.

Butterflies

Comparatively few gorgeous butterflies inhabit Hog Island. Of course, the small and bright yellow ones flit about in the sunshine, the big brown ones are frequent callers, and the tiny blue variety is conspicuous.

The Heronry

I have been to our amazing heronry! It was discovered accidentally a month or two since, but this was the first time I had actually visited it. Raucous sounds warned me of our nearness, and suddenly we stuck full into view of a wonderful community. The huge fathers and mothers were flying gracefully about high overhead, but the deserted babies were complaining loudly of their desertion. And the babies were just as large as their elders, practically three in each nest, and the number of nests seemed legion. I counted twenty-one, in each of which were standing three youngsters, while one unfortunate, trying to leave his stronghold untimely, had caught by his wing and hung there, high in an old spruce, calling intermittently for assistance. Probably an acre at least was occupied with the myriad nests, and there were many more than the ones I first counted. Beneath was a wilderness of raspberry bushes, whitened with the excreta of the birds, and the trees containing the nests were very ancient specimens of spruce, belonging to the ninety years old contingent, many of them really dead, and all the nests high in air.

Toward evening the parent birds take flight one by one from island shores, aiming in general to the northeast, their silent even majestic passing a feature of our nightly out-of-doors supper. Sometimes they return the same night, sometimes I see them sailing home in the early morning sunlight of my favorite rising time. But the heronry is here, on our own island, a wonderful curiosity not to be lightly investigated or carelessly shown to the uninitiated.

Shakespeare

The calm face of Shakespeare confronts me at every meal. And it is not a painting, either, but carved in the solid rock. He has been a silent friend for years, and seems ever contemplating, without sadness or expectancy, the varied nature pavement at his base. Sometimes the full tide comes even over his chin or above, and often it is out, many feet down the beach; in either case he is unmoved. The high forehead, rather abundant hair on both sides, his deep eyes, a mustache and small goatee, all resemble to an uncanny degree the best and most authentic portraits of the "elder brother of all humanity." It is as if some lover of the great bard had given me a fine representation of his earthly presentment as patron saint of the island.

Sometimes at low tide, I have had to search a bit for the dear and well-remembered countenance, which speedily is found again, placidly gazing downward in the familiar pose. I have called the attention of guests frequently to the remarkable face, who generally say, "Oh, yes! Isn't it curious!" and then speedily forget all about it. To me it is a permanent and trustworthy friend, always there, for years, with the patience of the centuries, waiting, waiting for some denouement as yet unknown to men.

What One Can See Without Turning One's Head

Our artist made the surprising suggestion the other day that he would like to paint my portrait. That had already been done some years since, when I am certain I was much better worth painting than in these latter years. Still, I was flattered, of course, and proceeded, one brilliant morning, to his studio. After studying my face for some time, and trying various positions, he was at last satisfied, and telling me to preserve the pose, proceeded to draw in his happy subject. After nearly an hour of good work, it came into my mind that I was greatly enjoying the view from his north window. I had noticed at first that the mass of superb spruces lay in delicate early morning sunlight which brought out their varied shades of living green, one kind blue-green, almost as beautiful as the Rocky Mountain blue spruce, the other a delightful shade of soft yellow-green, infinitely rich and lovely; while apparently to enhance these warm tints, the gnarled old branches already dead, and the many shades of gray and suggested purple and violet in the sturdy trunks, gave a variety to the silent picture quite unbelievable to one who only saw some trees in his landscape.

Very soon began some of the forest life. A mass of tiny warblers tilted across the big window, all in tints of soft gray, alighting among the heavy foliage for a moment in their morning game. Then, as the weeds were once more quiet, came two delightful little scarlet birds, who played about the great trees as decoratively as possible in apparent joy at the sunshine and gentle breeze. Several times they returned that morning, but between their gay visits arrived a gorgeous butterfly in tints of burnt sienna and white, which fluttered across in eager hurry for some unknown object. Hardly had he disappeared when my eye caught an old friend—a most wonderful spider's web stretched from one tree across an incredible space to another, its iridescent colors glistening in the sunshine as the breeze gently waved its beautiful architecture to and fro. By this time the sunshine had crept around in my picture, illuminating still more woodland spaces, into the depths of which I peered, seeing more and more beauty in every farther glimpse.

Suddenly tilted into view a great dragon fly, his colors almost as varied as those in the cobweb, his irregular flight startlingly swift. As speedily he disappeared. And over the masses of spruce-green swept in dignified slowness three immense shadows, the counterfeit presentment of three gulls in one of their temporary visits to the forests. Later, one of the deliciously snow-white great birds came into actual view, as he flew very quickly across the window, apparently startled by his singular environment. Deep in the forest spaces a blue figure came in sight, the man who serves the island community in a dozen necessary capacities, going this morning to cut and bring into the studio some huge logs for the big stone fireplace. A group of sandpipers almost came in sight, veering off just as they touched the picture in one corner, and a dark brown, this-year's gull tumbled into sight briefly. A flight of tiny yellow birds careened across the view, just as a lovely cloud shadow gently turned the greens into more sombre shadow, and as the sun came out almost immediately, my eye caught the flutter of a long green moss, attached to a nearby tree. In this part of the island there is very little of the picturesque moss which makes of its northeast groves a ghostly gray retreat, residence one could readily believe of many a wood pixie, or subdued nymph, in her old age. The lichens are beautiful here, on tree trunks, and I unconsciously compare and study their varying forms as the shadows change. The sun had warmed all the lovely view into brilliant tints, other warblers were flitting across the trees, the intense blue sky with its freight of deliciously changing white clouds high above, was growing deeper—when suddenly the painter, who had been industriously at work without my conscious apprehension, said, throwing down palette and brushes, "There, that's enough for today," and getting up in surprise from my big chair, I found the first day's results surprisingly like the sitter, whose morning had been so happily filled that she did not know her likeness was actually proceeding all the time.

Hog Island Neighbors

The main shore, across by a ten minutes' row from the island, is inhabited chiefly by retired sea captains or master fishermen and their families. They are all friendly and good companions, I get milk and eggs from them, late in the season fresh vegetables, and apples, but none of the finer fruits, which have to be brought from farther away. Their kitchens are sunny and cheerful apartments, a tea kettle singing domestically on the wood stove, the views almost unbelievably splendid, and the housekeepers glad to see me, and hospitably anxious to give me something very good to eat—which is especially welcome, always. Also I sometimes get fresh fish from these neighbors, or lobsters from the pots all around. Their lives have been lonely, in a sense, and they are really glad to see someone from away, although their experience has made them rather silent of habit. And each is a character, as we call all those who are somewhat different from the average run of commonplace society folk. Cap'n Elisha King, whose vegetables are the best for miles around, is certainly a "character," whose comments on life in general and the peculiarities of humanity are worthy of permanent recording. Moreover, he has his likes and dislikes in the way of food for the body. "Why," he said one day, "I suppose you folks likes riz bread! For me, I'shd jest as soon eat fawg!" And his bright and brisk little old wife has to make baking powder biscuit at every meal for this epicure! And they are exceedingly good rolls, too. But think of it! Every meal!

They make hay in its season, and they go out on the sea, but now only for short runs. And their women are uniformly afraid of boats. They would call on me at once at the island, only that it would involve a row across, and that they wish to avoid. Hereditary fear, I suppose, from the generations of sea experience behind them. One of the men has the voice of a child, as if some little chorister had failed to let his voice descend to its proper tone when the time came. But he is an expert in the ways of the sea, and says he never needs a compass, that he can always "smell out" where he is even in thickest fog or night. We have proved that contention....

[**Editor's note:** *End of this essay lost*]

Near Camp

Very near the living room on Hog is a huge rock, the pride and delight of all the dwellers in the enchanted isle. Like a little hill in the landscape, it stands like the guardian spirit of the inhabitants. Several roots of fine ferns are caught in crevices, greening from year to year, and growing splendidly large. A little spruce has coyly rooted itself on the ultimate apex, a delicate wood daughter, prettily green and graceful. A lovely variety of greenest moss covers most of the rock, and the whole makes a perfect adjunct to the Camp.

Just beyond grow two small spruces, apparently forming the entrance to the large wood beyond, a tiny path passing between them. For years, now, those two little trees have been a joy to me, for on them grows a variety of lichen which has a curious significance. In sunny, dry days it is hardly noticeable, a flat dull gray, appealing little even to me—who loves every manifestation of native growth on the whole big island— but as soon as a fog come up from the sea, and a lovely damp softness embraces every tree in sight, then the mysterious lichen comes at once into its own, for what was an uninteresting drab becomes almost immediately vivid green, and the two little trees are lovely with a sort of ruffled green garment, standing out in relief from their trunks, and turning momently a darker and richer tint. When it really rains it seems absolutely triumphant and grows more beautiful with every passing hour.

I have stood close by those little trees, while the rain softly trickled down my neck, watching the unfolding of the exquisite growth. How I wish that I had made a specialty of lichens, studying them with a delightful old professor whose happy theme they were long years ago!

Mushrooms

In August the mushrooms come, a mighty army, beginning modestly in July, and sprinkling dark recesses in the woods with wonderful colors especially if much rain prevails. But as the season advances, and hot August days come on, so many varieties spring up in a night that I am half bewildered with the amount.

Of course we have them on the Camp table, but I am sure of only three varieties, the most delicious being the dark yellow chanterelles which can be cooked in many delightful ways, and, as health experts tell us, a handful are equal to a pound of beefsteak; and the fairy white coral variety, which we do not so often use, while the big white puffballs make a most succulent third in our list of known edible mushrooms.

But for merely decorative effect, there are literally hundreds filling the wood spaces. Around old stumps grow dozens of tiny brown ones, differing in size; and a still smaller kind grow trustfully in masses where sunshine occasionally comes. The gorgeous red and yellow umbrellas lighten dark nooks where no flowers blossom, opening their canopies gradually in two or three days, from tiny ones their umbrellas almost closed, to the wide, flat glories of color; and beautiful scarlet ones of the same shape are diversified by shades of pink and dull crimson. Some huge ones, which turn dark brown as they reach maturity, really startle one with their giant shades through the otherwise innocent woods. The "fairy ring" mushroom, with the pretty name which indicates its usual growth in a circle, is also edible. Indeed, there are so many more of the edible variety than of the non-delicious or poisonous kinds, that one is practically certain not to venture upon dangerous ground, at least here in the island. But we do have the deadly amanita ("destroying angel," or *Amanita verna*), the pure white, apparently friendly mushroom, which is of such intensely poisonous character that death after eating is practically certain. I give it a wide berth in our lovely woods. The beautiful non-edible yet not deadly poisonous "Jack-o-lantern," a beautiful yellow cluster, is popularly named from its curious habit of emitting light, like phosphorescent wood, actually giving out light in a dark room; and a Japanese kind of *Pleurotus* of which family our so-called oyster mushroom is a member, gives so generously of its mysterious light that it is quite possible to read by its luminosity.

But my three kinds, certainly known, we do enjoy eating, though some of my guests suspect everything in the mushroom line, and although I point out distinctly that I have not died yet, after twenty years or more of eating them, they always continue to look at them very questioningly, if not with real suspicion.

Several dead trees are the basis of most picturesque and woody parasitic growths, pushing out from the side like well carpentered shelves. From year to year they increase in size, and one set in particular, I have happily preserved as a sort of natural memorial to my dear father, who cut the tree and took a pardonable pride in seeing it depart after being dead and not pretty for several years. Now it is really beautiful, with nature's attempts at carpentering.

Sometimes in the woods the beautiful soil all covered with soft brown "needles" I see a curious lifting of this carpet, and each day it swells a little more, until suddenly emerges a lovely mushroom from its little bed and stars the wood with one more colorful umbrella.

Iceland Moss*

Algae are interesting, always, but the kinds are few here. The "Iceland moss" is comparatively frequent, and I have collected it during many summers, for use in *blancmange*. I have learned in the passage of many valuable years, however, several things about Iceland moss. When a bride I went from Washington to live at Amherst College, where my husband had been made a professor, we did not at once keep house, but boarded luxuriously. So many students called upon us, however, and so many kind things were done for us by faculty and town people, that it seemed to me, after two or three years, it was incumbent upon us to take a house and become householders. So we went to Boston one fine day, and made a call upon a certain wholesale grocer whom we had met and who had politely said that if we desired at any time to supply our pantry with edibles, all we had to do was call upon him. We did, and the resulting large pile of eatables seemed to me rather formidable. However, we were just starting away when it occurred to me that Iceland moss would be a good addition to our list.

"How much of that ought we to order?" said I, in a housewifely ardor.

"Oh, I do not know," replied my very young husband, and consulting together feverishly, we decided at first that ten pounds would be all right, when my husband said, "I do not think we should be small in our orders—remember this is a wholesale establishment, and it is only by personal favor that we are allowed to purchase here," to which I agreed, neither of us knowing much about our selection. The salesman looked somewhat astonished at our order, and half a dozen men were at once dispatched in search for the amount. After some time they all returned with reports, and our particular man, while quite ashamed apparently at the result, said they were sorry they had not so much, but they had found twenty-four pounds, which had been put with our various things. When we reached the scholastic shades of Amherst and our own dwelling that Irish moss filled a box of enormous dimensions. For indefinite years we had it for blancmange, and our little daughter reported that until she was at least fifteen years old it was impossible for her to open any box or barrel in the kitchen regions without coming upon Irish moss in vast amounts. So we never required any more! Somehow now it does not fascinate me on the beach even at the present day.

The heavy, bulbous yellow sea weed which fringes the shore is distinctive and at times handsome, when the setting sun, for instance, is lighting all the shore line at low tide. Then it is in color a rich yellow, but at some times it is almost black, and repellant in suggestiveness. I used to make pretty necklaces from its bulbs, and even now it is like an old friend.

[***Editor's note:** Mrs. Todd first writes of Iceland moss (lichen), then changes to Irish moss (algae). Both have very similar appearances and are used in food preparation, but it is believed here she is referring to the seaweed (algae) variety that is common in Hog Island's lower intertidal zone.]

Appendix B

Hog Island Flora ca. 1912

In the botanizing tradition of Henry David Thoreau, the Todd Bingham effort following carries on that practice by listing common names of all wildflowers they found on Hog Island. The list offered here is a composite of two unpublished typewritten documents. The first typewritten list was hand dated 1911 by an unknown source while the other was dated via typewriter as exhibited here.

The handwritten note gives credit for the origins of the list to Mabel Todd, though her name was not recorded on the 1912 version. It should be noted that according to her diary, she did not arrive at Hog Island until August 10 in the summer of 1912. No mention was made of Millicent being on the island then, either. Therefore, dates of botanizing and the precise family compiler remain unclear. The list may be the product of a family project over their first summers on Hog Island.

The 1912 version of the list bears an indication it was revisited in 1953. Many flowers have the expression *'53* penciled in to the right of each, while others are blank, and yet others are crossed out for unknown reasons. Those random and unclear marks are omitted here.

FLOWERS NATIVE TO HOG ISLAND

List taken July 1–August 12, 1912
Nomenclature from
Fieldbook of American Wildflowers by F. Schuyler Mathews

Canada Hawkweed
Tawny Hawkweed
Crimson Clover
White Clover
Alsike Clover
Buttercup
Daisy
Daisy Fleabane
Wild Virginia
   Strawberry
American Wood
   Strawberry
Blue-eyed Grass
Four-leaved
   Loosestrife
Heal-all
Sundrops Pumila
Sundrops Fustiosa
Blackberry
Cow Wheat
Ladies Slipper
Blue Flag
Pink Yarrow
White Yarrow
Cinquefoil

Canada Mayflower
Bristly Sarsaparilla
Linnea borealis (Twin
   Flower)
Norway Cinquefoil
Evening Primrose
Cireasa Alpina
Rudbeckia
Fire Weed
Dwarf Sumac
Thistle
Canada Thistle
Wood Sorrel
Gold Thread
Star Flower
Long-leaved
   Stitchwort
Pyrola (Shinleaf)
Lysimachia Stricta
Tear Thumb
Wood Lily
Pearly Everlasting
Wild Lettuce
Dwarf Cornel
Great Mullen

Skunk Cabbage
Indian Tobacco
Sow Thistle
Bugleweed
Mustard
Field Sorrel
Chickweed
Meadow Sweet
Hardhack
Wild Rose
Shepherd's Purse
Wild Peppergrass
Snap Dragon
Sweet Cicely
Rough Bedstraw
Climbing False
   Buckwheat
Burdock
Convolvulus
Pin weed
March Cudweed
Bladder Campion
Fall Dandelion
Agrimony
Narrow Dock

Epilobium Coloratum
Hop Clover
Wild Mint
Wild Parsnip
Water Pennywort
Catnip
Lady's Thumb
Ladies Tresses
Silvery Cinquefoil

Rough Stemmed
    Goldenrod
Showy Goldenrod
Seaside Goldenrod
Lance-leaved
    Goldenrod
Ladies Tobacco
Marsh Rosemary
Cow Parsnip

Golden Dock
Boneset
Clintonia
Michelmas Daisy
White Aster
Purple Aster
Hobble bush

Appendix C

Preliminary Notes on Behavior and Ethnology
of *Homo Sapiens Audubiensis*
in the Muscongus Bay Region

A speech given by Walter Van Dyke
Bingham to an Audubon gathering in
New York City on October 22, 1937

Of all the forms of wildlife for which the Todd Sanctuary on Hog Island provides a refuge, to me the most fascinating are not the baby Parula Warblers in their mossy nests, nor the soaring Ospreys, nor the Great Blue Heron, nor the fawns, not even the *Sciuridae*, but the primates. Here I have seen, for example, specimens of *Hominidae*, notably, in recent summers, flocks of the rare species *Homo sapiens Auduboniensis*.

What is this species like? How does it differ from other species of the genus *Homo*? What are its distinctive markings, its flight pattern, its song, its feeding habits, its behavior in caring for its young? How is it most readily distinguished from the birds of the vicinity with which it is often found in a close association?

My notes suggest that in two respects *Auduboniensis* is strikingly like the Phalarope. Among the Phalaropes, which last summer visited Muscongus Bay literally by the thousands, you recall that it is the female who wears the brighter, more conspicuous plumage; also during court-ship it is the female who makes the advances.

The song of the male *Auduboniensis* can easily be distinguished from that of the female. It is an octave lower in pitch and more robust in timbre. I have heard it often in the early morning, about six o'clock, at which time it sounds like that of the common Crow. Later in the day it resembles rather the chattering of Magpies, interspersed with cries like those made by the Laughing Gull, while at dusk it rivals the Hermit Thrush in lyric beauty and variety of melody.

One of their songs which last summer could be heard each evening toward sunset, punctually as the hoot of the Great Horned Owl, is like this: "O du mein holder Abendstern." Listeners with vivid imaginations have suggested that this song resembles a Wagnerian melody. On moonlit evenings *Auduboniensis* could be heard singing in chorus, like bullfrogs. At such times their song sounds this way: "Good night ladies." These unforgettable notes have a tender, plaintive quality when heard across the water, and indeed grow lovelier to the ear the more remote they are.

The habitat of *Auduboniensis* covers an almost unparalleled range. Specimens have been reported nesting as far north as Acadia, as far south as Florida, and as far west as the Pacific coast; while on Admiral Byrd's second expedition to the Antarctic, one migrant was seen in the Bay of Whales, in close association with a flock of Emperor Penguins—a bird to which the *Hominidae* are said to bear a curiously striking resemblance, not only in general appearance but in their quaint manner of locomotion and solemn dignity of attitude. Like the Penguin, *Auduboniensis* cannot fly but can ambulate rapidly over the land. It has been seen slowly and somewhat tentatively wading on mudflats, where it delves for worms. It is also at home in the water. Toward high noon its plumage sometimes undergoes a chameleon-like transformation, after which it utters a loud scream and plunges headlong into the sea.

The species is both herbivorous and carnivorous. It lives partly on the flesh of other vertebrates, partly on crustaceans, partly on seeds, fruits, and succulent herbs, but chiefly on an oleaginous, saccharine exudate of the *Theobroma cacao* known locally in Maine as chocolate bars.

Appearing as migrants during the summer months, as many as fifty to sixty have been seen descending upon Hog Island in a single day. They were first observed in considerable numbers on June 9, 1936. Since that date they have often been noted, particularly on the northernmost point of the island and on the waters of Muscongus Bay. They have sometimes stayed within this area for two weeks, or even longer, before continuing their migration. Scarcely has one flock disappeared before another arrives, rapidly molting its spring plumage and appearing almost immediately in pinfeathers and down of variegated but unpredictable colors.

Of 223 specimens banded in 1936, twenty-two were observed again in the summer of 1937.

These migrants have been traced to remote parts of the country. Wherever found, it has been discovered that they behave like leaders among the *Hominidae* of their several localities. Many are engaged in the care of the young, training them to act in an intelligent and friendly way toward other forms of wildlife, for *Auduboniensis* seems to appreciate the mutual interdependence of different forms of life and to understand the forces of the natural environments in which they thrive or perish.

It is obviously desirable that more and more *Audubonienses* should, in future summers, find their way to the Todd Wildlife Sanctuary. But since the environment there has only limited coverage for protecting them from predators and storms, the wardens of this sanctuary must take steps to see that these haunts are not appropriated by other species of *Hominidae*. I am especially apprehensive of the *Summer-vacationistoria*, partly because this less active and more self-indulgent species is not always easy to distinguish from the true *Auduboniensis*. And so I shall try to describe more precisely the distinctive characteristics of this latter species.

It must be confessed that I have had to abandon all attempts to identify *Auduboniensis* by its plumage alone, or its form, or its external markings. It can be recognized only by its behavior.

1. *Auduboniensis* exhibits, while still immature, a strong preference for woods, marshes, streams, prairies, wilderness—in other words, for the out-of-doors. (This trait persists into maturity, instead of dying out as it does with many other species of *Homo.*)

2. It is not to be deterred from its pursuits by discomforts and difficulties—by mosquitoes or swamps or storms.

3. It exhibits an absorbing curiosity regarding certain forms of vegetation and wildlife. It watches them closely and examines them in great detail.

4. It is peculiarly sensitive to the beauty and the worth of different forms of life. It cherishes them.

5. It gathers and brings to its lair choice specimens of certain forms, but not if these forms are rare or in danger of extinction.

6. It excels in the ability to observe slight differences among these forms: differences of color, sound, size, and shape; differences in markings, texture, pattern; differences of behavior.

7. It can describe these differences accurately with words, pencil, brush, or camera.

8. It also excels in noting similarities, even though these similarities may be obscure. In other words, it has highly developed powers of observing, classifying, abstracting, and generalizing; that is, an aptitude for scientific thinking.

9. Its curiosity extends to questions of relationships between different forms of life and the connections between events. It is a rational animal, with a strong proclivity for exercising its mind on problems presented by the world of nature.

10. But it is capable of retaining, in the presence of nature, an attitude of wonder.

These ten characteristics seem to be peculiarly in evidence among naturalists, young and old. Those who most greatly benefit their species are endowed with yet another characteristic—*the capacity to make their interests and enthusiasms contagious.*

These are the leaders. It is primarily to shelter and encourage such potential leaders that the Audubon Nature Camp exists. It is our privilege to discover them when we can and to stimulate their flight in the direction of Muscongus Bay.

This preliminary report of observations on the characteristics of nature students has been offered, not only because the natural history of the *Hominidae* is in itself a topic of absorbing interest but more especially because this particular species, *Auduboniensis*, plays a vital role in the great drama of conservation. Before many years have passed, it will be recognized as performing one of the key functions in maintaining the balance of nature on this continent.